Cary F. Goulson is a member of the Faculty of Education at the University of Victoria.

This is a comprehensive primary reference to a rich and often neglected storehouse of information on Canada's educational background.

As the boundary between full-fledged royal commissions and other official governmental inquiries is not always clear - and many legislative committee inquiries and special department of education investigations have been as significant in educational development as regular commissions - Goulson has included all major ministerial-level governmental inquiries in Canadian education between 1787 and 1978.

More than 300 inquiries are included, among them general, special interest, judicial, legislative, parliamentary, and other governmental committees. The information provided for each includes the type of commission or committee, its size, chairman, purpose, dates of appointment and reporting, and primary source references, as well as a selection of its major conclusions and/or recommendations.

Official governmental records and documents including the Reports themselves, Legislative Journals, House Debates and Hansard, Sessional Papers, Statutes, and Department of Education records were used as the resource base.

This volume will be of specific interest to teachers and students of the history of education, and most educators, no matter what their fields, will find it useful.

A Source Book of Royal Commissions and Other Major Governmental Inquiries in Canadian Education 1787-1978

CARY F. GOULSON

University of Toronto Press
Toronto Buffalo London

Toronto Buffalo London
Reprinted in paperback 2017
ISBN 978-0-8020-2408-4 (cloth)
ISBN 978-1-4875-9912-6 (paper)

Goulson, Carlyn Floyd.
A source book of Royal Commissions and other major governmental inquiries in Canadian education 1787-1978

Includes bibliographical references and index.
ISBN 978-0-8020-2408-4 (bound) ISBN 978-1-4875-9912-6 (pbk.)
1. Governmental investigations - Canada - History.
2. Education - Canada - History. 3. Education and state - Canada - History. I. Title.
LA411.G68 379.71 C81-094660-2

This book has been published with the help of a grant from the Social Science Federation of Canada, using funds provided by the Social Sciences and Humanities Research Council of Canada.

To Jean

Contents

Preface

The present study began as an examination of the use of royal commissions in Canadian education. However, as my research progressed, I found that the boundary between full-fledged royal commissions and other official governmental inquiries was not always clear. Moreover, many of the more important legislative committee inquiries and special department of education investigations have played as significant a role in educational development as have the regular commissions. Therefore, my topic was broadened to include other major (that is, ministerial level) governmental inquiries in Canadian education. A very few non-governmental inquiries have been added to the 'special committee' category because of their particular relevance.

I have included an introductory chapter, but the heart of the publication is the sequence of 367 inquiries. These are presented chronologically by province, beginning on the eastern seaboard as did Canada's story.

The type of 'commission' or 'committee' is shown for each inquiry, and also the dates of appointing and reporting, the size of the commission/committee, the chairman (and his or her position), the purpose, and the primary reference sources. In addition major conclusions/recommendations have been given. These of course represent editorial choice, sometimes from very long formal listings. I have tried always to include those items that have seemed of major educational importance up through the years, and I have endeavoured to reflect all findings as accurately as possible. In every case I have conformed closely to the wording of the original.

For the most part my sources have been official government records and documents - the Reports themselves,

Legislative Journals, House Debates and Hansard, Sessional Papers, Statutes, Department of Education records. Contemporary newspapers have also proven very useful. I have been in correspondence with each province's Department of Education and each Attorney General's Department, and I have visited the Legislative Libraries in all eleven capital cities. For the invaluable assistance everywhere rendered, I am most grateful.

Cary F. Goulson

Victoria, British Columbia
December, 1980

Introduction

> *Inquiries are well-fitted for overloading every question with ten or fifteen times the quantity of matter necessary for its consideration.* (W. E. Gladstone)
>
> *Inquiries are pregnant with prudent and sagacious suggestions for the improvement of the administration of affairs.* (B. Disraeli) [1]

The use of official fact-finding commissions goes back a long way in English governmental history. Some authorities cite the Domesday survey as the first royal commission, having a similar intent and function but differing in form from those of modern times. Others, perhaps more precisely, name the Commission on Enclosures in 1517 as the first real royal commission.

In the days of crown control, the king's commissioners were often given blanket authority with powers that were at once investigative, judicial, and administrative. Under the Tudors and the early Stuarts especially, such practices led to notorious abuses, and the seventeenth century was one long constitutional struggle against such extraordinary powers and courts. Sir Edward Coke, the outstanding jurist of those centuries, pronounced strongly against the legality of government by commission. An ascendant Parliament strengthened by such judgments, stifled commission procedures throughout the eighteenth century. Not until well into the nineteenth century when the misery and corruption of industrial England made it absolutely necessary once again to make use of governmental investigative techniques did the royal commission overcome its stigma of disrepute and gain recognition as a legitimate function of modern democratic government.

Harried governments discovered that 'royal' commissions had many inherent advantages not possessed by parliamentary committees. Select committees were always sorely pressed for time. Their background investigation, their travel, their study of evidence, their report writing, all of these had to be rushed to meet sessional deadlines. The appointees were often inexpert in the area of investigation and were further hampered by party representation and loyalties. Furthermore, because they were a part of government, it was difficult to escape completely the suspicion of prejudice and puppetry.

By comparison, royal commissions had the prestige of monarchical appointment neatly coupled with the efficacy of government choice from nonpartisan ranks. Outstanding scholars, recognized experts, men above reproach could be named, and often such were found who, for altruistic rewards alone, were willing to serve until the job was done.[2] Their conscientious and unhurried reports, often the result of extensive travel, provided members of parliament and the public with documented facts and informed opinions so badly needed in the crusade against social wrong.

Paving the way for the humanitarian reform acts of the 1800s were the ever-multiplying commissions of inquiry. Professor Redlich in his study of the British House of Commons stated in 1908, 'Almost all the great reforms of the nineteenth century in internal administration, taxation, education, labour protection and other social questions, have been based on the full investigations made by royal commissions, often continued over a space of many years, and on their reports which, with the evidence collected, are laid before Parliament.'[3]

This latter-day revival of commissionism was not without opposition. Critics viewed with alarm the encroachment of commissioners into every cranny of everyday life. 'They would, in fact, put the whole earth in commission, and delivery over the whole human race saved from the flood....' Thus wrote Toulmin Smith, Barrister-at-Law in 1849.[4] Smith saw the spreading use of government by commission as an illegal device to dodge responsibility, to parcel out patronage and to whitewash Whigs.

Probably the most devestating and certainly the most entertaining criticism of royal commissions came from the pages of *Punch*. Sir Alan P. Herbert's poem 'Pageant of Parliament' appeared in 1934 and read in part as follows:

The necessity for action was clear to everyone,
But the view was very general that nothing could be done,
And the Government courageously decided that the Crown
Should appoint a score of gentlemen to track the trouble down --
Which always takes a long, long time.

I am the Royal Commission on Kissing,
Appointed by Gladstone in '74;
The rest of my colleagues are buried or missing;
Our Minutes were lost in the last Great War.
But still I'm a Royal Commission,
My task I intend to see through
Though I know, as an old politician,
Not much will be done if I do.[5]

In spite of good natured or venomous barbs such as these the golden age of British royal commissions flourished well into the twentieth century. And when the practice seemed somewhat on the wane in the Mother Country the British Dominions were making extravagant use of this investigative technique. Royal commissions of inquiry were passed on to the British colonies and later dominions as part of their constitutional heritage. In the early years Britain appointed colonial commissions autocratically as befitted a worthy imperialistic power, but after the evolution of self-governing colonies and dominions, no British commission was sent out except by consent or invitation.

Interestingly, though the commission technique was enthusiastically adopted by Canada, there appeared distinctive differences in formation and use. The federal government and each of the provinces passed a Public Inquiries Act in some form, giving much more sweeping powers to Canadian commissioners than had their British counterparts.[6] The right to demand papers, to summon witnesses, to hear evidence under oath with the potential threat of legal penalties, all these have become automatic in Canada. Britain, perhaps because of a centuries-old conscience nagged by memories of autocratic misuse, gives such powers only by special statute for exceptional circumstances.

There are other differences as well. Canada has tended to appoint fewer persons to each commission. Three has been a common number, and one also has been very popular; the latter, of course, having the built-in advantage of no minority report. Smaller commissions may be a studied attempt to get closer agreement (leaving the widely diverse views to the witness chair), or it may be the realization that group representation in Canada would become a hopeless process, or it may be that there is a dearth of available experts, or it might simply be that Canadian commissioners expect recompense for their services. In the words of J. E. Hodgetts, '...The British tradition of unpaid commissioners and a chairman who is prepared to settle for the Queen's gift of a silver inkstand has obviously not caught on in Canada.'[7]

The purposes for which commissions are appointed are many and varied. A royal commission may be formed to pave the way for legislative action already decided upon by the government. This sets the public mind into positive, sympathetic motion. Or the government may be considering an important line of action but it wishes to test and gauge public opinion. A royal commission here acts as a sort of trial balloon, an indication as to whether policy in this direction would flush out unknown and perhaps overwhelming opposition. Or a commission of inquiry may be just *that* -- a painstaking investigation to get a wealth of facts and knowledge which might lead to eventual solution of some important public problem.

The afore-mentioned purposes are all examples of the party in power having a relatively free choice as to whether or not to institute a royal commission. Often, however, the government is under pressure by the opposition, by the press, by the public, or by influential factions to take investigative action. Not infrequently the hint of maladministration or scandal is the catalyst. In such instances the role of a commission of inquiry might be to clear the name of an individual or department -- or to 'whitewash', depending upon the viewpoint. The government of course might move early to forestall potential criticism or it might move late to stall hostile developments purposely and to gain time, the great healer of political maladies.

Education, because of the division of powers in 1867, is a provincial right, and so nearly all of the post-confederation governmental inquiries into education have emanated from provincial capitals. The 1910 Royal Commission on Industrial Training and Technical Education is an exception. In addition there have been federal commissions such as the Royal Commission on National Development in the Arts, Letters and Sciences (1949-1951) and the Royal Commission on Bilingualism and Biculturalism (1963-1970) that have important educational overtones.

For this study, 367 major inquiries into Canadian education have been considered. These have included investigations into education generally, into certain aspects of education in particular, and into other matters that were of significance to education in some way. Nearly all have been governmental investigations of some form or another, but a very few special inquiries sponsored from without government ranks have been noted. Even these have entailed indirect governmental involvement, whether through initial instigation, or interest and encouragement, or obvious repercussions.

Of the 367 inquiries, 127 can be considered 'royal commissions' since they were issued in the name of the Crown under a Great Seal and carried with them powers authorized by 'public inquiries' acts or by special acts. This group can be further divided into royal commissions having general educational significance, royal commissions in other areas but having special educational significance, and royal commissions of a judicial nature that were appointed to investigate a person or incident. These three divisions have been designated 'R1', 'R2', and 'R3', respectively, for the 'Bibliography-Index' in the Appendix and for the tabulation which follows. The decision as between R1 and R3 (that is, general and judicial) was not always clearcut, and the writer had to use editorial discretion. For instance, the 1861 Royal Commission on Affairs and Financial Conditions of Toronto University and University College; the 1893 Commission of Inquiry into Charges Relating to the Bathurst Schools and Other Schools in Gloucester County; and the 1924 Commission of Inquiry into the Extension of the Powers of the Board of Roman Catholic School Commissioners of Montreal, the Education of Jewish Children in Protestant Schools or in Others, and the Financial Situation of the Protestant Schools of Verdun, were included in the first broad grouping because it was felt that the findings and ramifications of commissions such as these were of wide interest rather than narrow. There were, then, 47 general royal commissions, 48 related commissions, and 32 judicial commissions.

The remaining 240 inquiries were also divided into three groups: legislative or parliamentary committees of various kinds (designated 'L'); departmental and other governmental committees ('D'); and special committees ('S'). In these divisions, 44 legislative committees were considered, 158 departmental committees, and 38 special committees. An index listing all 367 commissions and committees is provided in the Appendix, but a tabulation summary is presented at this point for clarification.

TABULATION OF INQUIRIES IN CANADIAN EDUCATION

	R1	R2	R3	L	D	S	TOTAL
Nfld.	3	6	1	1	3	2	16
N.S.	5	1	2	4	10	3	25
P.E.I.	4	-	2	8	1	2	17
N.B.	6	2	1	3	13	6	31
Que.	4	6	1	2	21	1	35
Ont.	7	9	14	8	38	3	79
Man.	6	2	2	3	9	4	26
Sask.	2	5	1	1	21	3	33
Alta.	4	3	2	4	15	3	31
B.C.	5	4	6	7	19	5	46
Canada	1	10	-	3	8	6	28
	47	48	32	44	158	38	367

Obviously all provinces (and the federal government as well) have made much use of fact finding techniques in the field of education. Outside of Ontario, which has been much the busiest, the inquiries are spread rather evenly among the other provinces.

Although legislative committees on education were much more widely used in pre-confederation days, it would be wrong to discount the importance of such in later periods. The 1934 Legislative Committee appointed to make a comprehensive survey and study of education in the rural districts of Alberta faced a formidable task (see Item 269). Ten years later, the 1944 Special Select Committee on Education in Manitoba undertook an inquiry as comprehensive as any royal commission -- and with 'powers of 'Commissioners' under Part V of the Manitoba Evidence Act' as well (Item 215). Ontario in 1962 appointed a Select Committee on Manpower Training, and two years later, a Select Committee on Youth. And there were many others.

The large group of 158 departmental and other governmental committees showed wide variance in manner of appointment. Some were very similar in power and scope to royal commissions, and indeed some were appointed under authority of a sub-section of a public inquiries act. However, if a Minister of Education (or other departmental minister) did the appointing rather than a Lieutenant Governor in Council, and if the resultant report was returned to the Minister, then it was adjudged a departmental committee or 'commission' rather than a royal commission. Examples of this type include the 1881 Ontario Commission of Inquiry 'to investigate certain charges against Dr. Samuel May of the Education Department', and the 1919 Manitoba Commission on Status and Salaries of Teachers.

Also within this broad category fell such significant inquiries as the Putman-Weir Survey of the School System in British Columbia in 1924, and the 1934 Commission on School Finance in the same province. Still another type of investigation was placed here -- that of the department official touring other provinces and other lands in search of new educational ideas. Ryerson's journeys in the mid 1800s and the technical education surveys of John Seath and Dr. Merchant in the early 1900s are examples. Not included at all in this study are the regular departmental reports representing ordinary departmental procedures. It should be noted that departmental committees have been very widely used as an investigative technique in recent years -- over one hundred of the 158 total dating from the mid 1960s.

Of particular interest are the 18 inquiries classified as 'special'. For some of these, international educators of high repute were brought in to view dispassionately the Canadian scene. In 1917, Harold W. Foght, Specialist on Rural School Practice from Washington, D.C., made a survey of education in the Province of Saskatchewan (Item 234). In 1933, C.A. Richardson, Inspector of His Majesty's schools in London, prepared a report on 'certain aspects of the educational system of Newfoundland' (Item 3). And in 1937, W.A.F. Hepburn, Director of Education from

Ayrshire, Scotland, headed the Quebec Protestant Education Survey Committee (Item 99).

In some instances philanthropic organizations have made their resources available. In 1921 (Nova Scotia) and again in 1923 (Manitoba), the Carnegie Foundation for the Advancement of Teaching sent personnel to assess higher education (see Items 20 and 210). The Ford Foundation rendered financial assistance to two 'commissions' investigating university affairs in the mid 1960s. These were the Duff-Berdahl Commission on university government and administration and the Bladen Commission on university finance (Items 352 and 353). There was also the Royal Institute of International Affairs which sponsored a Supervisory Committee on Newfoundland Studies from 1941 to 1946 (Item 5).

A very few non-governmental inquiries have been added to the 'special committee' category because of their particular relevance. Examples are the 1968 British Columbia Teachers' Federation Commission on Education (Item 317) and the 1975 Study of Northern People and Higher Education (Item 363).

Quite understandably the 32 judicial royal commissions were involved in investigations of a more personal and specific nature than were met with elsewhere in education. These inquiries resulted almost always from incidents and situations that deteriorated into sweeping accusations and wild charges played up usually by a grateful press. Since public officials or public institutions were involved, the Government eventually was forced to take action, and an objective commission of inquiry was an acceptable disinterested means. It is not surprising that by far the greatest number of these investigations were placed in the hands of legal experts -- usually a sole commissioner. Charges under consideration ranged from the obviously serious to the seemingly insignificant. Among them were depletion of funds, examination irregularities, mismanagement, excessively severe discipline, improper textbook contracts, mishandling of construction, and unacceptable art drawing books.

It is in the area of general royal commissions (R1) that particular attention should be paid, for it is here that the findings of widest interest and the recommendations of most lasting consequence are to be found. As can be seen in the previously presented tabulation, these 47 commissions have been spread fairly evenly across the land. Saskatchewan shows only two, but the 1952-57 Royal Commission on Agriculture and Rural Life in that province included an important survey of education.

These 'general' commissions have tended to come in waves. Depression lack-of-wherewithal was no doubt one reason for the few commissions in the 'Thirties , because there were most certainly educational woes in this period. No such commission was appointed in World War I, and during World War II only two were launched, and these in the closing months of the struggle. Obviously the nation's energy in these times of stress was being directed to other fronts.

Through the years, twelve of the 47 commissions have been directed to look at education generally. Twelve have dealt with university affairs and higher education; six with school taxes and educational finance;[8] three with agricultural, technical and industrial education; two with teachers' salaries; two with textbooks; and the remaining nine with other miscellaneous matters.

The number of members appointed to these several commissions shows wide divergence. Most popular have been 3, 5, 1, and 7 in that order. Here is the tabulation for the 47 noted.

Number of Commissioners	Number of Commissions	Number of Commissioners	Number of Commissions
1	5	8	2
2	1	9	2
3	14	10	1
4	1	12	1
5	9	21	1
6	3	22	1
7	5	25	1

Again, men of legal background have been popular choices for chairman -- seventeen such being named. Eighteen chairmen were from college or university life of some kind (governors, administrators, deans, professors); four of these being university presidents. Five of the chairmen were department of education officials (three superintendents, a secretary of education, and a former deputy minister). Also heading commissions were an industrialist, an engineer, a newspaper editor, a minister of the church, an assistant-deputy attorney general, and two senators.

Widely representative have been the remaining personnel. The Prairie Provinces in particular have appointed office-holders of influential citizen groups such as 'home and school', farm leagues, and women's organizations. Rarely have practising school teachers been made members. Illustrative of the breadth of background are the senator, past-president of the Federation of Home and School Associations, past-president of the Farm Women's Union, lawyer, department store manager, and university professor who made up the 1957 Alberta Royal Commission on Education.

As the writer read through the reports represented in this study he was impressed in general by the aspirations of the Commissioners, the eloquence of their presentations, and the intrinsic value of their findings. Here was a valuable source of reference material for the educational researcher, yet it lay largely unused. Report after report included historical summaries and statements of philosophies in clear, untechnical prose -- for these represented public commissions of inquiry. Tables of statistics, facts and figures, thoughtful suggestions, major recommendations were advanced. Taken in sequence they provide a thread of educational development in each province, and taken together they produce a comparative or composite picture, nationwide.

Trends and patterns are discernible in retrospect. From the first there has been conspicuous effort on the part of every province to lift up its own standards -- to look at the systems of education elsewhere and to endeavour not to be found too far wanting. Since the turn of the century, large district consolidation has been an ever recurring issue. In the early years of the 1900s, agricultural and technical education were stressed, and at mid-century, studies were suggesting ways and means of providing more diverse programmes to meet the age of automation and individual differences.

Through the years, teacher training, teacher supply, teachers' salaries have been high in problem priority. The raising of teaching standards and teacher status has been regarded as a hopeful solution. After World War II many general commissions favoured university degree programmes for all teachers, which meant an advance towards professional parity for elementary and secondary levels. More and more attention has been paid to higher education and to continuing education -- and in the 'Seventies , cultural fulfilment, minority group needs, and declining enrolments have been recurring topics. Undoubtedly the one matter of greatest urgency in all periods and at all levels has been educational finance. Equalization of assessment and equalization of opportunity has been the cry -- a widespread desire, apparent in all the provinces, to provide a maximum opportunity for all children. And the costs have spiralled ever upwards.

Now, to assess in general, and in brief, the place of royal commissions in the development of Canadian education! Assignment of direct cause and effect can rarely be done with certainty. Inferences, however, can be drawn, and these show wide divergence in practice. There have been major commissions shelved with little thanks. There have been successive studies finding the same facts and recommending the same remedies to the same province with few apparent results. By contrast there have been many instances of governments working with remarkable speed to institute commission proposals. British Columbia put into effect in a matter of months the main features of the 1945 Cameron Report, and the ink was hardly dry on the Chant Report of 1960, before a full scale educational overhaul was begun by the same province.

Subsequent implementation of ideas is not the only contribution of commissions, however. Whether there is immediate action, later action, or no action, the accumulation of information and the directing of public attention are of very real value. Conscientious scrutiny and objective reassessment are good things to do on occasion. 'Education is everybody's business' is an overworked maxim which nonetheless points up an inescapable truth. Royal commissions and formal governmental inquiries permit individuals and groups to have their say. A commission is an excuse and a reason for channelling extraordinary attention to education.

Reference Notes

[1] Cited in Hugh McDowall Clodie and J. William Robinson. *Royal Commissions of Inquiry: The Significance of Investigations in British Politics*. Palo Alto, Stanford University Press, 1937, p. 80.

[2] The letter of commission setting up the 1919 Royal Commission on Oxford and Cambridge Universities is a

good example of the calibre of person appointed in Britain. See Appendix, p. 377.

[3]Josef Redlich. *The Procedure of the House of Commons: A Study of Its History and Present Form.* (Translated from German by A. Ernest Steinthal) London, Archibald Constable, 1908, vol. II, p. 193.

[4]J. Toulmin Smith. *Government by Commissions: Illegal and Pernicious.* London, S. Sweet, 1849, p. 13.

[5]A.P.H., 'Pageant of Parliament', *Punch,* vol. 186, June 27, 1934, p. 708.

[6]See Appendix, p. 379 for listing of Canadian Public Inquiries Acts.

[7]John Edwin Hodgetts, 'Should Canada be De-Commissioned? A Commoner's View of Royal Commissions', *Queen's Quarterly,* vol. LXX, no. 4, Winter 1964, p. 477.

[8]To these six should be added several related 'R2' commissions on assessment and taxes.

Checklist

NEWFOUNDLAND

1 SELECT COMMITTEE ON THE PRESENT SCHOOL SYSTEM
(Legislative Committee)

Appointed May 8, 1890

Reported February 12, 1891

Committee Nine members; James Murray (Member for Burgeo and LaPoile) chairman

Purpose To take evidence upon the subject of the present school system and its operation.

Conclusions/Recommendations

That no change be made at present in the basis of the educational system as a whole;

That no alteration be made in the number or personality of the school inspectors;

That the education committee do all in their power to promote uniformity in the management and practice of the schools;

That the whole subject of placing the teachers' salaries on a reasonable and satisfactory basis be considered;

That a metropolitan college or normal school for the examination and grading of teachers be established as soon as possible;

That future appointments of school inspectors whenever practicable be made from the ranks of school teachers in the colony.

References

Newfoundland, *Journals of Newfoundland House of Assembly*, 1890 & 1891.

2 BRITISH ROYAL COMMISSION ON THE FUTURE OF NEWFOUNDLAND (Related Commission)

Appointed February 17, 1933

Reported October 4, 1933

Commission Three members; William Warrender Mackenzie (Baron Amulree, King's Counsel) chairman

Purpose To examine into the future of Newfoundland and in particular to report on the financial situation and prospects therein.

Conclusions/Recommendations

That existing forms of government be suspended until such time as the Island may become self-supporting again;

That a special Commission of Government take the place of the existing Legislature and Executive Council;

That the Commission of Government be composed of six members (exclusive of the Governor) -- three from Newfoundland and three from the United Kingdom;

That the United Kingdom assume general responsibility for the finances of the Island until it may become self-supporting again;

That as soon as the Island's difficulties are overcome, responsible government, on request from the people of Newfoundland, would be restored;

That the hope that any new educational curriculum, while giving an equal opportunity to all school children and meeting the requirements of students of exceptional promise, will better equip the average boy and girl for the only avenues of employment likely to be available to them in the Island.

References

British House of Commons, *Sessional Papers*, 14, 1933-34.

3 REPORT ON CERTAIN ASPECTS OF THE EDUCATIONAL SYSTEM OF NEWFOUNDLAND
(Special Committee)

Appointed 1933

Reported October 18, 1933

Committee One member; C.A. Richardson (H.M. Inspector of Schools)

Purpose To study the subject of the curriculum in Newfoundland schools.

Conclusions/Recommendations

That the educational curriculum is very largely artificial and divorced from the actual experience and needs of the child;

That the freedom of the teacher is severely restricted making it difficult to use any special talent or ability;

That practically nothing is done, or can be done, to foster self-reliance and independent activity on the part of children.

References

Newfoundland, *Certain Aspects of the Educational System of Newfoundland*, 1933.

4 COMMISSION OF ENQUIRY INTO THE PRESENT CURRICULUM OF THE COLLEGES AND SCHOOLS IN NEWFOUNDLAND
(General Commission)

Appointed October 18, 1933

Reported May 19, 1934

Commission Ten members; Vincent P. Burke (Secretary for Education) chairman

Purpose To reconsider the present curriculum of the public schools in Newfoundland, and to make suggestions or recommendations.

Conclusions/Recommendations

That it is unsound to give a utilitarian emphasis to the work of the elementary school which must be informative and cultural without much regard to future vocational tendencies;

That local school boards be required to test popular feeling on the matter of compulsory education;

That one-teacher schools be restrained from preparing candidates for Grade XI examinations;

That an advisory body be appointed to draw up scales of salaries that would be equitable and attract to the teaching profession a sufficient number of qualified men and women;

That the length of the teacher training course be at least one year, preferably two;

That all women teachers who expect to teach in elementary schools be qualified to teach needlework and knitting.

References

Newfoundland, *Report of the Commission of Enquiry into the Present Curriculum of the Colleges and Schools in Newfoundland*, 1934.

5 SUPERVISORY COMMITTEE ON NEWFOUNDLAND STUDIES
(Special Committee)

Appointed June, 1941

Reported 1946

Committee Nine members; Sir Campbell Stuart (Chairman Imperial Committee, Royal Institute of International Affairs) chairman

Purpose To supervise a research study of the economy and external relations of the Island.

Conclusions/Recommendations

That it is clear that the basic difficulties facing Newfoundland in the educational field in the past, as in other fields of public welfare are economic, and that if Newfoundland is to carry itself in the future the total funds available for public services are likely to be severely limited.

References

Newfoundland: Economic, Diplomatic, and Strategic Studies, 1946. [Sponsored by the Royal Institute of International Affairs]

6 NATIONAL CONVENTION EDUCATION COMMITTEE
(Departmental Committee)

Appointed 1946

Reported 1946

Committee Ten members; Malcolm Hollett (Magistrate) chairman

Purpose To survey the status of education with particular attention to economic questions.

Conclusions/Recommendations

That education is no longer regarded as a luxury for those who can afford it, but a necessity for all, whether they can afford it or not;

That none of the existing services should be abolished or reduced and that the trend towards extension and improvement should be continued.

References

Newfoundland, 'Report of Committee on Education', 1946.

7 ROYAL COMMISSION FOR THE PREPARATION OF THE CASE OF THE GOVERNMENT OF NEWFOUNDLAND FOR THE REVISION OF THE FINANCIAL TERMS OF UNION
(Related Commission)

Appointed December 3, 1953

Reported May 13, 1957

Commission Five members; Philip Joseph Lewis (Queen's Counsel) chairman

Purpose To review the financial position of the Province of Newfoundland since Union.

Conclusions/Recommendations

That in the case of Newfoundland the isolation of the outports, the lack of communications and the want of means of the people, combine to deprive many an able child of his fundamental human right to develop his mind and his skills to the full extent of his capacities.

References

Newfoundland, *Report of the Newfoundland Royal Commission for the Preparation of the Case of the Government of Newfoundland for the Revision of the Financial Terms of Union*, 1957.

8 COMMISSION OF INQUIRY INTO THE QUESTIONS RELATING TO THE IMPOSITION OF THE SCHOOL TAX AT CORNER BROOK
(General Commission)

Appointed March 5, 1956

Reported April 11, 1956

Commission Three members; Beaton J. Abbott (District Magistrate, Grand Falls) chairman

Purpose To enquire into the questions relating to the imposition of the school tax at Corner Brook.

Conclusions/Recommendations

That after long and close study of the evidence submitted there is no doubt whatever that the School Tax is quite justified;

That the heartbreak, the disappointments in trying to build classrooms to meet an influx of children amounting to sometimes alarming propositions will not be swept aside and forgotten by the continuance of the School Tax.

References

Newfoundland, 'Report of the Commission of Enquiry into the Questions Relating to the Imposition of the School Tax at Corner Brook', 1956.

9 ROYAL COMMISSION OF NEWFOUNDLAND FINANCES UNDER THE TERMS OF UNION OF NEWFOUNDLAND WITH CANADA
(Related Commission)

Appointed February 21, 1957

Reported May 31, 1958

Commission Three members; John Babbit McNair (Chief Justice of New Brunswick) chairman

<u>Purpose</u> To review the financial position of the Province of Newfoundland and to recommend the form and scale of additional financial assistance, if any.

<u>Conclusions/Recommendations</u>

That without voluntary contributions by the public and financing by religious denominations, a system of local taxation or higher provincial government expenditure would be necessary in Newfoundland.

<u>References</u>

Newfoundland, *Royal Commission on Newfoundland Finances Under the Terms of Union of Newfoundland with Canada,* 1958.

10 ROYAL COMMISSION ON EDUCATION AND YOUTH (General Commission)

<u>Appointed</u> December 11, 1964

<u>Reported</u> Volume One, January 15, 1967; Volume Two, October 23, 1967

<u>Commission</u> Twelve members; P.J. Warren (Faculty of Education, Memorial University) chairman

<u>Purpose</u> Generally to enquire into all aspects of education in the province.

<u>Conclusions/Recommendations</u>

That the Department of Education be reorganized on a functional rather than a denominational basis;

That consolidation be undertaken to reduce the number of school districts from 230 to approximately 35;

That long-range plans be undertaken for the upgrading of teachers qualifications;

That immediate efforts be made to improve and diversify

the school curriculum;

That a systematic effort be made to improve the validity and reliability of public examinations;

That a province-wide 'Foundation Programme' be established with the entire cost to be borne by the Provincial Government.

References

Newfoundland, *Department of Education News Letter*, Dec., 1964, Vol. 16, No. 4.

Newfoundland, *Report of the Royal Commission on Education and Youth*, 1967.

11 ROYAL COMMISSION ON MUNICIPAL GOVERNMENT IN NEWFOUNDLAND AND LABRADOR
(Related Commission)

Appointed August 23, 1972

Reported September 18, 1974

Commission Four members; Hugh J. Whalen (Political Science Department, Memorial University) chairman

Purpose To enquire into and to make recommendations with respect to:

a) the legislation presently in effect relating to local government and the policies of financial assistance to municipalities by the Province;

b) the improvement of the structure and administration of local government;

c) the establishment of criteria and procedures for the creation of new municipalities;

d) the sources of revenue available to municipalities with particular reference to taxation;

e) the levels of service that should be provided in municipalities;

f) the establishment of adequate financial controls over municipal expenditures.

Conclusions/Recommendations

That school finance in Newfoundland is the responsibility of the denominational school boards and of the Province, and unlike New Brunswick and Prince Edward Island, and to a lesser extent British Columbia, the Province does not levy a real property tax generally for school purposes;

That due to the substantial provincial fiscal responsibility for education in Newfoundland, local ratepayers contribute toward education at levels far below those prevailing in most Canadian provinces; but Newfoundland's school boards not only receive substantial funds from government, school tax authorities and direct assessment levies, they also receive a substantial benefit from municipal services supplied to their tax-exempt schools by local ratepayers;

That, upon the establishment of regional municipal authorities, these units should become the tax billing and tax collection agencies for all school boards within their boundaries.

References

Newfoundland, *Royal Commission on Municipal Government in Newfoundland and Labrador*, 1974.

12 ROYAL COMMISSION ON LABRADOR
(Related Commission)

Appointed October 23, 1972

Newfoundland / 13

Reported February, 1974

Commission Four members; Donald Snowden (Director of Extension Services, Memorial University) chairman

Purpose To inquire into the economic and sociological conditions of life in Labrador; including all phases of education in Labrador (including pre-school, primary, secondary and high school, adult education, vocational and technical training, arts and crafts programmes and life skills) and all matters related to teaching and teachers.

Conclusions/Recommendations

That supervisory personnel with school boards whose jurisdiction is in part or wholly in Labrador be required to visit district schools at least three times a year;

That the Department of Education begin a thorough examination of the present curriculum with a view to developing courses with local relevance;

That immediate provision be made for employment of bilingual teacher aides in schools with native populations;

That kindergartens be established in all schools with native populations in Labrador;

That teacher training at Memorial University offer Indian and Eskimo cross-cultural courses to teachers who are considering teaching native children in Labrador schools;

That programmes which assist student travel and exchange for educational purposes be extended to include travel and exchange within Labrador.

References

Newfoundland, *Recommendations of the Royal Commission on Labrador*, 1974.

13 COMMISSION OF ENQUIRY INTO THE ST. JOHN'S URBAN REGION STUDY
(Related Commission)

Appointed January 7, 1974

Reported October 25, 1974

Commission Three members; Alec G. Henley (St. John's businessman) chairman

Purpose To make an enquiry into:

a) the adoption of a Regional Plan for the St. John's Urban Region;

b) the precise boundaries of the Region;

c) the standards and levels of municipal services and policies required in the Region;

d) the form of local government structure most suitable for adoption in the Region;

e) the possible future regional and municipal tax base for the Region and proposals for Federal and Provincial financial involvement in this field.

Conclusions/Recommendations

That if the proposed policies were to be applied rigidly over the Region, it is conceivable that there would be no schools beyond junior grades in the local centres, and there was fear that the acceptance of this particular policy would mean that all major school facilities would be located in the downtown St. John's central area;

That school facilities for the whole Region be examined by the appropriate authorities so that all areas are provided with adequate and proper school facilities in relation to their needs and that regional school facilities should not be substituted for a more decentralized system of schools which could realistically be provided in local centres within the Region.

References

Newfoundland, *Commission of Enquiry: St. John's Urban Region Study*, vol. 1, 1974.

14 COMMISSION OF INQUIRY INTO THE CLOSING OF UPPER GULLIES SCHOOL
(Judicial Commission)

Appointed	November 5, 1974
Reported	May 20, 1975
Commission	One member; Terrence J. Corbett (Placentia Magistrate)
Purpose	To make an enquiry into and concerning the events which led to the closing of the Upper Gullies Elementary School, and in particular the circumstances surrounding the installation, approval, inspection, operation and maintenance of the water and sewage systems.

Conclusions/Recommendations

That special consideration be given to the approval of plans and construction by the Department of Education, and that precise and detailed legislation be enacted which would ensure that school building projects would be carried out in conformity with approved plans and specifications;

That arrangements be made for the training of Board maintenance supervisors and of building caretakers;

That School Principals, Board Superintendents and Business Managers have sufficient appreciation of such material as to be aware of proper performance in care and maintenance of the school and its equipment;

That some form of routine checking or inspection be established to assure that reasonable standards of safety are maintained in school buildings.

References

Newfoundland, *Commission of Inquiry into the Closing of Upper Gullies School,* 1975.

15 MINISTER'S ADVISORY COMMITTEE ON GRADE XII
(Departmental Committee)

Appointed 1977

Reported December, 1978

Committee Nine members; C. Roebothan (Deputy Minister of Education) chairman

Purpose To examine the question of introducing Grade XII in High Schools.

Conclusions/Recommendations

That an immediate decision be taken to add a twelfth grade to the Newfoundland secondary school system;

That planning for the implementation of that decision be commenced at once with a view to a phased introduction commencing with the Grade X class of 1980.

References

Newfoundland, *Report of Minister's Advisory Committee on Grade XII,* December 1978.

16 TASK FORCE ON DECLINING ENROLMENT IN EDUCATION
(Departmental Committee)

Appointed May 1, 1978

Reported June 30, 1978

Committee — Two members; R.K. Crocker (Director, Institute for Educational Research and Development, Memorial University) and F. Riggs (Department of Curriculum and Instruction, Memorial University) co-chairmen

Purpose — To conduct a survey of declining enrolments by School Districts and the impact of this decline on individual school programs, class size, teacher deployment and class and grade organization in each School District for the school year 1978-79; and to formulate recommendations concerning appropriate and realistic courses of action which Government and administrative groups in education should adopt in order to take advantage of declining enrolments to improve the quality of education.

Conclusions/Recommendations

That present teacher salary unit allocations be adjusted to provide for additional full-time or specialist teachers.

References

Newfoundland, *Perspectives on Declining Enrolments in the Schools of Newfoundland and Labrador*, Interim Report, 1978.

NOVA SCOTIA

17 JOINT COMMITTEE OF COUNCIL AND ASSEMBLY ON EDUCATION (Legislative Committee)

Appointed 1825 (?)

Reported March 7, 1825

Committee Eight members; Charles Fairbanks (Member for Halifax) chairman

Purpose To review the whole system of common school education and to make recommendations for the future.

Conclusions/Recommendations

That education ought to be general throughout the Province in order that none, even in the remotest and poorest settlement, may be without some provision for the instruction of their youth;

That it should be compulsory in every place because too many are found insensible of the just value of education;

That it should not be gratuitous because what costs nothing is generally valued at nothing;

That it cannot be supported from the Provincial Treasury because the expense would surpass the disposeable income of the Colony;

That its funds should be raised by a general and equal

assessment on the whole population, according to each man's ability;

That the respectability and talents -- and consequent usefulness -- of the teachers should be secured by the adequateness and permanency of their salary.

References

Nova Scotia, *Journals of the House of Assembly of Nova Scotia*, 1825.

18 SELECT COMMITTEE ON EDUCATION
(Legislative Committee)

Appointed January 31, 1848

Reported March 23, 1848

Committee Five members; George R. Young (Member for Pictou) chairman

Purpose To enquire into the state of education of schools generally throughout the Province.

Conclusions/Recommendations

That Normal Schools for the training of a higher class of Masters be introduced, and that an Inspector or Superintendent be employed.

References

Nova Scotia, *Journals*, 1848, App. 77.

19 COMMISSION FOR THE PURPOSE OF INVESTIGATING THE BEST METHODS OF TEACHING ENGLISH IN THE SCHOOLS SITUATE IN THE FRENCH-SPEAKING DISTRICTS OF THE PROVINCE
(General Commission)

Appointed April 18, 1902

Reported April 28, 1902

Commission Eight members; W.E. MacLellan (Halifax Barrister, Editor of Morning Chronicle) chairman

Purpose To investigate the best methods of teaching English in the schools situate in the French-speaking districts of the Province.

Conclusions/Recommendations

That the French-speaking sections of the Province have been and continue to be at a very serious disadvantage in the matter of education;

That English can be best and most effectively taught in the French-speaking school sections of Nova Scotia by the daily use in speaking and writing of that language, taught according to the most approved methods, from the pupils' first entrance into school;

That as long as necessary French-speaking pupils should, while learning English, be taught the other subjects of the curriculum in French, provided, however, that the use or study of French shall be optional with every pupil;

That as far as practicable, in the French-speaking schools of the Province, only bilingual teachers should be employed.

References

Nova Scotia, 'The Acadian Commission', 1902.

20 REPORT ON EDUCATION IN THE MARITIME PROVINCES OF CANADA (Special Committee)

Appointed 1921

Reported 1922

Committee William S. Learned (Carnegie Foundation) and Kenneth C.M. Sills (President, Bowdoin College)

Purpose To consider a policy for aid to institutions of higher education in the Maritime provinces.

Conclusions/Recommendations

That there be a complete reconstruction and the use of funds, not to strengthen one institution at the expense of others, but to bring together into one new organization at Halifax several institutions with their endowments and equipment.

References

William S. Learned and Kenneth C.M. Sills, *Education in the Maritime Provinces of Canada,* 1922.
[Sponsored by The Carnegie Foundation for the Advancement of Teaching]

21 COMMITTEE ON SCHOOL STUDIES
(Departmental Committee)

Appointed 1930

Reported March, 1933

Committee Nine members; F.H. Sexton (Director of Technical Education) chairman

Purpose To examine fully into the subject of school studies as related to the present social, ecnomic and intellectual needs of this Province.

Conclusions/Recommendations

That new text books be recommended for use in the Common and High School grades.

References

Nova Scotia, *Journals*, 1931 & 1934.

22 COMMISSION ON THE LARGER SCHOOL UNIT
(Departmental Committee)

Appointed November 19, 1938

Reported October 17, 1939

Committee Six members; Henry P. Munro (Superintendent of Education) chairman

Purpose To study the larger school unit.

Conclusions/Recommendations

That there be a provincial plan whereby district boards would be replaced by municipal school boards, and property and income would be properly reassessed;

That an immediately feasible transition plan be adopted which would make the municipality a unit for school finance and certain administrative functions.

References

Nova Scotia, *Report of the Committee on the Larger School Unit*, 1939.

23 ROYAL COMMISSION ON PROVINCIAL DEVELOPMENT AND REHABILITATION
(Related Commission)

Appointed May 12, 1943

Reported 1944

Commission One member; Robert MacGregor Dawson (Political Science Department, University of Toronto)

Purpose To investigate problems of rehabilitation and development in Nova Scotia.

Conclusions/Recommendations

That in order to obtain the more thorough and intelligent utilization of resources the province needs above everything else more and more knowledge of all kinds -- the education in the common schools, the technical training of the vocational institute, and the broader and more advanced knowledge of the university;

That money was the most urgent need of education in Nova Scotia, and the Dominion should give substantial assistance (based on need) to the poorer provinces for educational purposes;

That salaries of teachers, which in Nova Scotia were deplorably low, be raised so that a better calibre of person would be drawn into and kept in the profession;

That teachers' qualifications and training be upgraded;

That without losing the necessary quota of traditional studies there be a wider and more flexible offering of courses to meet individual needs and abilities;

That the academic load in rural schools be lightened, and consolidation be considered where feasible;

That at the university level some form of federation be instituted.

References

Nova Scotia, *Royal Commission on Provincial Development and Rehabilitation*, 1944.

24 COMMISSION TO INVESTIGATE AND REPORT ON ALL MATTERS AFFECTING TEACHERS SALARIES
(Departmental Committee)

Appointed [ ]

Reported [1946]

Committee Six members; John A. MacGregor (Mayor of Westville) chairman

Purpose To investigate and report on all matters affecting teachers' salaries.

Conclusions/Recommendations

References

Nova Scotia, *Journals*, 1946.

25 COMMISSION ON TEACHER EDUCATION
(Departmental Committee)

Appointed May 1, 1950

Reported November, 1950

Committee Twelve members; Charles E. Phillips (Ontario College of Education) chairman

Purpose To make recommendations for the training of elementary school teachers, high school teachers, and teachers of special subjects.

Conclusions/Recommendations

That support be given to three established trends in teacher education: first a movement towards parity of professional status for elementary school and high school teachers; second, a movement towards a longer minimum period of teacher education for the elementary school teacher; and third, a movement towards teacher preparation of a truly professional character at the university level.

References

Nova Scotia, *Report of the Commission on Teacher Education*, 1950.

26 SURVEY PROJECT OF THE JOINT COMMITTEE ON PUBLIC ATTITUDES TOWARDS OUR SCHOOLS
(Special Committee)

Appointed September, 1952

Reported 1954 (?)

Committee Three members; Mortimer V. Marshall (Director, School of Education, Acadia University) chairman

Purpose To survey public attitudes towards teachers, teacher-parent-pupil relationship, finance and administrative responsibility, physical facilities, and the school program.

Conclusions/Recommendations

(The 'General Conclusions' tabulated public opinion regarding teachers, parent-teacher-pupil relationship, finance and administration, and the program of the school.)

References

Nova Scotia, *A Survey Project of the Joint Committee on Public Attitudes Toward Our Schools*, 1952.

27 ROYAL COMMISSION ON PUBLIC SCHOOL FINANCE IN NOVA SCOTIA
(General Commission)

Appointed March 2, 1953

Reported November 25, 1954

Commission One member; V.J. Pottier, (Judge, Halifax County Court)

Purpose To inquire into and report upon all matters relating to the financial support of schools established and operated under the Education Act, the Vocational Education Act, and special acts relating to the education of handicapped children.

Conclusions/Recommendations

That every child in Nova Scotia be entitled to an education in accordance with his abilities and needs;

That teachers should receive higher salaries, but they must respond with an awakened interest, rekindled enthusiasm and improved professional competence;

That every municipal unit should pay according to its ability by equalized assessment.

References

Nova Scotia, *Report of the Royal Commission on Public School Finance in Nova Scotia,* 1954.

28 ROYAL COMMISSION ON SCHOOL CONSTRUCTION IN NOVA SCOTIA (General Commission)

Appointed October 18, 1957

Reported December 29, 1958

Commission Three members; Ira P. Macnab (Civil Engineer) chairman

Purpose To inquire into matters related to school construction.

Conclusions/Recommendations

That the prime purpose of a school building should be to supply accommodation and facilities that will permit adequate and proper education for children;

That schools must have all the facilities necessary, with the minimum of non-essentials.

References

Nova Scotia, *Royal Commission on School Construction in Nova Scotia*, 1958.

29 SURVEY REPORT ON HIGHER EDUCATION IN NOVA SCOTIA (Special Committee)

Appointed	January 7, 1963
Reported	January 9, 1964
Committee	Three members; Norman A.M. MacKenzie, (former President, University of B.C.) chairman
Purpose	To enquire into and to advise the Government of the Province of Nova Scotia concerning aspects of higher education in the Province.

Conclusions/Recommendations

That grants totalling $1,500,000 be distributed to the universities and colleges, as outlined in interim reports of May 27, July 10 and December 5, 1963;

That to qualify for entrance to university in Nova Scotia a candidate must meet the university entrance requirements of his own province or country, provided that they are at least equal to the Nova Scotia requirements;

That increases in tuition fees be seriously considered by the universities, along with a system of bursaries;

That the ordinary requirement for admission to university be set as Nova Scotia Grade 12 rather than Grade 11;

That serious consideration be given to the institution of a year-round university calendar;

That some appropriate body, such as the Associated Atlantic Universities or the Central Advisory Committee, assume responsibility for ensuring the most effective cooperation among universities and colleges in the Atlantic;

Nova Scotia / 28

That teacher education in Nova Scotia be given thorough study.

References

Nova Scotia, *Higher Education in Nova Scotia,* 1964.

30 ROYAL COMMISSION ON THE SAFE TRANSPORTATION OF SCHOOL PUPILS
(General Commission)

Appointed August 22, 1963

Reported February 10, 1964

Commission One member; C. Roger Rand (Queen's Counsel, Yarmouth)

Purpose To enquire into measures designed to ensure the safety of pupils and other persons while being transported to and from schools.

Conclusions/Recommendations

That the value of any safety legislation is largely dependent upon its intelligent and sympathetic acceptance, understanding and use by school bus drivers, pupil passengers and the motoring public.

References

Nova Scotia, *Royal Commission on the Safe Transportation of School Pupils,* 1964.

31 TRIBUNAL ON BILINGUAL HIGHER EDUCATION IN NOVA SCOTIA
(Departmental Committee)

Appointed March 25, 1969

Reported November 13, 1969

Committee Three members; David C. Munroe (Faculty of Education, McGill University) chairman

Purpose To assess the needs, present and future, of higher education in western Nova Scotia, with special reference to those needs as related to the Acadian community of the Province, and others who may desire a bilingual education.

Conclusions/Recommendations

That a Bilingual Community College, to be known as the Community College of the Southwest -- College Communautaire du sud-ouest -- be established at Meteghan, in the District of Clare;

That the Community College, being situated in an Acadian community, give special consideration to the preservation and development of Acadian culture;

That immediate action be taken in providing training for teachers specialized in the teaching of French and English, so that the standards of language training may be improved.

References

Nova Scotia, *Tribunal on Bilingual Higher Education in Nova Scotia,* 1969.

32 ROYAL COMMISSION ON SECTION 3 OF THE EXPIRED COLLECTIVE AGREEMENT BETWEEN THE SYDNEY SCHOOL BOARD AND THE NOVA SCOTIA TEACHERS' UNION, SYDNEY LOCAL
(Judicial Commission)

Appointed October 14, 1969

Reported December 11, 1969

Commission One member; Arthur Moreira (Barrister)

Purpose To deal with one residual question remaining unsettled after mediation.

Conclusions/Recommendations

That the $200.00 item in Section 3 of the expired collective agreement made between the Sydney School Board and the Nova Scotia Teachers' Union, Sydney Local, is a salary differential, and not a bonus.

References

Nova Scotia, *Report of Royal Commission on Section 3 of the Expired Collective Agreement between the Sydney School Board and the Nova Scotia Teachers' Union,* Sydney Local, 1969.

33 SURVEY OF DIGBY SCHOOL SYSTEM
(Departmental Committee)

Appointed February, 1970

Reported March 26, 1970

Committee Three members; Maurice Keating (Superintendent of Schools) chairman

Purpose To inquire into the administration and operation of the public school system in the District of Digby.

Conclusions/Recommendations

That the role of the Superintendent of Schools be primarily that of an educator;

That the Digby School Boards study carefully their functions as laid down in the Education Act;

That all sales and purchases of school buses, and all other substantial sales and purchases be made by tender;

That the public have ready and easy access to School Board records, financial statements, budgets, and minutes.

References

Nova Scotia, *Survey: Digby School System*, March 1970.

34 COMMUNITY COLLEGE PLANNING COMMISSION
(Departmental Committee)

Appointed June 1, 1970

Reported March 31, 1971

Committee Three members; Alphonse B. Gaudet (Faculty of Education, University of Moncton) chairman

Purpose To make and carry out a plan for the establishment in Southwestern Nova Scotia of a post-secondary bilingual community college.

Conclusions/Recommendations

That a Bilingual Community College be established at a place in Southwestern Nova Scotia to meet the needs of both Francophone and Anglophone students in the tri-county area: Shelburne-Digby-Yarmouth;

That the Programs of the Bilingual Community College include courses for both degree and non-degree requirements;

That the Administration and Personnel of the Bilingual Community College be functionally bilingual;

That Anglophone and Francophone students integrate at least one-third of their courses in the other official language for degree or non-degree requirements;

That a strong French Department be established at the Nova Scotia Bilingual Community College, in liaison with department of education officials, with responsibilities for curriculum revision in the teaching of French, particularly in French Acadian schools;

That the establishment of the Bilingual Community College in Southwest Nova Scotia in its Philosophy, Programs, and

Site Requirements be determined, once and for all, on the basis of Southwestern Nova Scotia community needs and not 'through, by and for' political expediency.

References

Nova Scotia, *Nova Scotia Bilingual Community College: Report of the Community College Planning Commission,* March 1971.

35 ROYAL COMMISSION ON EDUCATION, PUBLIC SERVICES AND PROVINCIAL-MUNICIPAL RELATIONS
(General Commission)

Appointed — March 31, 1971

Reported — June 27, 1974

Commission — Three members; John F. Graham (former Head, Department of Economics, Dalhousie University) chairman

Purpose — To inquire generally into the provision of education and other public services in the Province of Nova Scotia.

Conclusions/Recommendations

That the Education Act define the general goals of education for the schools of Nova Scotia

1) to develop competence in effective communication, particularly through language, in accordance with standards established by the province;

2) to develop competence in basic arithmetic and understanding of the basic principles of mathematics, in accordance with standards established by the province;

3) to develop the practice and methods of critical and disciplined thinking;

4) to provide in school programs and activities

opportunities for students:

a) to express and exercise originality and imagination;

b) to develop civic, social, and moral responsibility and judgement;

c) to have their curiosity encouraged and to develop knowledge and understanding of themselves, their fellowmen, their environment, and the relationship among the three;

d) to acquire habits, attitudes, and intellectual skills that will be helpful in employment and in training for employment.

References

Nova Scotia, *Royal Commission on Education, Public Services and Provincial-Municipal Relations; Volume I, Summary and Recommendations*, 1974.

36 COMMITTEE ON PRE-SCHOOL EDUCATION AND SOCIAL DEVELOPMENT PROGRAMS
(Departmental Committee)

Appointed August 16, 1973

Reported May, 1974

Committee Seven members; G.W. MacKenzie (Director of Inspection Services) chairman

Purpose To examine the training and teaching patterns being followed in the various pre-school programs; to determine whether or not common standards of practice should be developed in these pre-school programs; and to examine means by which the easy transfer of children from pre-school classes, Day-Care and Head Start Programs into the regular school situation could be facilitated.

Conclusions/Recommendations

That the age at which school boards in Nova Scotia are required to accept children in school be reduced by one year, from the present five years on October 1 of the school-year to four years on October 1 of the school-year;

That the lower age limit for compulsory attendance at school in Nova Scotia be reduced from six years to five years;

That the cost of educating the four-year old pupils be included in the Foundation Program of Education and thus be a shareable cost between school boards and the Department of Education under the Foundation Program cost-sharing formula.

References

Nova Scotia, *Report of the Committee on Pre-School Education and Social Development Programs*, May 1974.

37 FEDERAL-PROVINCIAL STUDY OF EDUCATIONAL TECHNOLOGY IN NOVA SCOTIA
(Departmental Committee)

Appointed March 6, 1974

Reported 1975 [to Deputy Minister Responsible for Communications and to Department of Education]

Committee Five members; Gaylen A. Duncan (Coordinator of Communications Policy, Province of Nova Scotia) chairman

Purpose To examine educational technology to identify principles and procedures which could lead to enhancing the educational process in the Province of Nova Scotia through the cost-effective application of educational technology.

Conclusions/Recommendations

That the Minister of Education assert the principle of the provision, by the Department of Education, of basic supportive services related to educational technology in order to meet present and anticipated needs throughout the province;

That the Minister of Education assert, as a principle, the integration and coordination of existing departmental programs and activities;

That by March 31, 1977, the Nova Scotia Minister of Education implement minimum levels of materials, equipment and facilities, and resolve issues related to copyright and distribution;

That the Nova Scotia Minister of Education and the Nova Scotia Minister Responsible for Communications agree, subject to the development of an acceptable work plan, to undertake Phase II of the Educational Technology Program for Nova Scotia, until June 30, 1977.

References

Nova Scotia, *Educational Technology Program for Nova Scotia: Initial Phase*, 1975.

38 SELECT COMMITTEE ON EDUCATION, PUBLIC SERVICES AND PROVINCIAL-MUNICIPAL RELATIONS
(Legislative Committee)

Appointed June 28, 1974

Reported June, 1975

Committee Eight members; Fraser Mooney (Minister of Municipal Affairs) chairman

Purpose To consider and to report upon Education, Public Services and Provincial-Municipal Relations, with particular reference to the Report of the Royal Commission on Education,

Public Services and Provincial-Municipal Relations tabled in the House on 27 June, 1974.

Conclusions/Recommendations

That the Royal Commission recommendation that Nova Scotia be divided into 11 new municipalities called counties, each covering both urban and rural areas, be considered unacceptable;

That there is, understandably, widespread support for the recommendation of the Royal Commission that the general services of education, including libraries, health, social services and housing, administration of justice and certain transportation services should be provided and financed entirely by the Province;

That there appears to be no consensus on the recommendations of the Royal Commission in regard to education.

References

Nova Scotia, *Report of the Select Committee of the House of Assembly on Education, Public Services and Provincial-Municipal Relations*, June, 1975.

39 SELECT COMMITTEE ON THE NOVA SCOTIA TECHNICAL COLLEGE ACT (Legislative Committee)

Appointed November 26, 1974

Reported 1975

Committee Seven members; Melinda MacLean (Member for Colchester) chairman

Purpose To assess the Nova Scotia Technical College Act.

Conclusions/Recommendations

That the powers of the Board of Governors of Nova Scotia

Technical College be enlarged to authorize that Board, subject to the approval of the Governor in Council, to enter into and carry out agreements with any college or university whereby the College may, for consideration or otherwise, transfer to such college or university all or any part of the undertaking, property, assets or liabilities of the College, including the College's contracts of employment with its staff and including any assets held in trust by the College provided the college or university agrees to assume such trust.

References

Nova Scotia, *Report to the House of Assembly of the Select Committee on the Nova Scotia Technical College Act*, [1975].

40 COOPERATIVE EDUCATIONAL SURVEY
(Departmental Committee)

Appointed 1976

Reported 1977

Committee Eleven members; Dorothy Walker (School Board Supervisor) coordinator

Purpose To provide an in-depth assessment of facilities, staff and services in the Kings County System after five years of amalgamation; an assessment of testing and grading practices compared provincially and/or nationally; and a comparison of results in standard projects between Kings County and the rest of Nova Scotia, or national norms over a period of at least three years.

Conclusions/Recommendations

That the Board assign or appoint a senior administrative officer who would be primarily responsible for educational programs and curriculum;

That the Board ensure that the unique needs of the junior

high student are met by providing a school program to meet the needs of *all* students at their identified ability level; providing the students with teachers who understand adolescents and respect them as individuals; and provide adequate guidance services;

That the Department of Education improve and increase its analytical research and reporting capacities;

That the Board initiate and continue as policy, meetings of teachers to discuss methodology, curricula, marking standards and pupil evaluation policies;

That the Board acquire the services of consultants in core subject areas to advise, monitor and supervise curricula and standards of academic achievement;

That the Board undertake a review of the attendance patterns and dropout rate of students;

That an official of supervisory status be appointed whose sole duties will be with continuing education for adults.

References

Nova Scotia, *Cooperative Educational Survey*, Kings County Amalgamated School Board and Department of Education, 1977.

41 ROYAL COMMISSION ON THE BOARD OF SCHOOL COMMISSIONERS FOR THE TOWN OF MULGRAVE
(Judicial Commission)

Appointed May 25, 1976

Reported November 15, 1976

Commission One member; W.E. Moseley (former Deputy Minister of Municipal Affairs)

Purpose To inquire into and concerning the manner in which the Board of School Commissioners of the Town of Mulgrave has carried out its duties and responsibilities.

Conclusions/Recommendations

That for a variety of fairly obvious reasons, no report can hope to solve the situation which the evidence has disclosed.

References

Nova Scotia, *Report of W.E. Moseley, Q.C., Commissioner, in the matter of The Board of School Commissioners for the Town of Mulgrave*, [November 1976].

PRINCE EDWARD ISLAND

42 SPECIAL COMMITTEE ON EDUCATION
(Legislative Committee)

Appointed February 7, 1834

Reported February 20, 1834

Committee Six members; George Dalrymple (Member for Queen's County) chairman

Purpose To report their opinion as to the expediency of renewing or amending the Act of 11th Geo. 4th, Cap. 3, for the Establishment and Support of Schools.

Conclusions/Recommendations

That an improved System of Education is the most effectual means for preventing crimes and promoting the welfare of the community;

That too much attention cannot be bestowed to insure the selection of persons duly qualified to instruct the young and form their morals as it has been invariably felt and acknowledged that the expectations of the framers of the present School Act have been in too many instances defeated by the appointment of improper and incompetent persons to the District Schools.

References

Prince Edward Island, *Journal of the House of Assembly of*

Prince Edward Island / 41

Prince Edward Island, 1834.

43 SPECIAL COMMITTEE ON EDUCATION
(Legislative Committee)

<u>Appointed</u> March 28, 1839

<u>Reported</u> March 9, 1840

<u>Committee</u> Twelve members; A. Rae (Member for Prince County) chairman

<u>Purpose</u> To acquire information during the Recess, touching such amendments as it may be expedient to make to the Act for the encouragement and support of District and other Schools.

<u>Conclusions/Recommendations</u>

That at all times the expense of instructing youth in the higher branches must, in the counties, chiefly devolve on the parents whose children are expected to be enabled thereby to reap in after years emolument and honour -- and that in the meantime the whole of the public money that can be spared from the Treasury for educational purposes should be devoted to the establishment of common schools.

<u>References</u>

Prince Edward Island, *Journals*, 1840, App. K.

44 JOINT COMMITTEE OF COUNCIL AND ASSEMBLY ON EDUCATION
(Legislative Committee)

<u>Appointed</u> February 8 (Council) and February 10 (Assembly), 1842

<u>Reported</u> February 26, 1842

<u>Committee</u> Three members from Council, six from Assembly;

D. MacDonald, (Member for King's County) chairman

Purpose — To examine into and report upon the state of the Central Academy, and upon general education.

Conclusions/Recommendations

That the moneys arising from the sale of school land endowments be invested in the public Treasury of the Colony, and that the annual legal interest arising therefrom be applied to the gratuitous instructions in the District Schools of the children of the destitute poor, under the direction of the Legislature of the Colony.

References

Prince Edward Island, *Journals*, 1842.

45 SPECIAL COMMITTEE TO ENQUIRE INTO THE EXPEDIENCY OF MAKING EDUCATION FREE THROUGHOUT THE ISLAND
(Legislative Committee)

Appointed — April 26, 1851

Reported — February 16, 1852

Committee — Twelve members; G. Coles (Member for Queen's County) chairman

Purpose — To enquire into the expediency of making education free throughout the Island.

Conclusions/Recommendations

That unless School Masters' salaries are wholly paid by the Government, and a system of Free Education established, many settlements will not be able to reap the benefits of Education for the rising generation under the present system.

References

Prince Edward Island, *Journals*, 1852.

46 COMMISSION TO INVESTIGATE THE CASES OF TEACHERS WHOSE SALARIES WERE IN DISPUTE
(Judicial Commission)

Appointed January 25, 1873

Reported March 13, 1873

Commission Three members; Peter Sinclair (Member of Prince Edward Island Executive Council) chairman

Purpose To enquire into the cases of teachers whose salaries have been intercepted by the late Secretary of the Board of Education and to report the facts connected with each case to the Government.

Conclusions/Recommendations

That upon the Secretary of the Board of Education depends, to a very great extent, the efficiency of the whole Free System of Education;

That the present salary is a very inadequate one and the services of a competent man are not likely to be had or retained for such an insignificant sum.

References

Prince Edward Island, *Journals*, 1873, App. T.

47 SPECIAL LEGISLATIVE COMMITTEE TO INVESTIGATE THE WORKINGS OF THE EDUCATION LAW
(Legislative Committee)

Appointed April 24, 1876

Reported April 29, 1876

Committee Five members; Louis H. Davies (Member for King's County) chairman

Purpose To investigate the workings of the Education Law.

Conclusions/Recommendations

That the Board of Education, as at present constituted, does not seem able, either to grapple with and remedy the evils or difficulties of the educational system of the Colony, or effectively to carry out the existing Law.

References

Prince Edward Island, *Journals*, 1876, App. AA.

48 ROYAL COMMISSION ON EDUCATION
(General Commission)

Appointed October 15, 1908

Reported February 14, 1910

Commission Three members; Duncan C. McLeod (King's Counsel, Charlottetown) chairman

Purpose Generally to deal with the whole matter of education in the Province.

Conclusions/Recommendations

That the schools of the Province be consolidated;

That Nature Study and Agriculture be given a considerable place in the school course;

That the new set of Readers published in Ontario be adopted;

That there be conscientious choosing and screening of

teachers;

That inspectors be of a very high calibre.

References

Prince Edward Island, *Report of the Committee on Education*, 1910.

49 ROYAL COMMISSION ON EDUCATION
(General Commission)

Appointed July 25, 1929

Reported December 31, 1929

Commission Three members; Cyrus J. MacMillan (Chairman, Department of English, McGill University) chairman

Purpose To examine and report upon the subjects relating to the consolidation of schools; the condition under which licenses are to be obtained; the question of promotion for long and distinguished service of teachers; pensions, salaries and proper means of providing for increase of same; the best text books and their costs; the underlying cause or causes of the large number of failures by students at the entrance examinations to Prince of Wales College and after admission thereto; and other matters respecting education.

Conclusions/Recommendations

That the administrative machinery of the Department of Education be completely reorganized in order to provide greater stability and continuity of policy, and to remove it from the vicissitudes of party;

That consolidation be effected and that instruction in grades nine and ten in one-roomed schools be discontinued as soon as possible;

That in an attempt to stem the drift to towns the programme of studies in the upper grades of the rural schools be reorganized to include optional courses in agriculture, elementary mechanics and bookkeeping;

That school buildings be at least fit for children to live and work in for a large part of the day;

That the role of the inspector be broadened to include constructive supervision as well as critical inspection;

That certain teachers of experience and proved efficiency act as travelling instructors or demonstrators to aid the beginning teachers;

That the granting of teaching permits to academically unqualified persons be wholly discontinued, and third-class licenses be abolished;

That in the interests of contentment and stability, teachers receive a living salary;

That the Board of Education and the Teachers Federation should formulate a plan to provide pensions.

References

Prince Edward Island, 'Report of the Royal Commission on Education', *Journals*, 1930, App. J.

50 COMMISSION ON SCHOOL DIVISION NO. 1
(Judicial Commission)

Appointed April 7, 1955

Reported July 12, 1955

Commission Three members; Walter E. Darby (Judge of Prince County Court) chairman

Purpose To investigate the dissatisfaction felt by

some ratepayers in School District No. 1 regarding consolidation.

Conclusions/Recommendations

That whereas the larger unit of school administration is providing much better educational facilities, a higher standard of academic training, and a better qualified teaching staff, School Division No. 1 should not be broken up, nor should any school district within the Division be permitted to withdraw;

That before any new Divisions are formed, considerable study should be devoted to laying a proper foundation so that an harmonious and working administration will result.

References

Prince Edward Island, 'Report of the Committee on School Division No. 1', 1955.

51 SELECT STANDING COMMITTEE ON EDUCATION
(Legislative Committee)

Appointed February 22, 1956

Reported March 14, 1956

Committee Five members; J. George MacKay (Member for Prince County) chairman

Purpose To consider problems in education generally, and in particular to give careful consideration to the problem of School District No. 1.

Conclusions/Recommendations

That School District Number 1 be broken up in conformity with the wishes of the people as expressed in the plebiscite.

References

Prince Edward Island, *Journals*, 1956.

52 SELECT STANDING COMMITTEE ON EDUCATION
(Legislative Committee)

Appointed March 13, 1957

Reported April 16, 1957

Committee Nine members; Frederic A. Large (Member for Queen's County) chairman

Purpose To hear representations from persons interested in presenting their ideas and opinions for educational change.

Conclusions/Recommendations

That a Government policy encouraging school districts to unite voluntarily into larger administrative units be undertaken;

That grades 9 and 10 be removed from one-room rural schools and channelled to regional high schools which are desperately needed;

That without losing sight of the fundamentals, a more diversified curriculum be presented;

That standards for admission to teacher training be raised with Grade 12 the minimum;

That a teachers' salary scale recognizing qualifications and experience be put into operation;

That because of the enormous power wielded by the Minister of Education, there be a return to the principle of a Board of Education;

That federal aid be sought for financing, and that local communities be expected to assume a fair share of the costs.

References

Prince Edward Island, 'Report of the Select Standing Committee on Education of the Legislative Assembly of Prince Edward Island', 1957.

53 SELECT STANDING COMMITTEE ON EDUCATION
(Legislative Committee)

Appointed March 12, 1958

Reported April 11, 1958

Committee Seven members; Morley M. Bell (Member for Prince County) chairman

Purpose To consider problems in education generally.

Conclusions/Recommendations

That satisfaction be expressed at the manner in which the recommendations of the Select Committee on Education of the 1957 Session of the Legislature have been implemented.

References

Prince Edward Island, *Journals*, 1958.

54 ROYAL COMMISSION ON EDUCATIONAL FINANCE AND RELATED PROBLEMS IN ADMINISTRATION
(General Commission)

Appointed October 15, 1959

Reported April, 1960

Commission One member; Melton Ezra La Zerte (former Dean of Education, University of Alberta)

Purpose To enquire into all matters relating to the administration and the financial support of schools established and operated under The Education Act and The School Act of the Province, the relative tax paying ability of the Province in comparison with that of the other provinces of Canada, and the financial problems in the training of teachers.

Conclusions/Recommendations

That Prince Edward Island adopt principles currently shaping educational practice in most Canadian provinces; including a foundation program, equal educational opportunity, and equality of responsibility for the support of elementary and secondary education;

That a larger percentage of the net general expenditure of the Province be spent annually on education;

That a foundation program supported by provincial grants and uniform local taxation be prescribed for the Province;

That local school boards be urged to form consolidated school districts;

That a minimum salary schedule be prescribed with increments based on qualifications and experience;

That diversified programs at secondary school level be available in the five composite schools;

That minimum requirements for teacher training be senior matriculation plus the completion of a two-year program of academic and professional subjects.

References

Prince Edward Island, *Report of the Commissioner on Educational Finance and Related Problems in Administration*, 1960.

55 ROYAL COMMISSION ON HIGHER EDUCATION
(General Commission)

Appointed July 9, 1964

Reported January 20, 1965

Commission Three members; J. Sutherland Bonnell (Presbyterian Minister) chairman

Purpose To make full inquiry and to indicate how the future requirements of the Province in the field of higher education may best be met and the available resources used in the most efficient manner.

Conclusions/Recommendations

That the provincial allocation of funds at the university level be increased;

That Prince of Wales College be made a degree granting institution at once;

That Grade 12 be established as the standard university entrance requirement;

That the Provincial Government cooperate in the federation of St. Dunstan's and Prince of Wales by the establishment of a University of Prince Edward Island with two colleges as components.

References

Prince Edward Island, *Report of the Royal Commission on Higher Education for Prince Edward Island*, 1965.

56 PROVINCE OF PRINCE EDWARD ISLAND: PROVINCIAL-MUNICIPAL FISCAL STUDY
(Special Committee)

Appointed September 12, 1968

Reported August, 1969 [to Provincial Treasurer]

Committee Touche, Ross, Bailey & Smart (Chartered

Accountants)

Purpose — To carry out a study of provincial and municipal taxation in Prince Edward Island.

Conclusions/Recommendations

That the major unit of local government in Prince Edward Island has been the school board, not the municipality;

That outside of Charlottetown and Summerside the School Act has provided not only for the levying of taxes but also for their assessment;

That the province now introduce a foundations program of public school education which would establish overall standards for such items as teachers' salaries, maintenance of school buildings, etc., for the entire Island (including Charlottetown and Summerside);

That the province assume the full cost of the financing of the public school foundation program;

That the province enter the real property tax field in order to assist it in the financing of the public school foundation program;

That the province continue its present policy of financing two-thirds of the cost of public school education from general revenues; the remaining one-third to come from a new province-wide uniform education rate on real property.

References

Prince Edward Island, *Province of Prince Edward Island: Provincial-Municipal Fiscal Study*, 1969.

57 COMMITTEE ON TEACHER EDUCATION IN PRINCE EDWARD ISLAND (Special Committee)

Appointed — April 16, 1970

Reported — April, 1971

Committee — Four members; Verner Smitheram (Department of Philosophy, University of P.E.I.) chairman

Purpose — To consider the current development of teacher education programs in Canada; the structure, objectives, principles and graduate study for teacher education at the University of P.E.I.; the local needs of teachers and problems of teacher training; the relation between the Faculty of Education and other departments in the University; the relationship between the Faculty of Education and external bodies such as the school system, the Atlantic Institute of Education, the Provincial Department of Education, the Teachers' Federation and the Association of School Trustees; and the professional status of elementary and secondary school teachers.

Conclusions/Recommendations

[Among the 91 recommendations were the following:]

That all teachers now entering the profession undertake a university program of studies leading to a baccalaureate degree;

That procedures for the upgrading of practicing teachers to degree level be established;

That Education students be required to meet the same or higher academic standards as students in other Faculties;

That elementary and secondary school teachers be recognized as peers, and that this be reflected in their preparatory programs, responsibilities, and pay;

That affiliation with the Atlantic Institute of Education be undertaken immediately so that graduate courses could be offered in P.E.I., research in education relevant to the Province could be coordinated, and U.P.E.I. have access to educational specialists.

References

Prince Edward Island / 54

University of Prince Edward Island, *Teacher Education: Perseverance or Professionalism*, 1971.

58 EVALUATION OF ELEMENTARY AND SECONDARY EDUCATION IN PRINCE EDWARD ISLAND
(Departmental Committee)

Appointed 1973

Reported 1974 [to Department of Development]

Committee Two members; Verner Smitheram (Department of Philosophy, University of P.E.I.) chairman

Purpose To evaluate elementary and secondary education in Prince Edward Island from 1969 to 1973.

Conclusions/Recommendations

That the general policy of school consolidation be pursued to full implementation;

That special measures be established to ensure that the educational opportunities of disadvantaged children are improved to the same degree as those of other types of children;

That a decentralized organization for curriculum design and development engaging the collaboration of all school interested persons be instituted as soon as possible;

That wherever possible, learning opportunities be organized to permit each individual to progress at his own rate rather than at a group rate;

That evaluation be continuous rather than periodic and the use of self-evaluation procedures be maximized.

References

Prince Edward Island, *An Evaluation of Elementary and Secondary Education in Prince Edward Island*, vol. I & II, [1974].

NEW BRUNSWICK

59 COMMITTEE ON EDUCATION
(Legislative Committee)

Appointed January 9, 1837

Reported February 14, 1837

Committee Five members; John A. Street (Member for Northumberland) chairman

Purpose To inquire into the Grammer School system in the Province.

Conclusions/Recommendations

That having taken the subject matter of these Petitions into their most serious consideration, the Committee cannot at present recommend the adoption of public assessments as a mode of supporting Grammar or other Schools.

References

New Brunswick, *Journal of the House of Assembly of New Brunswick*, 1837.

60 COMMITTEE ON EDUCATION
(Legislative Committee)

Appointed January 31, 1842

Reported March 31, 1842

Committee Twelve members; L.A. Wilmot (Member for York) chairman

Purpose To consider all matters brought before the House connected with the subject of Education throughout the Province.

Conclusions/Recommendations

That the present voluntary and therefore uncertain mode of local contribution for the support of Teachers and the erection of School Houses not be permitted to continue longer;

That he who has property and no children should be compelled to contribute towards the education of the children of those who may have no property.

References

New Brunswick, *Journals*, 1842.

61 GOVERNOR COLEBROOK'S ELABORATE INQUIRY INTO EDUCATION (Special Committee)

Appointed 1844

Reported February, 1845

Committee Three members; James Brown (Inspector of Schools) chairman

Purpose To inquire into the present condition and future improvement of the Parish Schools.

Conclusions/Recommendations

That the most effectual remedy for the evils arising from the apathy and backwardness of the people and the scanty and irregular attendance of the children will be the diffusion of information on the object and power of education.

References

New Brunswick, *Journals*, 1845.

62 SELECT COMMITTEE ON EDUCATION
(Legislative Committee)

Appointed February 3, 1845

Reported April 12, 1845

Committee Seven members; Lemuel Wilmot (Member for York) chairman

Purpose To report by Bill or otherwise on matters in His Excellency's Speech which relate to the Education of Youth.

Conclusions/Recommendations

That the Committee are deeply impressed with the importance of this great subject and hope that the Legislature will be prepared at the next Session to adopt such improvements in the present system as will carry with them the approbation and support of the country, and at the same time ensure those Educational advantages which are in a great measure denied by the present defective system.

References

New Brunswick, *Journals*, 1845.

63 ROYAL COMMISSION ON KING'S COLLEGE
(General Commission)

Appointed May 1, 1854

Reported December 28, 1854

Commission — Five members; John Hamilton Gray (Queen's Counsel) chairman

Purpose — To inquire into the present state of King's College, its management and utility, with the view of improving the same and rendering that Institution more generally useful, and of suggesting the best mode of effecting that desirable object.

Conclusions/Recommendations

That the system of Collegiate Education be at once comprehensive, special, and practical; that it ought to embrace those branches of learning which are usually taught in Colleges both in Great Britain and the United States -- and special courses of instruction adapted to the agricultural, mechanical, manufacturing, and commercial pursuits and interests of New Brunswick; and that the subjects and modes of instruction in science and the modern languages (including English, French, and German) should have practical reference to those pursuits and interests;

That the idea of abolishing or suspending the Endowment of King's College should not be entertained for a moment;

That a non-denominational plan with facilities for each persuasion to give weekly religious instruction be adopted;

That a provincial body under the style and title of 'The University of New Brunswick' be established.

References

New Brunswick, *Journals*, 1854.

New Brunswick, *Report of the Commission appointed under the Act of Assembly relating to King's College*, 1855.

64 COMMISSION OF INQUIRY INTO THE CONDUCT AND MANAGEMENT OF THE INSTITUTION FOR THE DEAF AND DUMB, FREDERICTON

(Judicial Commission)

Appointed   May 7, 1886

Reported   July 8, 1886

Commission   One member; James Mitchell (Surveyor General of New Brunswick)

Purpose   To inquire into the circumstances connected with the alleged misconduct and mismanagement at the Institution for the Deaf and Dumb, Fredericton.

Conclusions/Recommendations

That no grounds exist for the grave charges which have been made.

References

New Brunswick, *Journals*, 1887, Supplementary Appendix.

65 COMMISSION OF INQUIRY INTO CHARGES RELATING TO THE BATHURST SCHOOLS AND OTHER SCHOOLS IN GLOUCESTER COUNTY (General Commission)

Appointed   April 18, 1893

Reported   November 23, 1893

Commission   One member; John James Fraser (Supreme Court Justice)

Purpose   To inquire into and fully and thoroughly investigate any alleged infractions of the Law or Regulations on the part of the Teachers or Trustees in the Bathurst schools and other schools in Gloucester County.

Conclusions/Recommendations

That all sorts and kinds of irregularities may occur in the

carrying on of the schools in any county, but unless they are brought to the notice of the Inspector of Schools for the county, and through him to the notice of the Board of Education itself, it would be manifestly unjust to charge the Board of Education with any dereliction of duty in regard to such irregularities.

References

New Brunswick, *Journals*, 1893.

New Brunswick, *Report upon Changes Relating to the Bathurst Schools and Other Schools in Gloucester County*, 1894.

66 COMMISSION IN RESPECT TO THE SALARIES OF TEACHERS IN THE PUBLIC SCHOOLS OF THE PROVINCE
(General Commission)

Appointed April 17, 1919

Reported March 19, 1920

Commission Five members; W.S. Carter (Chief Superintendent of Education)

Purpose To take into consideration and make recommendations as to the best means to provide increased salaries for teachers in the public schools of the Province.

Conclusions/Recommendations

That the County Fund tax be doubled and a sliding scale instituted to give needy districts more assistance;

That the minimum salary, including Government grants, to be paid in the poorest districts be $500 per year; in the middle districts, $600; and in the more prosperous districts, $700;

That the Board of Education withhold County and Provincial Grants from trustees who engaged teachers at lower than the proposed minimum salaries;

That teachers who accepted less than the minimum be suspended for a designated period.

References

New Brunswick, *Acts of the Legislative Assembly of New Brunswick*, 9 George V., 1919, CAP. XXXIII.

New Brunswick, *Journals*, 1920, Supplementary Appendix.

67 ROYAL COMMISSION ON EDUCATION
(General Commission)

Appointed May 15, 1931

Reported March 1, 1932

Commission Twenty-two members; A.S. McFarland (Chief Superintendent of Education) chairman

Purpose To investigate the Educational system of the Province and particularly to consider: (a) the administration in co-operation of (i) common school, (ii) agricultural and (iii) vocational education; and (b) the method of raising money for the support of schools together with the area of school districts with a view to approximate equalization of school rates and especially to giving greater assistance to poor districts; (c) the relation of all branches of education in common, agricultural schools, vocational schools, to the universities in the Province, (d) such other subjects in relation thereto as the Council shall deem cognate to the inquiry.

Conclusions/Recommendations

That there be one central Board of Education to control all branches of education, including academic, vocational, agricultural education, and physical training if this could be done without additional cost;

That Third Class temporary teaching licenses be abolished and entrance requirements for Second Class training be raised to Grade Eleven within three years;

That more professional training and practice teaching with observation and criticism be given;

That entrance requirements for First Class be full High School with good standing;

That since 140,000 of New Brunswick's 408,000 people are of French origin, Normal Schools meet the increasing demand for teachers who can teach both English and French;

That a system of Helping Teachers similar to that already operating in Nova Scotia be introduced;

That a Provincial Tax Commission be appointed to insure equalization of assessment and educational taxes;

That a minimum standard of school service and a suitable schedule of minimum salaries be set up;

That the present County Grammar Schools and Parish Superior Schools be replaced by a system of High Schools;

That the Grammar School Course be maintained for those desiring matriculation but a modified programme be introduced;

That in order to improve the means of communication between the English and French races and provide a more sympathetic understanding of each other, book teachings in the first two grades be exclusively in the native language of the child, and special editions of text-books be made available up to grade eight with the two-languages on opposite pages.

References

New Brunswick, *Report of the Committee on Education for the Province of New Brunswick*, 1932.

(Special Committee)

Appointed 1937

Reported 1937

Committee Three members; William A. Plenderleith (British Columbia School Inspector) chairman

Purpose To survey the methods of administering and financing education in New Brunswick and to make suggestions.

Conclusions/Recommendations

That an immediate improvement be made in rural school conditions by following certain specific suggestions;

That greater financial responsibility for rural education be undertaken by the Provincial Government;

That a re-organization of the administrative system be undertaken.

References

New Brunswick, *The Plenderleith Report*, 1937.

69 COMMITTEE ON CURRICULUM AND TEXT BOOKS
(Departmental Committee)

Appointed February 12, 1937

Reported [Created as a standing committee]

Committee Fourteen members; Fletcher Peacock (Director, Educational Services) chairman

Purpose To make an exhaustive study of advances in science and educational methods as well as the requirements of a constantly changing social order and to recommend a suitable programme of studies.

Conclusions/Recommendations

References

New Brunswick, 'Report of the Director of Educational Services', 1937.

70 ROYAL COMMISSION ON THE FINANCING OF SCHOOLS IN NEW BRUNSWICK
(General Commission)

Appointed September 11, 1953

Reported January 26, 1955

Commission Three members; William Havelock McKenzie (Superintendent of Schools) chairman

Purpose To inquire into all matters proper to be considered for the disposition of government grants made available to and administered through the several school administrative units of the Province and the relative tax paying ability of the Province in comparison with that of the other provinces of Canada.

Conclusions/Recommendations

That the Federal Government participate, directly or indirectly, in the financial support of the public schools of New Brunswick, but in such manner, and only in such manner, that the provincial government retains its full control over the system; and further, that this participation be on the basis of fiscal need.

References

New Brunswick, *Report of the Royal Commission on the Financing of Schools in New Brunswick*, 1955.

71 ROYAL COMMISSION ON HIGHER EDUCATION IN NEW BRUNSWICK (General Commission)

Appointed May 9, 1961

Reported June 21, 1962

Commission Three members; John J. Deutsch (Vice-Principal, Queen's University) chairman

Purpose To make full inquiry and to make findings and recommendations consistent with the public interest and the general welfare of the Province of New Brunswick respecting the whole field of higher education, and to indicate how the future requirements of the Province may best be met by the various institutions, and the role which the said institutions should play in meeting those requirements so that the available resources of the Province can be used in the most efficient manner.

Conclusions/Recommendations

That there be only two degree-granting institutions in the province, one French-speaking and one English;

That the Legislative Assembly grant a charter to establish the University of Moncton as the sole degree-granting French-language institution of higher education in New Brunswick;

That to this institution, St. Joseph's, Sacred Heart, and St. Louis be affiliated for academic purposes but retain their own administrative autonomy;

That St. Thomas University be federated with the University of New Brunswick and transfer its operations to the Fredericton campus;

That a permanent branch of the University of New Brunswick be established in the Metropolitan Saint John area;

That Mount Allison continue its announced policy of remaining a liberal arts college of limited enrolment;

That no new degree-granting institutions be established in the province.

References

New Brunswick, *Report of the Royal Commission on Higher Education in New Brunswick*, 1962.

72 ROYAL COMMISSION ON FINANCE AND MUNICIPAL TAXATION (Related Commission)

Appointed	March 8, 1962
Reported	November 4, 1963
Commission	Five members; E.G. Byrne (Queen's Counsel, Bathurst) chairman
Purpose	To hold inquiry into and concerning the desirability and feasibility of maintaining or increasing the present revenues of municipal bodies, and relieving individuals and industry of some part of municipal tax burdens by the sbustitution or creation of new or other sources of revenue or bases of taxation.

Conclusions/Recommendations

That the Provincial Government assume full responsibility for administering and financing a uniform programme of elementary and secondary education, both academic and vocational;

That the province be reorganized into about sixty school districts, each with at least one central high school and with a number of feeder elementary and junior high schools;

That part of the costs be raised by a uniform provincially

imposed tax on an equally-assessed real property tax;

That a uniform salary scale be established for teachers, based at first on the high Saint John scale; and there be no more negotiation of salaries at the local level;

That adequate account be taken of the two main linguistic and cultural groups in New Brunswick, recognizing at the same time the essential unity of the educational aims of the two groups in a modern industrial society.

References

New Brunswick, *Report of the Royal Commission on Finance and Municipal Taxation in New Brunswick*, 1963.

73 ROYAL COMMISSION ON METROPOLITAN SAINT JOHN
(Related Commission)

Appointed — May 29, 1962

Reported — July 10, 1963

Commission — One member; H. Carl Goldenberg (Barrister of Montreal)

Purpose — To inquire into the form, method and manner of municipal government now existing in any of the units located in the County of Saint John, the feasibility of amalgamation, and the feasibility of alteration of boundaries.

Conclusions/Recommendations

That legislation be enacted to consolidate all school administration within the County of Saint John under a County Board of School Trustees, which shall be responsible for all public education in Grades 1 to 13;

That the Board of School Trustees be appointed, and that it be composed of twelve members, of whom four, including the chairman, shall be appointed by the Provincial Government, and eight by the Common Council, and that their term of office be three years, subject to re-appointment.

References

New Brunswick, *Report of the Royal Commission in Metropolitan Saint John,* [1963].

74 COMMITTEE ON THE FINANCING OF HIGHER EDUCATION IN NEW BRUNSWICK
(Departmental Committee)

Appointed February 9, 1966

Reported February, 1967

Committee Three members; John J. Deutsch (Vice-Principal, Queen's University) chairman

Purpose To study, in consultation with the universities of the Province and with due regard to the Province's resources, and to make recommendations to the government regarding the types and amounts of assistance to be required by both institutions and students, and to consider and report upon other related matters. [The Report was submitted to the Lieutenant-Governor in Council as a follow-up to the 1964 report of the Royal Commission on Higher Education.]

Conclusions/Recommendations

That further change must be made in the administrative structure of the University of Moncton in order to be equipped to meet successfully its growing responsibilities for providing advanced, specialized and professional education for the Province's French-speaking population;

That provision of adequate facilities for the Saint John branch of the University of New Brunswick needs to be accelerated;

That a permanent Commission on Post-Secondary Education should be established immediately which would have a continuing responsibility for advising the government on the needs and the appropriate pattern for future development.

References

New Brunswick, *Report of the Committee on the Financing of Higher Education in New Brunswick*, 1967.

75 STUDY OF TEACHER EDUCATION AND TRAINING
(Special Committee)

Appointed January 4, 1968

Reported 1969

Committee One member; Donald C. Duffie (President, St. Thomas University)

Purpose To consider the present and future roles of universities, teachers' colleges and other institutions in meeting the Province's needs in the field of teacher education and training; to assess the adequacy of the relationship and the forms of cooperative effort which now exist among the universities, teachers' colleges and other institutions concerned; and to recommend whatever changes may be required.

Conclusions/Recommendations

That Teacher Training be integrated into Higher Education, given over to the universities, and placed under the Higher Education Commission;

That admission requirements for candidates for teacher training be those of the university;

That there be a continuing selection of candidates for

teacher training;

That curriculum be developed by the university, without prejudice to certification;

That appointment of staff in education be made by the university;

That 'elementary' and 'secondary' teacher training be given in one and the same faculty of education;

That the faculty of education should be subject to the same academic procedures as other faculties of the university;

That practice teaching should be examined and expanded;

That the minimum program for those intending to teach academic subjects in high school should be five years beyond Junior Matriculation;

That the present minimum two year teacher training program for 'elementary' teachers should be increased to a minimum of three and later four years in university.

References

New Brunswick Higher Education Commission, *Teacher Education and Training: A Report*, 1969.

76 A STUDY OF HIGHER EDUCATION IN THE ATLANTIC PROVINCES FOR THE 1970's
(Special Committee)

Appointed 1969

Reported December, 1969

Committee Three members; John F. Crean, Michael M. Ferguson, Hugh J. Somers [no chairman designated]

Purpose To study the present state of higher education

in the three Maritime Provinces and its future prospects; and to assess existing forms of cooperative endeavour and new forms that may be required.

Conclusions/Recommendations

That universities and governments of the Atlantic Provinces plan to provide the numbers of university places that will be sought by students as indicated by increasing enrolments and that adequate financial support be provided;

That governments act with due respect for the autonomy and freedom necessary to the institutions of higher learning;

That the universities give the highest priority to the implementation of their agreement in regard to graduate studies and to a continued search for more effective means of cooperation and coordination in all areas of higher education;

That the public relations officers of the universities review critically their present use of the communications media, and formulate policies that would give full information on higher education to the taxpayer on whom the universities depend;

That, whether Maritime political union comes about or not, there be one university grants committee adequately staffed to serve the three provinces;

That each institution of higher education set definite targets of enrolments, not only in general but by faculties, for three to five-year periods.

References

Association of Atlantic Universities, *Higher Education in the Atlantic Provinces for the 1970's*, 1969.

[Prepared by the Association of Atlantic Universities for the Maritime Union Study]

77 TASK FORCE ON SOCIAL DEVELOPMENT AND SOCIAL WELFARE (Departmental Committee)

Appointed July, 1970

Reported September, 1971

Committee Eleven members; Emery Le Blanc (Former Editor of *L'Evangeline*) and H.L. Nutter (Dean of Christ Church Cathedral, Fredericton) co-chairmen

Purpose To initiate and promote public dialogue on problems in social development and social welfare, and on the objectives and proposed objectives of government; and to recommend broad guidelines to the Government to assist in the future development of program priorities and legislation in the field of social development and social welfare.

Conclusions/Recommendations

That the role of education be recognized as a major component of social development;

That provincial authorities accept in practice the stated principle that the purpose of public school education in New Brunswick is to 'provide educational opportunities for all educable children so that each may develop to the limit of his capacity and special abilities';

That orientation of the education system be broadened to 'preparation for living' rather than the narrower orientation of 'preparation for work' which appears predominant at present;

That in the course of teacher training programs, candidates for certification as teachers be continually assessed regarding their motivation, ability to relate to students, and potential effectiveness as teachers;

That since education must prepare a person for living, the curriculum be restructured at both the elementary and secondary levels to recognize the primary importance of instruction in social relationships and physical education; in addition, areas such as music, art, homemaking, and so on must be recognized as essential components of the educational process;

That a French-language section be created within the Department of Education, with full responsibility for the determination of the French-language curriculum, the adoption of French-language textbooks and materials, and the setting of personnel standards and equivalences in qualifications for French-speaking teachers.

References

New Brunswick, *Participation and Development: Report of the New Brunswick Task Force on Social Development*, 1971.

78 STUDY COMMITTEE ON AUXILIARY CLASSES
(Departmental Committee)

Appointed 1971

Reported 1972

Committee Nine members; G.E.M. MacLeod (Assistant Deputy Minister of Education) and Elizabeth J. Owens (Consultant in Special Education) co-chairmen

Purpose To study the present operation of Auxiliary Classes in New Brunswick; to study operational models in other provinces of Canada; to make recommendations with respect to the future operation of Auxiliary Classes and to establish and supervise pilot projects for evaluative purposes.

Conclusions/Recommendations

That the term 'trainable mentally retarded' be redefined; and that the term 'cerebral palsied persons' be replaced in the Auxiliary Classes Act with the term 'physically handicapped';

That the Auxiliary Classes Act provide for tutoring for handicapped persons upon application by the District Superintendent to the Minister;

That the Department of Social Services become the supporting agency for adult programs for the handicapped over age 18 years;

That school districts provide transportation for persons under the Auxiliary Classes Act;

That the Department of Education assume the financial responsibility for the maintenance of facilities which house Auxiliary Classes;

That the Interdepartmental Committee on Mental Retardation be charged with the immediate responsibility of investigating the cost-sharing arrangements for the handicapped with the Federal Government.

References

New Brunswick, *The Right to Choose and the Right to be Served: The Report of the Study Committee on Auxiliary Classes*, 1972.

79 COMMITTEE ON THE COMMUNITY USE OF SCHOOL FACILITIES (Departmental Committee)

Appointed December, 1971

Reported June, 1973

Committee Seven members; W.S. Ritchie (New Brunswick Department of Education) chairman

Purpose To determine, in consultation with school and municipal authorities, community groups, private agencies and the public at large, means by which school facilities may be best utilized; and to explore means whereby a closer liaison may be established between school authorities and community recreation councils, commissions, and departments, in the matter of the planning of new multi-use school-community facilities.

Conclusions/Recommendations

That all schools (public and trade) be made available for use by groups other than regularly scheduled classes;

That future schools be designed with community use in mind;

That school grounds be considered and developed as parks and/or playgrounds for use in after-school and vacation time;

That additional costs be borne 50% by the province and 50% by the local community;

That the control of facilities remain a responsibility of School Boards.

References

New Brunswick, *Report of the Committee on the Community Use of School Facilities*, 1973.

80 COMMITTEE ON SPECIAL EDUCATION
(Special Committee)

Appointed April, 1972

Reported January, 1973 [to Ministers of Education of New Brunswick, Newfoundland, Nova Scotia, and Prince Edward Island]

Committee Ten members; David Kendall (Professor of Special Education, University of B.C.) chairman

Purpose To inquire into present facilities and programs available in the Atlantic provinces for children requiring special educational consideration, with particular emphasis on those with impairment of sight and/or hearing; to recommend programs of study and training and procedures for assessment of these children; and to recommend to the governments of the Atlantic provinces further direction in this field, bearing in mind the educational systems of the four provinces.

Conclusions/Recommendations

That the governments of the Atlantic Provinces recognize and endorse the right of all handicapped persons to be educated to the maximum of their potential, and develop a comprehensive range of services and programs sufficient to meet the educational needs of all handicapped persons;

That wherever possible and practicable, handicapped persons be educated in regular public school programs, provided that the special needs of the child can be fully met through the service available in the public schools;

That the Governments, through their education systems, give priority to the establishment and development of diagnostic, remedial and special education services within the public schools at both elementary and secondary levels;

That for the purposes of educational administration the governments distinguish between two main categories of handicapped persons: (Category I: the severely handicapped, and Category II: the educationally handicapped).

References

Atlantic Provinces Report of the Special Education Committee to the Ministers of Education, January 1973.

81 COMMITTEE TO EXAMINE HUMAN RIGHTS EDUCATION IN NEW BRUNSWICK
(Departmental Committee)

Appointed March, 1973

Reported August, 1973 [to Department of Labour]

Committee — Four members; Russell A. McNeilly (Faculty of Education, University of New Brunswick) chairman

Purpose — To examine Human Rights Education in New Brunswick in particular, and other jurisdictions in general; to document the need for human rights education; to study the possibility of implementing human rights education in all segments of the school and in teacher education institutions; and to consider methods of approach in establishing human rights education.

Conclusions/Recommendations

That the Human Rights Commission of the Department of Labour along with the Department of Education form an inter-ministerial committee to examine textbooks used in the schools of the Province;

That, as soon as possible, the Human Rights Commission in co-operation with the Department of Education plan, design models and prepare guides for pilot programs on human rights education;

That summer projects utilizing a core of graduate students engage in research on the development of programs and curriculum strategies in human rights education for use in the schools;

That the Human Rights Commission consider the appointment of a part-time consultant in human rights education for the coordination of research activities and field developments;

That the Commission along with the Department of Education should organize workshops for teachers during the school year on human rights education and program planning.

References

New Brunswick, *Strategies for Human Rights Education in New Brunswick*, 1974.

82 COMMITTEE ON EDUCATIONAL PLANNING
(Departmental Committee)

Appointed March, 1973

Reported November 2, 1973

Committee Fifteen members; G.E. Malcolm MacLeod (Assistant Deputy Minister of Education) and Arthur A. Pinet (Regional Superintendent of Schools) co-chairmen

Purpose To review objectively the complete educational system in New Brunswick today and the role of the Department of Education.

Conclusions/Recommendations

That a selective pre-school education program be developed which would assure the readiness of all pupils to cope with and benefit from the basic program of the elementary school;

That a minimum of six years be recommended for the completion of the elementary school program while making provision for the gifted child;

That the philosophy of continuous progress be implemented in the junior high school;

That research be conducted regarding the effectiveness of the three-year junior high school as compared to other types of organization such as the middle school;

That a study be carried out immediately to evaluate the current junior and senior high summer school programs;

That second languages be taught by specialists;

That the Department at this time not adopt the policy of implementing immersion programs throughout the Province, but it be prepared to encourage such programs and offer assistance wherever possible;

That art, music, and physical education be studied with a

view to providing them with the same status as other parts of the basic program;

That the Department of Education assume the financial responsibility for the education of all special education children;

That the Department move towards a gradual decentralization of curriculum development;

That the Department of Education establish area resource centres.

References

New Brunswick, *Education Tomorrow: Report of the Minister's Committee on Educational Planning*, 1973.

83 TASK FORCE FOR KINDERGARTEN DESIGN
(Departmental Committee)

Appointed	June, 1974
Reported	December 20, 1974
Committee	Ten members; Cheryl C. Smith (Consultant, Department of Education) Anglophone chairman, and Rose Marie Roy (Consultant, Department of Education) Francophone chairman
Purpose	To propose a program which is not only viable for the province of New Brunswick but which also reflects a thorough study of the best in current research and practice within the field of early childhood education.

Conclusions/Recommendations

That the program have the three following basic characteristics;

That it provide rich and varied learning experiences for children;

That it be staffed by caring, informed and trained adults;

That it provide a physical environment which is safe as well as attractive and which promotes learning and healthy development.

References

New Brunswick, *Learning in the Play Environment: Report of the Minister's Task Force for Kindergarten Design (Anglophone)* and 'Vivre pour apprendre à Vivre': Rapport du Groupe de Travail Ministériel sur l'Étude des Maternelles (Section Francophone), December 1974.

84 COMMITTEE ON HIGHER EDUCATION IN THE FRENCH SECTOR OF NEW BRUNSWICK
(Special Committee)

Appointed — September 23, 1974

Reported — April 22, 1975

Committee — Three members; Louis Lebel (Judge, St. Quentin), chairman

Purpose — To study the present structure of Francophone higher education which originated with the Deutsch Report in 1962.

Conclusions/Recommendations

That there be a single French Language University for all francophones of New Brunswick;

That Université Acadienne not be responsible for any teaching in English Language, apart from language courses; and that it must however, be the only Institution with a mandate to provide French language education to students in New Brunswick;

That there be created a new university: that this new university replace, as from July 1st, 1976, the University of Moncton, St. Louis Maillet College, and Jesus Mary of

Shippagan;

That Université Acadienne be the legal entity which owns the land, buildings and equipment of the present University of Moncton, of St. Louis Maillet College, and of Jesus Mary College of Shippagan: and that Université Acadienne provide full-time university education on each of these three campuses.

References

Maritime Provinces High Education Commission, *Report of the Committee on Higher Education in the French Sector of New Brunswick*, 1975.

85 TASK FORCE ON SCHOOL FOOD SERVICE IN NEW BRUNSWICK (Departmental Committee)

Appointed 1975

Reported October, 1976

Committee Three members; Katherine Johnston (Home Economics Consultant) chairman

Purpose To survey present situations of school cafeterias with regard to funding, space, facilities, staff and service; to examine policies; to project an adequate school cafeteria policy; to project cost of implementation; and to look at various means of funding.

Conclusions/Recommendations

That the Department of Education in co-operation with other interested government departments develop a policy for school food service which would ensure adequate nourishment for students during the hours they are required to remain at school.

References

New Brunswick / 82

New Brunswick, *School Food Service in New Brunswick; Report of Department of Education and Department of Health*, 1976.

86 TASK FORCE ON PROVINCIAL TESTING AND EVALUATION (Departmental Committee)

Appointed November, 1975

Reported August, 1976

Committee Two members; Lionel Bruneau (Principal, Nepisiguit High School) and Barry E. Fontaine (Principal, Millidgeville North Senior High School) co-chairmen

Purpose To study the question of accountability as it relates to provincial responsibility for education and to make recommendations on the means to achieve it through provincial evaluation programs; to determine and make recommendations to the Minister on informational needs that should and could be met through a provincial testing program; and to study the need for and make recommendations on a Provincial Advisory Committee on Evaluation.

Conclusions/Recommendations

That the Department of Education continue to make every effort to ensure that the general public is made fully aware of the General Educational Development Tests Program;

That the Second Language Testing Program should be encouraged and supported by the Department of Education;

That the Francophone 3, 6 and 9 Testing Program be continued in some form;

That the criteria of the Co-operative School Evaluation

Program should be revised to focus more on good pedagogical practices rather than specific innovations;

That the current New Brunswick School Achievement Testing Program be discontinued;

That the Department of Education initiate the development of an annual criterion-referenced provincial testing program for grades 5, 8 and 11 with priority on First Language and Mathematics;

That the Department administer to students norm-referenced achievement tests at the end of the 6th, 9th and 12th years every three years.

References

New Brunswick, *Task Force on Provincial Testing and Evaluation Report*, 1976.

87 TASK FORCE ON SCHOOL LIBRARIES
(Departmental Committee)

Appointed November 20, 1975

Reported March 4, 1977

Committee Nine members; Dale Aiken (New Brunswick Library Council) chairman

Purpose To examine present methods of staffing and supporting school libraries, the relationships between extension libraries at the regional level and school libraries, present expenditures on school libraries; to make recommendations and to consider costs.

Conclusions/Recommendations

That a comprehensive, systematic plan for the development of school libraries in New Brunswick be formulated;

That, on a one-year pilot basis, library co-ordinators or

supervisors be appointed immediately in two Superintendencies, one Anglophone and one Francophone, responsible to the District Superintendents;

That Provincial library consultants within the Program Development and Implementation Branches of the Department of Education and directly responsible to the Directors of those branches be appointed immediately.

References

New Brunswick, *Report: Task Force on School Libraries*, 1977.

88 SPECIAL COMMITTEE ON STUDENT AID
(Departmental Committee)

Appointed February 9, 1976

Reported March 26, 1976

Committee Three members; (No chairman designated; Fernand Arsenault, University of Moncton, first listed)

Purpose To review the Student Aid Program as it applied to the province and to make recommendations.

Conclusions/Recommendations

That a Loan Rebate Schedule as outlined be adopted;

That the Loan Rebate formula apply only to students graduating from New Brunswick institutions or outside the province where the discipline is not offered;

That the special bursary program called post-graduate grants administered by the Department of Youth be altered to assist needy students at the post-graduate level;

That there be a student advisory body on Student Aid.

References

New Brunswick, *Report to the Cabinet by the Special Committee on Student Aid*, March, 1976.

89 TASK FORCE ON SCHOOL YEAR (Departmental Committee)

Appointed June 14, 1976

Reported February 28, 1977

Committee Ten members; Madeleine Girouard (New Brunswick School Trustees' Association) and A.H. Kingett (New Brunswick Teachers' Association) co-chairmen

Purpose To make a complete study of school year organization with a view to making recommendations, both short-term and long-term, relative to the school year in school districts throughout the Province.

Conclusions/Recommendations

That the year round operation of schools in the province of New Brunswick is not desirable at this point of time, and although there is some evidence to support the conclusion that economic savings might be realized, the evidence is by no means conclusive;

That there is considerable evidence that the year round operation of schools is neither socially nor educationally acceptable;

That the school year consist of 195 days;

That the school year begin on the last Monday in August;

That of the 195 days, thirteen days be available for professional development activities and administrative purposes.

References

New Brunswick, *Report of Task Force on School Year*, 1977.

QUEBEC

90 COMMITTEE OF THE COUNCIL ON THE SUBJECT OF PROMOTING THE MEANS OF EDUCATION
(Legislative Committee)

Appointed May 31, 1787

Reported 1790

Committee Nine members; William Smith (Chief Justice) chairman

Purpose To investigate the education of youth throughout the province and to report, with all convenient speed, the best mode of remedying the defects, an estimate of the expense, and by what means it may be defrayed.

Conclusions/Recommendations

That parish or village free-schools be erected in every district of the province at the determination of the Magistrates of the district;

That each district have a free-school in the central or county town of the district;

That the tuition of the village schools be limited to reading, writing, and cyphering;

That the instruction in the district or county schools extend to all the rules of Arithmetic, the Languages, Grammar, Book-keeping, Gauging, Navigation, Surveying and the practical branches of the Mathematics;

That a collegiate institution be erected for cultivating the liberal arts and sciences usually taught in the European Universities; the Theology of Christians excepted, on account of the mixture of two Communions, whose joint aid is desirable, as far as they agree, and who ought to be left to find a separate provision for the candidates in the ministry of their respective churches;

That a society be incorporated for the purpose, and that the charter wisely provide against the perversion of the institution to any sectarian peculiarities, leaving free scope for cultivating the general circle of the sciences.

References

Quebec, *Report of the Committee of the Council on the Subject of Promoting the Means of Education*, 1790.

91 ROYAL COMMISSION FOR THE INVESTIGATION OF ALL GRIEVANCES AFFECTING HIS MAJESTY'S SUBJECTS OF LOWER CANADA (Related Commission)

Appointed 1835

Reported 1836

Commission Three members; Earl of Gosford, chairman

Purpose To inquire, to deliberate, and to report on the state of education in Lower Canada with a view to the best means of promoting the more general diffusion of sound learning, religious knowledge, and Christian principle.

Conclusions/Recommendations

That a control authority be created;

That trustees and inspectors be elected by the ratepayers in each parish or school district;

That funds for elementary education come from three sources: first, from a general assessment on all property within the parish or school district (on the principle that as education is a matter in which the public good is concerned, every inhabitant ought to contribute to it in proportion to his means); secondly, by a provincial grant (which should never exceed the amount of what is levied by local assessment); and thirdly, by payment from the parents of the children in school (for the reason that what people get for nothing they are apt not to value highly).

References

Great Britain, Despatches from Lord Glenelg, Colonial Secretary, July 17, 1835, *Imperial Blue Books*, vol. 51, 1814-37.

Great Britain, 'General Report', *Imperial Blue Books*, vol. 63, 1837-40.

92 ROYAL COMMISSION ON THE AFFAIRS OF BRITISH NORTH AMERICA (Related Commission)

Appointed March 31, 1838

Reported January 31, 1839

Commission One member; Earl of Durham

Purpose To inquire into, and, as far as may be possible, to adjust all questions depending in the said Provinces of *Lower* and *Upper* Canada, or either of them, respecting the Form and Administration of the Civil Government thereof respectively.

Conclusions/Recommendations

That a scheme be provided by which the children of these two antagonist races should be brought together (were it only for purposes of play would be preferable to one by which they receive a good education apart) by which both union and instruction were assured to them; such a scheme to be divested altogether of political and sectarian tendencies;

That there be some religious instruction in areas on which all Christians agree, and that different denominations be afforded the opportunities of still further and more exclusive religious instruction which they might enjoy without offending or interfering with each other;

That financial support be based on the American system of local assessment at least equal to state grants;

That both normal and model schools be provided to supply competent teachers;

That explicit provisions be made for inspection and supervision, in which the vitality of every system of education must eventually reside.

References

Great Britain, Despatch from Lord Glenelg, April 21, 1838, *Imperial Blue Books*, vol. 10.

Great Britain, 'Durham's Report on the Affairs of British North America', *Imperial Blue Books*, vol. 10.

Great Britain, Report by Arthur Buller, assistant commissioner, 'Durham's Report', App. D.

93 SELECT COMMITTEE OF THE LEGISLATIVE ASSEMBLY, APPOINTED TO ENQUIRE INTO THE STATE OF EDUCATION AND THE WORKING OF THE SCHOOL LAWS IN LOWER CANADA
(Legislative Committee)

Appointed February 22, 1853

Reported June 7, 1853

Committee Nine members; L.V. Sicotte (Député de Saint-Hyacinthe) chairman

Purpose — To enquire into the state of Education in *Lower Canada*, the working of the School Law, the efficiency of the Education Department in *Lower Canada*, and the means of rendering more effective the Legislative enactments adopted for the advancement of Education in *Lower Canada*.

Conclusions/Recommendations

That there be an active, energetic, intelligent management having the right to both advise and enforce;

That there be much closer surveillance by inspectors conjointly with local authorities, each to help control the other;

That a Council of Instruction be formed to decide finally all contestations and difficulties;

That the local authorities be composed of men qualified by at least an elementary education;

That normal schools be provided;

That teachers receive sufficient payment, and assistance in old age to such as have been engaged in teaching for at least thirty years;

That education be divided into two categories; elementary education as a foundation for all men in society, and secondary instruction for specialization in classics or the professions;

That there be more generous expenditure on education.

References

United Canada, *Journals of the Legislative Assembly of the Province of Canada*, 1853.

United Canada, *Report of the Select Committee of the Legislative Assembly, Appointed to Enquire into the State of Education and the Working of the School Laws in Lower Canada*, 1853.

94 COMMISSION OF INQUIRY INTO THE SCHOOL TRUST IN THE CITY OF MONTREAL
(General Commission)

Appointed September 1, 1882

Reported June 30, 1883

Commission Five members; Charles Joseph Coursol (Queen's Counsel, Montreal) chairman

Purpose To hold an investigation: (1) into the administration of the offices of the School Commissioners of the city of Montreal since their organization, (2) into the alleged necessity of increasing the school tax in the said city, and (3) generally into all matters of public interest respecting such schools and the school system in the said city.

Conclusions/Recommendations

That there be a complete change in the personnel of the Catholic Board even though the Commissioners did not find anything proved which could in any way, even in the slightest degree, impeach the honor and integrity of the individual members of the Board or of Mr. Principal Archambault;

That there be an increase in the school tax in Montreal from two-tenths of a cent on the dollar to three-tenths;

That the number of commissioners on each school board (Catholic and Protestant) be increased to at least nine, and that of these, three should be appointed by the government, three by the city council (chosen from each of the three electoral divisions of Montreal), and three should be elected directly by the people (Roman Catholics and Protestants voting separately);

That a concise financial statement be published half-yearly in the principal newspapers.

References

Quebec, *Journals*, 1884, Sessional Papers, No. 39.

95 COMMISSION OF INQUIRY INTO ALL DEPARTMENTS OF THE GOVERNMENT
(Related Commission)

Appointed 1883

Reported 1883 (?) [Sessional Papers destroyed by fire]

Commission

Purpose To make a general and searching investigation into the organization of all the public departments.

Conclusions/Recommendations

References

Quebec, *Journals*, 1883.

96 COMMITTEE ON AGRICULTURAL EDUCATION
(Departmental Committee)

Appointed 1891

Reported May 26, 1891

Committee Five members; Gédéon Ouimet (Superintendent of Public Instruction) chairman

Purpose To investigate agricultural education at two colleges; Ste. Anne de la Pocatière and l'Assomption.

Conclusions/Recommendations

That there be government compensation to enable a part of the farms to be consigned exclusively to student use so that on the spot farming operations can be used.

References

Québec, *Le Journal d'Agriculture Illustre*, Juin, 1891.

97 COMMISSION OF INQUIRY INTO THE POSSIBILITY OF CREATING A BOARD OF ROMAN CATHOLIC SCHOOL COMMISSIONERS FOR THE CITY OF MONTREAL AND ITS *BANLIEUE*
(General Commission)

Appointed	July 29, 1909
Reported	January 9, 1911
Commission	Three members; Raoul Dandurand (Senator) chairman
Purpose	To enquire into the best means to be taken to organize a board of Roman Catholic School Commissioners having jurisdiction over the city of Montreal.

Conclusions/Recommendations

That the idea of dividing the present school board of the city of Montreal into parochial boards be rejected, and that the amalgamation into a single board of all the school municipalities comprised within the present limits of the city of Montreal be considered.

References

Quebec, *Statutes of the Province of Quebec*, 1909, 9 Ed VII, c.8.

Quebec, *Sessional Papers*, 1911, No. 68.

98 COMMISSION OF INQUIRY INTO THE EXTENSION OF THE POWERS OF THE BOARD OF ROMAN CATHOLIC SCHOOL COMMISSIONERS OF MONTREAL, THE EDUCATION OF JEWISH CHILDREN IN PROTESTANT

SCHOOLS OR IN OTHERS, AND THE FINANCIAL SITUATION OF THE PROTESTANT SCHOOLS OF VERDUN
(General Commission)

Appointed	July 30, 1924
Reported	December 22 and December 27, 1924
Commission	Nine members; (three Roman Catholic, three Protestant, three Jewish); Lomer Gouin (former Minister of Justice) chairman
Purpose	To investigate the extension of the powers of the Board of Roman Catholic School Commissioners of Montreal; the education of Jewish children in Protestant schools or in others; and the financial situation of the Protestant schools of Verdun.

Conclusions/Recommendations

That the Act of 1903 be repealed since it might be unconstitutional;

That further legislation be enacted to clearly define and determine the rights of non-Protestants and non-Catholics, to provide for and assure the undivided control and administration of the Protestant schools by Protestants as contemplated by the British North America Act, and to make provision for the equitable distribution of the cost of the education of non-Protestants and non-Catholics on the whole population;

That both the Catholic and Protestant school systems be maintained in the city of Montreal, and no third system be created provided that a satisfactory solution can be found;

That the legal questions be put to higher courts;

That pending further developments in the municipality of Verdun, the system used for the Catholic schools be followed;

That within this framework there be a Central Board (the

present Board of Protestant School Commissioners of the City of Montreal) and four local boards representing the four districts.

References

Quebec, *Sessional Papers,* 1925, vol. 58, No. 60.

99 QUEBEC PROTESTANT EDUCATION SURVEY
(Special Committee)

Appointed November 26, 1937

Reported December, 1938

Committee Eleven members; W.A.F. Hepburn (Director of Education, Ayrshire, Scotland) chairman

Purpose To inquire into and report to the Protestant Committee of the Council of Education on all matters affecting Protestant education in the Province of Quebec.

Conclusions/Recommendations

That the Protestant Committee as now constituted be dissolved and a new Protestant Committee reconstituted with carefully designated representation and powers;

That Protestant district boards of education be organized for the administration and control of all schools outside the area of Montreal;

That school attendance be made compulsory to age fourteen, and, as soon as circumstances permit, be raised to fifteen;

That throughout the Province the length of the school year be ten months;

That teacher training be upgraded and that those responsible never relax their efforts to assemble and retain in their service a staff of gifted, cultured and highly-trained men and women;

That the practice of admitting into teacher training those who have completed Grade X be discontinued;

That the aim be to reach a stage when completion of Grade XII could be insisted upon as minimum qualifications;

That approximately a third of teacher training consist of observing teachers at work and of practising the art of teaching in different types of schools;

That time, money and teaching skill be freely spent in an endeavour to give as many as possible of the English-speaking children of the Province a speaking, reading and writing command of the French language.

References

Quebec, *Report of the Quebec Protestant Education Survey*, 1938.

100 SOUS-COMITE DE COORDINATION DE L'ENSEIGNMENT A SES DIVERS DEGRES AU COMITE CATHOLIQUE DU CONSEIL DE L'INSTRUCTION PUBLIQUE
(Departmental Committee)

Appointed 1951

Reported November, 1953

Committee Thirteen members; Omer-Jules Désaulniers (Surintendant du Département de l'instruction publique) chairman

Purpose To investigate the multiplicity of institutions and educational streams existent in the province.

Conclusions/Recommendations

That there be uniform terminology;

That all programmes give more consideration to what was being done at each educational level and by other institutions;

That more attention be paid to educational psychology and to individual differences;

That there be special classes for the gifted child in order to permit continuous acceleration;

That the differences between complementary and secondary schools be reduced;

That technical specialization not begin too early;

That without betraying their essential character, secondary schools be aware of newer subjects and other courses;

That colleges keep their classical emphasis, but experimental sciences be introduced to all sections;

That universities distinguish very carefully between full university courses and those under university auspices at a lower level;

That certification for degree be consistent.

References

Québec, *Rapport du Sous-Comité de Coordination de L'Enseignment à ses Divers Degrés au Comité Catholique du Conseil de L'Instruction Publique*, 1953.

101 ROYAL COMMISSION OF INQUIRY ON CONSTITUTIONAL MATTERS (Related Commission)

Appointed	February 12, 1953
Reported	1956
Commission	Six members; Thomas Tremblay (Judge in Chief, Quebec) chairman
Purpose	To inquire into constitutional problems, and submit recommendations as to steps to be taken

to safeguard the rights of the Province and those of municipalities and school corporations; and as part of its mandate, to study the problem of the distribution of taxes between the central power, the provinces, municipalities and school corporations.

Conclusions/Recommendations

That the remedy for provinces that are unable to meet their financial obligations in the field of education not be sought in any multiplying or increasing of federal subsidies, but rather in a distribution of fiscal powers which would assure to each class of government the financial means necessary to the fulfilment of its obligations.

References

Quebec, *Report of the Royal Commission of Inquiry on Constitutional Problems*, 1956.

102 COMITE D'ETUDE SUR L'ENSEIGNEMENT AGRICOLE ET AGRONOMIQUE (Departmental Committee)

Appointed October 5, 1960

Reported 1961

Committee Neuf membres; Louis-Marie Regis (ex-doyen de la Faculté de philosophie de l'Université de Montréal) président

Purpose Pour enquêter sur les problèmes de l'enseignement agricole et agronomique dans la province, y compris la recherche et la vulgarisation, lui faire un rapport de ses constatations et opinions et lui soumettre ses recommandations quant aux mesures à prendre pour réorganiser l'enseignement agricole et agronomique et l'adapter aux exigences nouvelles de l'agriculture.

Conclusions/Recommendations

References

Québec, *Rapport du Comité d'Etude sur l'Enseignement Agricole et Agronomique*, 1961.

103 COMITE D'ETUDE SUR L'ENSEIGNEMENT TECHNIQUE ET PROFESSIONNEL
(Departmental Committee)

Appointed January 10, 1961

Reported 1962

Committee Neuf membres; Arthur Tremblay (Directeur adjoint de l'Ecole de Pédagogie et d'orientation de l'Université Laval) président

Purpose Pour étudier les problèmes relatifs:

(a) à la structure de l'enseignement technique et professionnel, ses méthodes d'enseignement et ses programmes d'études;

(b) au recrutement, à la formation et aux conditions de travail du personnel dirigeant et enseignant;

(c) à la sélection et a l'orientation des élèves, au placement des diplômés et a leur intégration au monde du travail;

(d) à la coordination des institutions d'enseignement technique et professionnel avec les écoles de formation générale et les autres types d'institutions de formation professionnelle.

Conclusions/Recommendations

References

Québec, *Rapport du Comité d'Etude sur L'Enseignement*

Quebec / 101

Technique et Professionnel, 1962.

104 ROYAL COMMISSION OF INQUIRY ON EDUCATION IN THE PROVINCE OF QUEBEC
(General Commission)

Appointed April 21, 1961

Reported April, 1963; October, 1964; March, 1966

Commission Eight members; Alphonse-Marie Parent (Vice-Rector, Laval University) chairman

Purpose To have a thorough and impartial study of the state of education in the Province.

Conclusions/Recommendations

(Included in the 576 recommendations were the following:)

That a Minister of Education be appointed whose function shall be to promote and coordinate educational services at all levels, including the private and public sectors;

That a Superior Council of Education be created whose function is to advise the Minister;

That a Ministry of Education be established by merging the Department of Education and the Ministry of Youth;

That in the Ministry of Education there be an Associate Deputy Minister of the Protestant faith;

That the services of the Ministry of Education be grouped in three Divisions, each headed by a Director General: the Division of Instruction, the Division of Administration, the Division of Planning;

That the higher officials of the Ministry of Education be bilingual;

That all laws concerning education be completely revised;

That a Roman Catholic Committee and a Protestant Committee be established to make regulations concerning the teaching of religion and morals, to assure the religious character of the schools, and to offer suggestions to the Council on problems which may arise when teaching certain subjects;

That a Commission for Elementary and Secondary Education, a Commission for Higher Education, and a Commission for Technical and Specialized Education be established;

That the Department of Education use every means to encourage the training of teachers specialized in education;

That a system of public kindergartens and nursery schools, free, coeducational and of good quality, be developed;

That the organization of elementary education be conceived in accordance with the spirit, the principles and the techniques of the activist (that is, active experience) school;

That the elementary school be of six years duration divided into two equal cycles;

That coeducation in the elementary school be reestablished;

That elementary school discipline be so conceived as to develop a spirit of initiative and sense of responsibility in the pupils;

That the secondary course be of five years' duration; two years devoted to general education, and three years which would allow students to begin to specialize;

That Secondary education be organized in composite schools offering a variety of courses and services corresponding to the varied talents, tastes and needs of young people between twelve and sixteen or seventeen years of age;

That the advisability of establishing coeducation in all public institutions of secondary education be seriously examined in the light of the moral, pedagogical and economic factors involved;

That higher education be revised;

That teacher training be under the jurisdiction of higher education and be revised;

That the school curriculum be revised;

That the public educational system of Quebec respect differences in the religious options of parents and pupils and offer a choice of Roman Catholic, Protestant and non-confessional education, insofar as the requirements for quality in education can be satisfied in each instance;

That the unified school system for Quebec be made up, by law, of both French and English schools;

That a special service for the education of Indian children and adults be instituted;

That Canadian history textbooks be radically amended and corrected in such a way as to make the Amerindian civilization better known and to present a truer picture of American Indians;

That local and regional administration be revised;

That regulations for private educational institutions be revised;

That educational financing be revised;

That elementary and secondary teachers unite in a single professional association in order to promote the coordination of these two stages in education;

That as soon as possible the salaries of men and women teachers be made equal;

That teachers and students, as members of the community of scholars, devote themselves to the continuous growth of dedication to the spirit of research, of regard for competence and of concern for intellectual honesty.

<u>References</u>

Quebec / 104

Quebec, *Report of the Royal Commission of Inquiry on Education in the Province of Quebec,* Part One, 1963.

105 COMITE D'ETUDE SUR L'EDUCATION DES ADULTES
(Departmental Committee)

Appointed February 20, 1962

Reported 1964

Committee Sept membres; Claude Ryan (Editeur, *Le Devoir*) président

Purpose
1. faire le relevé du travail accompli par les divers organismes publics et privés;
2. inventorier et reclassifier les besoins;
3. proposer les grandes lignes de la politique du gouvernement;
4. définir les structures d'organismes provinciaux devant régir l'éducation des adultes.

Conclusions/Recommendations

References

Québec, *Rapport du Comité d'Etude sur l'Education des Adultes,* 1964.

106 COMITE D'ETUDE SUR LES LOISIRS, L'EDUCATION PHYSIQUE ET LES SPORTS
(Departmental Committee)

Appointed February 20, 1962

Reported 1964

Committee — Huit membres; René Bélisle (Surintendant de la division de la récréation du service des parcs de la Ville de Montréal) président

Purpose — To study the broad field of leisure, physical education, and sports.

Conclusions/Recommendations

That because of the growing importance of leisure, adequate recreation services be provided;

That proper legislation establish minimum standards for recreation organizations;

That care be taken to ensure adequate control of professional sports.

References

Québec, *Rapport du Comité d'Etude sur les Loisirs l'Education Physique et les Sports*, 1964.

107 COMMISSION D'ENQUETE SUR L'ENSEIGNEMENT DES ARTS AU QUEBEC
(Related Commission)

Appointed — 31 mars 1966

Reported — août 1968

Commission — Six membres; Marcel Rioux (Professeur de sociologie à l'Université de Montréal) président

Purpose — Pour étudier toutes les questions relatives à l'enseignement des arts, y compris les structures administratives, l'organisation matérielle des institutions affectées à cet enseignement et la coordination de ces institutions avec les écoles de formation générale.

Conclusions/Recommendations

Que l'enseignement public des arts, à quelque niveau que ce soit, relève exclusivement du Ministère de l'Education;

Que le Ministère de l'Education assume toute la responsabilité de la réforme générale de l'enseignement des arts;

Que soit reconnu, en principe et dans les faits, le droit de l'enfant à l'éducation artistique;

Que l'éducation artistique au niveau préscolaire soit considéreé comme la base même de la formation de l'enfant;

Que l'éducation artistique à l'élémentaire soit l'une des bases essentielles de la formation de l'enfant; que les matières suivantes soient inscrites aux programmes: la rythmique et la danse, le jeu dramatique, les activités plastiques et la musique; et qu'une durée hebdomadaire d'environ sept heures et demie leur soit consacrée;

Qu'au niveau secondaire l'éducation artistique soit considérée comme l'un des champs fondamentaux de l'enseignement polyvalent;

Que l'éducation artistique devinne l'une des formes de l'éducation permanente et qu'elle soit considérée selon les perspectives suivantes:

(a) comme une éducation essentielle aux études de formation générale;
(b) comme une reconversion professionnelle des adultes désirant faire carrière dans les arts, ainsi qu'un perfectionnement des artistes desireaux de parfaire leur formation;
(c) comme une reconversion et un perfectionnement d'ordre culturel pour tout individu.

References

Québec, *Rapport de la commission d'enquête sur l'enseignement des arts au Québec,* août 1968.

108 COMITE INTERMINISTERIEL SUR L'ENSEIGNEMENT DES LANGUES AUX NEO-CANADIENS
(Departmental Committee)

Appointed [ ]

Reported 27 janvier 1967 [au Ministère de l'Éducation et Ministère des Affaires Culturelles]

Committee Dix membres; Réné Gauthier (Directeur général de l'Immigration) président

Purpose D'examiner l'orientation et l'option linguistique des Néo-Québécois, à la lumière notamment de l'étude du français par les adultes et du type d'école fréquentée par les enfants.

Conclusions/Recommendations

D'assumer désormais la responsabilité totale de l'organisation des cours de langues aux immigrants et de prendre sans délai toutes les mesures utiles pour que de tels cours soient efficacement mis à la disposition des immigrants dans tout le Québec;

De faire en sorte que ce service spécialisé soit assuré de la collaboration la plus large des commissions scolaires locales et régionales;

De créer un comité pédagogique interministeriel dans lequel les Ministères de l'Education et des Affaires Culturelles (et tous autres ministères intéressés éventuellement) collaborerait à l'établissement des programmes, à la définition des méthodes, à la sélection des enseignants, au choix des manuels et du matériel didactique et à l'octroi des attestations;

Qu'il soit clairement reconnu que la responsabilité et la mise en oeuvre d'une politique scolaire pour les enfants néo-canadiens incombent directement et exclusivement au gouvernement du Québec, notamment à son Ministère de l'Education agissant, en l'occurrence, en étroite liaison avec la Direction générale de l'Immigration;

Que tous les moyens d'information, d'accueil et d'incitation soient employés, avec le concours actif du gouvernement et de tous les organismes publics, afin d'amener les immigrants à opter pour l'école de langue française;

D'établir concrètement et d'appliquer rigoureusement, dans les plus courts délais, une politique dynamique de priorité du francais, particulièrement comme langue du travail, de l'affichage et de la communication.

References

Québec, *Rapport: Comité interministériel sur l'enseignement des langues aux Néo-Canadiens*, janvier 1967.

109 CONSEIL DE RESTRUCTURATION SCOLAIRE DE L'ILE DE MONTREAL (Departmental Committee)

Appointed 30 septembre 1967

Reported 28 octobre 1968

Committee Dix-huit membres; Joseph L. Pagé (Vice-président de la Commission des écoles catholiques de Montréal) président

Purpose De promouvoir la régionalisation et la démocratisation de l'administration scolaire dans l'île de Montréal.

Conclusions/Recommendations

Qu'il soit reconnu que tout corps public qui a une responsabilité dans l'administration scolaire sur l'île de Montréal, a pour objectif premier d'assurer, à tous les élèves sans distinction, un enseignement de bonne qualité et favorable au plein épanouissement de la personnalité de chacun dans un juste respect de pluralisme religieux et de la dualité linguistique et culturelle qui caractérisent la région métropolitaine de Montréal;

Que le gouvernement adopte une législation fixant le statut des droits linguistiques au Québec, qu'il établisse une politique de la langue et de l'immigration, et que ces dispositions s'accompagnent de mesures propres à favoriser la priorité concrète du français;

Que, sur l'île de Montréal, les programmes d'études puissent conduire tout élève terminant ses études secondaires à parler couramment la langue officielle que n'aura pas été sa langue principale d'instruction et que, normalement, pour obtenir un diplôme de fin d'études il doive réussir au préalable un examen oral et écrit en langue seconde.

References

Québec, *Rapport au Ministre de L'Education: Conseil de Restructuration Scolaire de l'île de Montreal*, octobre 1968.

110 COMMISSION D'ENQUETE SUR LE DIFFEREND ENTRE LES PARTIES A LA NEGOCIATION ... DANS LE SECTEUR SCOLAIRE
(Judicial Commission)

Appointed 2 avril 1968

Reported 1968

Commission Un membre; Jean-Charles Simard (Juge de la Cour provinciale)

Purpose Pour faire enquête sur le différend; cette commission ne peut rendre une décision ni formuler de recommendations mais seulement constater les faits pertinents.

Conclusions/Recommendations

Les parties se sont buteés a un sérieux obstacle: celui de la définition de 'membre du personnel enseignant'. L'obstacle est d'autant plus sérieux qu'il infère tout le problème de la juridiction ou du champ d'application de la convention collective.

References

Quebec / 110

Québec, *Rapport de la Commission d'enquête constituée en vertu de l'article 16 de la Loi assurant le droit de l'enfant à l'éducation et instituant un nouveau régime de convention collective dans le secteur scolaire (15-16, Elizabett II, chapitre 63)*, 1968.

111 COMMISSION OF INQUIRY ON THE POSITION OF THE FRENCH LANGUAGE AND ON LANGUAGE RIGHTS IN QUEBEC
(Related Commission)

Appointed	December 9, 1968
Reported	December, 1972
Commission	Five members; Jean-Denis Gendron (Vice-doyen de la Faculté des lettres à l'Université Laval) président
Purpose	To make an inquiry into and submit a report on the position of French as the language of usage in Québec, and to recommend measures designed to guarantee the linguistic rights of the majority as well as the protection of the rights of the minority; and the full expansion and diffusion of the French language in Québec in all fields of activity and also at the educational, cultural, social and economic levels.

Conclusions/Recommendations

That the Government of Québec proceed to legislate forthwith to proclaim French as the Official Language of the Province of Québec, and to proclaim French and English as the two National Languages of the Province of Québec; thus making French the Provincial *Official Language* in Québec, and French and English the Provincial *National Languages* in Québec;

That the Government of Québec proceed, -- by legislation, administrative decrees and practice, and also voluntary, persuasive or facultative, community measures -- to make French a language that is useful and necessary in communications within all fields of activity in commerce and industry and the work *milieu* in general, in the Province of Québec;

That the Government of Québec require all children enrolled in English-speaking schools in the Province of Québec to acquire a mastery of French from the earliest possible age, and all children enrolled in French-speaking schools to acquire a mastery of English from the earliest possible age.

References

Québec, *Report of the Commission of Inquiry on the Position of the French Language and on Language Rights in Québec*, vol. 2 'Language Rights', December 1972.

112 COMMISSION D'ETUDE DE LA PROPAGANDE POLITIQUE DANS L'ENSEIGNEMENT
(Departmental Committee)

Appointed 19 novembre 1970

Reported 15 mars 1971

Committee Un membre; Gérard Dion (Professeur au département des relations industrielles à la Faculté des Sciences sociales de l'Université Laval)

Purpose Pour étudier les plaintes qui lui parvenaient touchant la propagande politique et l'endoctrinement auxquels se seraient indûment livrés certains professeurs dans l'exercice de leurs fonctions auprès des élèves.

Conclusions/Recommendations

Qu'on établit un code d'éthique professionnelle pour les enseignants et la création d'un poste permanent d'ombudsman dans le domaine de l'éducation.

References

Québec, *Rapport au Ministre de l'Éducation: Le Commissaire - Enquêteur Gérard Dion,* mars 1971.

113 COMITE INTERMINISTERIEL POUR ENTREPRENDRE L'ETUDE DU PROBLEME DE LA DISTRIBUTION DES IMPRIMES, PERIODIQUES ET LIVRES DE POCHE
(Departmental Committee)

Appointed octobre 1972

Reported 15 janvier 1973

Committee Cinq membres; Pierre de Grandpré (Conseiller culturel à la Délégation générale du Québec à Paris) président

Purpose D'examiner à fond les conditions dans lesquelles s'opère au Québec la diffusion des périodiques et des livres de poche et de présenter au Ministre des Affaires culturelles des recommandations propres à améliorer la situation.

Conclusions/Recommendations

Que le développement d'une véritable industrie québécoise de biens culturels constitue la meilleure garantie de l'indépendence et du développement culturel des citoyens du Québec.

References

Québec, *Rapport sur la distribution des périodiques et du livre de poche au Québec,* janvier 1973.

114 COMMISSION D'ETUDE DE LA TACHE DES ENSEIGNANTS DE L'ELEMENTAIRE ET DU SECONDAIRE
(Departmental Committee)

Appointed 15 décembre 1972

Reported mars 1975

Committee Huit membres; Jean-Noèl Faucher (Ministère de l'Education) coordonnateur

Purpose De proposer des méthodes et/ou systèmes pouvant permettre une utilisation optionale des ressources humaines actuellement affectées au système d'éducation, compte tenu des orientations pédagogiques du Ministère, des dispositions financières et des priorités collectives du Québec; et d'examiner les existants tant au Québec qu' à l'étranger.

Conclusions/Recommendations

Que le ministère de l'Education et les commissions scolaires fassent connaître et vulgarisent les orientations et les objectifs pédagogiques, qu'ils identifient clairement ceux qu'ils imposent et ceux qu'ils proposent et qu'ils en évaluent au préalable les implications sur les tâches des enseignants;

Que le ministère de l'Education, au niveau élémentaire (incluant l'enfance inadaptée), mette en application graduellement les recommandations du Conseil supérieur de l'éducation et du groupe COMMEL concernant l'implantation de spécialistes en langue seconde, en éducation physique et en musique, libérant ainsi les enseignants l'équivalent d'une période journalière d'enseignement (environ 45 minutes) leur permettant de se consacrer à d'autres activités professionnelles et d'améliorer la qualité de leur enseignement.

References

Québec, *Rapport de la C.E.T.E.E.S.: Commission d'étude de la tâche des enseignants de l'élémentaire et du secondaire*, mars 1975.

115 COMITE PROVINCIAL DE L'ENFANCE INADAPTEE
(Departmental Committee)

Appointed 15 décembre 1972

Reported 2 septembre 1976

Committee Sept membres; Thérèse Baron (Sous-ministre adjoint à l'éducation) présidente

Purpose De préparer des recommandations relatives à une meilleure coordination régionale et provinciale des ressources publiques et privées en éducation de l'enfance inadaptée; et de préparer, pour le bénéfice du ministère de l'Education, des recommandations relatives aux politiques générales qui régissent l'éducation des enfants en difficulté d'apprentissage et d'adaptation.

Conclusions/Recommendations

Que le ministère de l'Education adapte, en concertation avec les organismes concernes, et rende publique une politique officielle d'éducation de l'enfance en difficulté d'adaptation et d'apprentissage;

Que cette politique favorise le développement intégral et optimal de l'enfant en difficulté d'adaptation et d'apprentissage par l'utilisation d'une approche pédagogique axée sur le potentiel de l'enfant et par l'établissement d'une communication harmonieuse et d'un fonctionnement intègre entre tous les services et toutes les personnes responsables de l'enfant.

References

Québec, *L'Education de l'enfance en difficulté d'adaptation et d'apprentissage au Québec,* 1976.

116 COMMISSION D'ETUDE SUR LA CLASSIFICATION DES ENSEIGNANTS (Departmental Committee)

Appointed 8 février 1973

Reported février 1975

Committee — Quatre membres; Roger Laberge (Ministère de l'Education) président

Purpose — A étudier les systèmes de classification des enseignants des autres provinces canadiennes ainsi que de certains états américains.

Conclusions/Recommendations

Que le gouvernement crée une commission provinciale qui, à la lumière des travaux de la commission d'étude, aurait comme mandat d'établir et de reviser au besoin les principes et le plan de classification des enseignants, d'élaborer les règles nécessaires à l'évaluation des études faites hors du Québec et des compétences particulières;

Que les membres de cette commission soient issus des organismes d'éducation et des associations qui sont concernés par cette question, soit les commissions scolaires, les collèges, le gouvernement, les universités et les associations d'enseignants.

References

Québec, *Rapport de la commission d'étude la classification des enseignants*, février 1975.

117 CONSEIL SUPERIEUR DE L'EDUCATION SUR L'ETAT ET LES BESOINS DE L'ENSEIGNEMENT COLLEGIAL
(Departmental Committee)

Appointed — 15 février 1973

Reported — juillet 1975

Committee — Vingt-quatre membres; Jean-Marie Beauchemin (Sous-ministre associé au ministère de L'Education) président

Purpose — De demander au Conseil supérieur de l'Education un avis, dans le cadre de la loi qui le régit, sur l'état et les besoins de l'enseignement collégial, c'est-à-dire sur les résultats atteints à ce jour, sur les problèmes qu'il suscite et sur les orientations à retenir pour son développement ultérieur, tant sur le plan administratif que pédagogique.

Conclusions/Recommendations

Que le ministère de l'Education considére l'identification des besoins éducatifs comme une priorité et comme une condition préalable à la definition des objectifs de formation post-secondaire et de ses divers programmes;

Que l'organisation de l'enseignement post-secondaire dispensé par les collèges permette aux étudiants de réaliser les objectifs de leur programme dans des temps variables ajustés à leurs possibilités et à leur rythme;

Que l'on reconnaisse que pour atteindre les objectifs qu'il poursuit, l'étudiant puisse choisir ses activités ou dans l'institution qui offre le programme ou en dehors de celle-ci;

Que le collège soit structuré sur le module, unité de base qui administre le programme.

References

Québec, *Le Collège: Rapport sur l'état et les besoins de l'enseignement collégial*, 1975.

118 COMITE D'ETUDE SUR LA RECHERCHE ET L'ENSEIGNEMENT EN TECHNOLOGIE DU BOIS
(Departmental Committee)

Appointed janvier 1974

Reported octobre 1974

Committee Six membres; Jean Poliquin (faculté de Foresterie et de Géodésie, université Laval) président

Purpose De définir les objectifs de la province concernant la recherche et l'enseignement en technologie du bois; de déterminer le plus clairement possible les carences actuelles dans ce domaine; et de définir les principaux moyens nécessaires pour répondre aux besoins fixés et pour régler les principaux problèmes existants.

Conclusions/Recommandations

Que le ministère de l'Education et les universités s'emploient à assurer la priorité qu'il importe d'accorder à ce secteur de façon à ce que le programme puisse être accessible aux étudiants aux trois cycles universitaires.

References

Québec, *L'Enseignement et la recherche en sciences et technologie de bois*, octobre 1974.

119 COMITE D'ETUDE SUR LA CREATION DE L'INSTITUT DES SPORTS DU QUEBEC
(Departmental Committee)

Appointed 7 février 1974

Reported 24 mai 1974 [au Ministre d'Etat responsable du Haut-Commissariat à la Jeunesse, aux Loisirs et aux Sports]

Committee Quinze membres; Claude Bouchard (Directeur, Laboratoire des sciences, de l'activité physique, de l'Université Laval) président

Purpose D'étudier l'ensemble de la question de la création de l'Institut des Sports du Québec et d'émettre des recommandations au sujet de tous les aspects importants de son développement.

Conclusions/Recommandations

Quebec / 118

Que les organismes et les institutions du Québec reconnaissent, pour les fins de leurs programmes de sport, les quatre catégories suivantes de participants: le débutant, l'espoir, l'élite québécoise, l'élite canadienne et internationale;

Que le loi spéciale créant l'Institut des Sports du Québec assure la participation des institutions universitaires, des collèges et des municipalités au niveau décisionnel de l'Institut des Sports du Québec.

References

Québec, *Comité d'étude sur la création de l'institut des sports du Québec*, mai 1974.

120 GROUPE DE TRAVAIL SUR L'EDUCATION PHYSIQUE ET LE SPORT A L'ECOLE
(Departmental Committee)

Appointed mars 1974

Reported avril 1975

Committee Onze membres; Claude Beauregard (Bureau des sous-ministres) président

Purpose D'élucider et d'articuler au moins sommairement les concepts de sport scolaire, d'éducation physique, d'activité physique, d'activité de mouvement et d'activité de plein air pour les fins des niveaux élémentaire et secondaire; et de proposer un plan de développement du sport scolaire et de l'éducation physique aux niveaux élémentaire et secondaire dans la perspective d'un developpement prioritaire au niveau élémentaire.

Conclusions/Recommendations

Que le groupe de travail ministériel mandate le Comité d'étude sur les objectifs de l'éducation physique et du sport en milieu scolaire afin que ce dernier développe et élabore des taxonomies particulières aux objectifs de l'éducation physique d'ordre cognitif, social et affectif, culturel et esthétique et qu'il donne au Comité d'étude les moyens financiers de mener ses travaux à bonne fin.

References

Québec, *Rapport du groupe de travail sur l'éducation physique et le sport à l'école*, avril 1975.

121 COMITE D'ETUDE SUR LA READAPTATION DES ENFANTS ET ADOLESCENTS PLACES EN CENTRE D'ACCUEIL (Departmental Committee)

Appointed 1 février 1975

Reported 22 décembre 1975

Committee Huit membres; Manuel G. Batshaw (Directeur Général, Services Communautaires Juifs, Montréal) président

Purpose D'étudier les méthodes couramment utilisées ou qui pourraient l'être pour la réadaptation des pensionnaires reçus dans les centres d'accueil de transition et de réadaptation pour jeunes mésadaptés sociaux, tout en tenant compte de la coordination optionale avec les activités professionnelles pouvant être assumées par les Centres de Services Sociaux.

Conclusions/Recommendations

Que le Ministère de l'Education du Québec voit à ce que le développement des Services à l'Enfance Inadaptée tant au niveau primaire que secondaire ne soit pas uniquement des projets-pilotes ou émargeant au budget inadmissible des commissions scolaires, mais fasse bien partie des priorités budgétaires du Ministère;

Que conjointement avec le Ministère des Affaires Sociales, des Centres de Jour soient organisés pour les mésadaptés socio-affectifs graves tant au niveau primaire que secondaire;

Que les écoles aient le personnel nécessaire pour assurer la récupération scolaire, la compréhension des comportements difficiles des jeunes et l'attitude adéquate pour les aider à se contrôler et se développer normalement, et que les programmes appropriés à ces fins soient disponibles sans déplacer l'enfant.

References

Québec, *Rapport du comité d'étude sur la réadaptation des enfants et adolescents placés en centre d'accueil*, décembre 1975.

122 GROUPE DE TRAVAIL SUR L'INSTITUT D'HISTOIRE ET DE CIVILISATION DU QUEBEC
(Departmental Committee)

Appointed 23 juin 1976

Reported 21 février 1977

Committee Huit membres; Guy Frégault (Sous-ministre aux Affaires culturelles) président

Purpose De présenter des recommandations sur l'opportunité d'établir un Institut d'histoire et de civilisation du Québec; et d'indiquer, s'il y a lieu, ce que pourrait être un tel institut et, notamment: son statut; son mandat; sa composition; son mode de fonctionnement; les pouvoirs qui lui seraient utiles ou nécessaires; la participation éventuelle des organismes, tant publics que privés, oeuvrant dans les secteurs de l'histoire, des sciences humaines et des sciences physiques.

Conclusions/Recommendations

Que l'implantation de cet Institut québécois de recherche

sur la culture s'impose;

Que cette originalité s'inscrit en premier lieu dans les trois principales fonctions qu'il assumera: (1) poursuivre des recherches à long terme sur la nature et l'évolution de la culture québécoise; (2) conduire des investigations sur le développement culturel du Québec; (3) aménager la concertation des études québécoises et contribuer à une meilleure diffusion des travaux qui en résulteront.

References

Québec, *Rapport du groupe de travail sur l'institut d'histoire et de civilisation du Québec*, février 1977.

123 COMITE D'ETUDE SUR LA SITUATION DES ENSEIGNANTS RELIGIEUX (Departmental Committee)

Appointed 6 octobre 1976

Reported 15 juillet 1977

Committee Dix membres; Guy Monfette (Directeur général, Commission administrative du régime de retraite) président

Purpose D'étudier la situation dans laquelle se trouvent les religieux enseignants et les religieux enseignants laïcisés depuis le 1er juillet 1965 par rapport aux autres enseignants à qui le Régime de retraite des fonctionnaires de l'enseignement était applicable.

Conclusions/Recommendations

Que le Gouvernement du Québec accorde, pour chaque année d'enseignement en excédent des années rachetées en vertu de l'article 81 du Régime de retraite des employés du gouvernement et des organismes publics, un crédit de rente égal à 1% du traitement admissible annuel au 30 juin 1977, aux enseignants religieux et aux enseignants religieux laïcisés après le 30 juin 1965 qui cotisent audit Régime et qui rachètent ou ont racheté la totalité des années d'enseignement que leur permet l'article 81 audit Régime.

References

Québec, *Rapport du comité 'ad hoc' constitué pour étudier la situation des enseignants religieux et des enseignants religieux laïcisés après le 30 juin 1965 en regard de leur protection à la retraite*, juillet 1977.

124 COMMISSION D'ETUDE SUR LES UNIVERSITES
(Departmental Committee)

Appointed 20 juillet 1977

Reported 31 janvier 1978

Committee Huit membres; Pierre Angers (Professeur à l'Université du Québec à Trois-Rivières) président

Purpose De déterminer et analyser les indicateurs de l'avenir qui permettront de mieux cerner les choix qui s'offrent, de formuler les hypothèses, de dégager des problèmes prioritaires, d'indiquer des voies de solutions.

Conclusions/Recommendations

Si l'une des principales fonctions de l'université est de jouer un rôle dans l'évolution de la culture, elle devra envisager de former un type d'homme qui, au-delà des langages disjoints de la réussite matérielle, puisse se faire entendre de la collectivité et participer au gouvernement des hommes. Comment toutefois, établir cette nouvelle perspective pédagogique sans que ne s'engage également une discussion sur le discours politique et social sans lequel tout projet éducatif demeure vain? Nous souhaiterions donc que l'université soit en mesure de restaurer l'idéal qui lui permettrait de donner un sens à l'accumulation et à la diffusion des connaissances, et de les maîtriser avant justement que l'homme n'en devienne la victime;

Si l'université refusait d'éclairer la société dans la mesure de ses moyens et acceptait de se faire dicter son avenir sans participer à l'effort pour la définir, bref si elle faisait passer ses fonctions de formation avant ses fonctions critiques, elle ne pourrait guère demeurer longtemps encore 'le lieu où se poursuit sans contrainte l'expérience de l'esprit'.

References

Québec, *Commission d'étude sur les universités: Document de consultation,* janvier 1978.

125 COMMITTEE ON EDUCATION
(Legislative Committee)

Appointed April 10, 1835

Reported February 25, 1836

Committee Three members; Charles Duncombe (Member for Oxford) chairman

Purpose To obtain the best plans and estimates of a Lunatic Asylum and such information as may be considered relative to the management and good government of such institutions, and also respecting the system and management of Schools and Colleges.

Conclusions/Recommendations

That education of youth be provided in direct reference to the wants of the world;

That teachers in colleges be prepared to work as long hours as those in high schools and academies and primary schools;

That women be encouraged to make a career in teaching;

That religious training be provided in separate schools if this is the only way to guarantee a moral man;

That teachers be better qualified and better trained;

That normal schools be provided;

That competent common school teacher inspectors be appointed to prevent the disqualified from entering into the responsible profession of teaching;

That new areas of scientific study and of the inductive system whereby students collect facts and accumulate ideas from observation which is superseding the former arbitrary copying system learned from books alone be encouraged.

References

Upper Canada, *Journal of the House of Assembly of Upper Canada,* 1835.

Upper Canada, *Journals,* 1836, App. Vol. 1.

126 COMMISSION OF INQUIRY INTO THE PUBLIC DEPARTMENTS OF THE PROVINCE
(Related Commission)

Appointed October 21, 1839

Reported January 22, 1840 (Report of Education Committee)

Commission Nineteen members; Robert Baldwin Sullivan (Member of Legislative Council) chairman (Three education commissioners; John McCaul)

Purpose To investigate the business, conduct and organization of the several Public Departments in the Province, and to report on the state of the said several Departments, and what changes in the system of conducting the public business in the said several Departments would be beneficial;

And to ascertain the state of all School Funds; to examine into the past and present state of Education throughout the Province; to frame such a plan as will appear to be the best calculated to afford the best possible kind of Education to the community at the least possible expense; to institute an inquiry with reference to the constitution of King's College University, and also to the lands forming its endowment; and to investigate generally all matters of public interest.

Conclusions/Recommendations

That provision for professional education, that is, theology, law, and medicine, which is very deficient be improved;

That no grammar school master be appointed without an examination of his qualifications as a scholar and a teacher, for it often happens that excellent scholars are wholly unfit for the office of teachers;

That adequate salaries be paid to teachers;

That normal schools and model schools be provided;

That curriculum and textbooks be revised;

That a Board of Commissioners be provided;

That there be increased financial aid to education.

References

Upper Canada, *Journals*, 1839-40, App. Vol. 2.

127 RYERSON'S REPORT ON A SYSTEM OF PUBLIC ELEMENTARY INSTRUCTION FOR UPPER CANADA
(Departmental Committee)

Appointed 1844

Reported March 27, 1846

Committee One member; Egerton Ryerson (Assistant Superintedent of Education)

Purpose — To devise such measures as may be necessary to establish the most efficient system of Instruction.

Conclusions/Recommendations

That in adopting measures for the advancement of the education of the people, the Administration of Canada is but following the example of the most enlightened Governments, and, like them, laying the foundation for the strongest claims to the esteem of the country and the gratitude of posterity.

References

United Canada, *Report on a System of Public Elementary Instruction for Upper Canada,* [1846]

128 COMMISSION OF INQUIRY INTO THE AFFAIRS OF KING'S COLLEGE UNIVERSITY AND UPPER CANADA COLLEGE
(Special Committee)

Appointed — July 20, 1848

Reported — July 31, 1851

Committee — Three members; Joseph Workman (Physician) chairman

Purpose — To inquire into the affairs of King's College University and Upper Canada College.

Conclusions/Recommendations

That the business transactions of a wealthy corporation, extending over a period of twenty-two years, have been unravelled and brought from a state of unintelligible complexity and confusion into a proper business shape.

References

United Canada, *Journals,* 1849, App. Vol. No. 2, III.

Ontario / 128

United Canada, *Journals*, 1851, App. No. 4, EEE.

129 ROYAL COMMISSION ON AFFAIRS AND FINANCIAL CONDITIONS OF TORONTO UNIVERSITY AND UNIVERSITY COLLEGE
(General Commission)

Appointed October 28, 1861

Reported May 29, 1862

Commission Three members; James Patton (Vice-Chancellor, University of Toronto) chairman

Purpose To enquire into the affairs and financial conditions of Toronto University and University College.

Conclusions/Recommendations

That expenditure has been upon a scale disproportionate to its uses and requirements, as well as inexpedient when the necessity for public aid to sustain the higher educational interests of the country is considered;

That so long as the University and University College have no inducements to practice economy, there will, from the nature of things, be large expenditure without corresponding results; and so long as the other Colleges having University powers can see no advantage from affiliation, as is undoubtedly the case under the present system, they will not only decline to unite, but will inevitably continue to occupy a position of rivalry and of remonstrance;

That within a really National University all classes and denominations will be impartially provided with those opportunities for higher education which may be in accordance with their convictions, and none suffer wrong or disability because of their preference;

That the standard of University education will be uniform, and Degrees of equal value, because all will be tested by one curriculum and by one Board of Examiners, and endorsed by the same authority; although each Institution will be at liberty, without interference, to teach by such mode as the authorities thereof may deem best.

References

United Canada, 'Commission on Affairs and Financial Conditions of Toronto University and University College', Province of Canada *Sessional Papers,* 1863, No. 19.

130 SPECIAL REPORT ON POPULAR EDUCATION IN EUROPE AND THE UNITED STATES
(Departmental Committee)

Appointed 1866

Reported March 4, 1868

Committee One member; Egerton Ryerson (Superintendent of Education)

Purpose To make an educational tour of observation and enquiry into the working and progress of the systems of Public Instruction in the chief educating countries of America and Europe, that we might avail ourselves, as far as possible, of the experience of both Hemispheres in simplifying and improving our own system and methods of diffusing education and useful knowledge among all classes of the population.

Conclusions/Recommendations

References

United Canada, 'Special Report on Popular Education in Europe and the United States', *Journals,* 1867-68.

131 SELECT COMMITTEE TO ENQUIRE INTO THE MANAGEMENT AND WORKING OF THE EDUCATION DEPARTMENT
(Legislative Committee)

Appointed November 10, 1868

Reported January 19, 1869

Committee Twenty-three members; M.C. Cameron (Member for Toronto East) chairman

Purpose To examine into the working of the Common and Grammar School System of Ontario, together with the Department of Public Instruction.

Conclusions/Recommendations

That this report is an ample vindication of the Chief Superintendent, and all who assisted him, from the imputations long and recklessly thrown upon them by a portion of the public press and other parties; an unquestionable testimony to the fidelity, efficiency and economy with which the Department of Public Instruction has been conducted in its various branches and details.

References

Ontario, *Report on the Education Department by a Large Select Committee of the Legislative Assembly of Ontario*, 1869.

132 PROVINCIAL FARM COMMISSION
(Departmental Committee)

Appointed 1873

Reported January 31, 1874

Committee Eight members; David Christie (former President, Provincial Agricultural Association) chairman

Purpose To consider the whole subject of the future

organization and management of the newly acquired Provincial Farm.

Conclusions/Recommendations

(Forty-eight separate conclusions included everything from choosing a suitable name, to the best means of laying out the fields.)

References

Ontario, *Report of the Commissioner of Agriculture and Arts for 1873*, App. G.

133 LEGISLATIVE COMMITTEE TO ENQUIRE INTO THE MANAGEMENT OF THE AGRICULTURAL COLLEGE AND MODEL FARM
(Legislative Committee)

Appointed December 2, 1874

Reported December 19, 1874

Committee Five members; James Bethune (Member for Stormont) chairman

Purpose To enquire into the management of the Agricultural College and Model Farm.

Conclusions/Recommendations

That in the opinion of the Committee, the Government was fully justified, on the facts disclosed, in dispensing with the services of the Principal; present conditions and management seemed satisfactory; and it was not in the public interest to pursue the inquiry further.

References

Ontario, *The Daily Globe*, December 18, 1874.

134 COMMISSION OF INQUIRY INTO CHARGES AGAINST THE CENTRAL

COMMITTEE OF EXAMINERS OF THE EDUCATION DEPARTMENT
(Judicial Commission)

Appointed September 24, 1877

Reported December 31, 1877

Commission One member; Christopher Salmon Patterson (Justice of the Court of Appeal)

Purpose To enquire into and report upon charges that there is within the Central Committee a 'ring', the members of which have dishonorable relations with the publishing house of Adam Miller & Co., of Toronto; and that in the preparation of examination papers in connection with the Public and High Schools, there has been collusion between members of the Central Committee and other parties interested in the work or results of the examinations.

Conclusions/Recommendations

That the clear result of the whole evidence is that neither charge has any support from affirmative proof; that the charges have not been allowed to be disposed of as simply unproved, but that both have been conclusively rebutted.

References

Ontario, *Sessional Papers*, A1878, No. 11.

135 COMMISSION TO INVESTIGATE CERTAIN CHARGES AGAINST DR. SAMUEL MAY OF THE EDUCATION DEPARTMENT
(Departmental Committee)

Appointed December 30, 1881

Reported February 16, 1882

Committee One member; E.J. Senkler (Judge, Lincoln County)

Purpose — To enquire into certain charges preferred by a member of the Legislative Assembly of Ontario, against Samuel P. May, Doctor of Medicine, Superintendent of the Educational Museum and Library, and lately of the Depository of the Education Department.

Conclusions/Recommendations

That no evidence was given to support this charge, and it is not sustained.

References

Ontario, *Sessional Papers*, A1882, No. 55.

136 COMMISSION OF INQUIRY INTO AN INCIDENT AT THE AGRICULTURAL COLLEGE
(Judicial Commission)

Appointed — January, 1884

Reported — [ ]

Commission — One member; John Winchester (Inspector of Legal Offices)

Purpose — To inquire into and report in respect to an incident at the Agricultural College involving Mr. Hunt, the Assistant Master.

Conclusions/Recommendations

References

Handwritten entry dated 25 January 1884 in the Order in Council Book in the Executive Council Office, Toronto.

137 SPECIAL INQUIRY INTO CONDITIONS OF THE FRENCH SCHOOLS IN THE UNITED COUNTIES OF PRESCOTT AND RUSSELL

(Departmental Committee)

Appointed 1887 (?)

Reported March 25, 1887

Committee One member; O. Dufort (Assistant Inspector of Public Schools)

Purpose To investigate conditions of the French schools in the united counties of Prescott and Russell.

Conclusions/Recommendations

References

Ontario, 'Report of the Assistant Inspector of Public Schools upon the conditions of the French Schools in the United Counties of Prescott and Russell', 1887.

138 COMMISSION OF INQUIRY INTO THE FIRE AT THE GOVERNMENT FARM (Judicial Commission)

Appointed November, 1888

Reported [ ]

Commission Two members; Archibald Blue (Deputy Minister of Agriculture) and John Winchester (Inspector of Legal Offices)

Purpose To investigate the cause of the fire at the Government Farm.

Conclusions/Recommendations

References

Ontario, *Annual Report of the Agricultural College*, 1888.

139 SURVEY OF LEADING SCHOOLS OF TECHNOLOGY IN THE UNITED STATES
(Departmental Committee)

Appointed 1888

Reported February 4, 1889

Committee Two members; George Ross (Minister of Education) chairman

Purpose To survey the leading schools of technology in the United States.

Conclusions/Recommendations

That as a rule all the institutions visited in the United States were built with very little regard to architectural effect, and not one of them would compare with the University of Toronto in external appearances although they were all much superior in internal arrangements.

References

Ontario, *Report of the Minister of Education on the Subject of Technical Education*, 1889.

140 SPECIAL INQUIRY INTO THE SCHOOLS IN THE COUNTIES OF PRESCOTT, RUSSELL, ESSEX, KENT, AND SIMCOE
(Departmental Committee)

Appointed May 13, 1889

Reported August 22, 1889

Committee Three members; John J. Tilley (Inspector of County Model Schools) chairman

Purpose To visit the Public Schools of the Counties of Prescott, Russell, Essex, Kent and Simcoe, for the purpose of making full and careful enquiry by personal inspection and any other way that may be deemed expedient, into the teaching of

English in the Public Schools of the said counties in which the French language is taught, and the observance of the Regulations of the Education Department generally by teachers, trustees and other school officers therein; and to consider and report in what way the study of English may be most successfully promoted among those accustomed to the use of the French language as their mother tongue.

Conclusions/Recommendations

That there are some schools in which the time given to English and the use of that language in the school are too limited, but even in these, more attention is paid to English than formerly, and the use made of it in the work of instruction is greater than it was a few years ago;

That in dealing with these schools, in order to raise them to a higher standard, and to secure a satisfactory teaching of the English language in them, time must be allowed and patience must be exercised;

That there is reason to believe that whatever changes may be necessary to render these schools more efficient, and to advance the children more rapidly and intelligently in the knowledge of English, will be welcomed by the French people themselves; that on the whole the people take a deep interest in the education of their children;

That a special school be established for the training of French teachers in the English language;

That special institutes be held for the immediate benefit of the teachers now employed in the French Schools;

That the attention of the teachers be called at once to the necessity of making greater use of the oral or conversational method in teaching English;

That a bilingual series of readers -- French and English -- be provided for the French Schools in Ontario;

That the use of unauthorized text-books in the schools be

discontinued.

References

Ontario, *Sessional Papers*, 1890, No. 7.

Ontario, *Sessional Papers*, 1894, No. 4.

141 SPECIAL INQUIRY INTO THE SCHOOLS IN THE COUNTIES OF PRESCOTT, RUSSELL, ESSEX, KENT, AND SIMCOE (Departmental Committee)

Appointed May 29, 1893

Reported August 9, 1893

Committee Three members; John J. Tilley (Inspector of County Model Schools) chairman

Purpose To consider and report what progress, if any, has been made in the study of English since the date of the last report, and also as to what benefits, if any, have resulted from and by the establishment of the Model School.

Conclusions/Recommendations

That the backward condition of these schools which are described as inferior in their knowledge of English, must be attributed mainly to the inability of the teachers to speak the English language freely; and that the teacher who finds it difficult to express his thoughts in English to pupils who know even less English than himself, naturally uses the language which both he and they understand;

That a much larger number of teachers are now competent to make effective use of English in the work of instruction than was indicated in the former report; and that it is gratifying to notice the decided advance made by the schools as a whole during the past four years.

References

Ontario / 138

Ontario, *Sessional Papers*, 1894, No. 4.

142 COMMISSION OF INQUIRY AS TO THE ONTARIO AGRICULTURAL COLLEGE AND EXPERIMENTAL FARM
(Judicial Commission)

Appointed June 8, 1893

Reported July 29, 1893

Commission Three members; John Winchester (Inspector of Legal Offices) chairman

Purpose To inquire into the want of harmony said to prevail in the Agricultural College and Experimental Farm at the City of Guelph amongst the staff, officers and others connected with the said institution, or some of them, and into the conduct of said persons so far as the Commissioners may deem the interests of the institution to require.

Conclusions/Recommendations

That it is in the interest of the institution that the rules, regulations and by-laws in connection with the institution be rigidly enforced;

That it is absolutely necessary that there be only one head of the institution, and he alone responsible to the Minister for the proper discharge of the duties of all the staff and officers connected therewith.

References

Ontario, *Report of the Commission of Inquiry as to the Ontario Agricultural College and Experimental Farm*, 1893.

143 SPECIAL INQUIRY INTO THE SEPARATE SCHOOLS OF OTTAWA
(Departmental Committee)

Appointed 1895

Reported February 12, 1896

Committee Three members; William Scott (Toronto Normal School) chairman

Purpose To inquire into the charges made against Mr. Inspector White by the Rev. Mr. Flamien representing the Christian Brothers and to visit the Separate Schools of the City of Ottawa for the purpose of making full and careful inquiry by personal inspection, and any other way that may be deemed expedient, into the methods of teaching in the said schools, the training of pupils in the various subjects prescribed in the course of study, the text books used by the pupils, and the extent to which the English language is taught in the schools where the French language prevails.

Conclusions/Recommendations

References

Ontario, *Sessional Papers*, 1896, No. 1.

144 COMMISSION OF INQUIRY INTO THE DISCIPLINE AND OTHER MATTERS IN THE UNIVERSITY OF TORONTO
(General Commission)

Appointed April 6, 1895

Reported April 27, 1895

Commission Five members; Thomas Wardlaw Taylor (Chief Justice of Manitoba) chairman

Purpose To inquire into all complaints that may be submitted by any student, or by any person on behalf of any student, in respect to the discipline or exercise of authority by the Councils of the University of Toronto and University College, and into all causes that led to the friction alleged to exist between such students and the said Councils, and into all matters bearing thereon; also into the qualifications, conduct, teaching and efficiency of any member of the Faculties of the University of Toronto and University College against whom any charge or complaint may be laid before the Commissioners; and to inquire into the respective powers of the various governing bodies of the University of Toronto and University College, and, so far as may be deemed necessary, into all matters bearing on the administration of such bodies since the date of the proclamation of the Revised Statutes of the Province of Ontario, chaptered two hundred and thirty, and entitled 'An Act respecting the Federation of University of Toronto and University College with other Universities and Colleges', including their dealing with the discipline of students and the various societies and associations of students.

Conclusions/Recommendations

That the University Council and University College Council were within their jurisdiction in dealing with the case as they did;

That the statements were not properly facts, they were mere assertions;

That the students completely failed to show any justification for their alleged belief.

References

Ontario, *Report of the Commissioners on the Discipline and Other Matters in the University of Toronto*, 1895.

145 COMMISSION OF INQUIRY INTO COST OF TEXT BOOKS
(General Commission)

Appointed November 12, 1897

Reported January 10, 1898

Commission Three members; Edward Morgan (York County Judge) chairman

Purpose To enquire as to the cost of text books in the Province of Ontario and elsewhere, and to the royalty paid on all text books used in the Public and High Schools.

Conclusions/Recommendations

That, since experts were all united in speaking in terms of high praise as to the literary quality and educational value of all school books now in use in the Public and High Schools of Ontario, and since the Readers were of excellent and durable quality, attractive in appearance, selling for a retail price not excessive, and infinitely better adapted for use in Ontario schools than either the Irish or American series, there seemed little reason for recommending changes;

That the policy of publishers paying royalties to authors was considered the best way of obtaining a book of acceptable calibre and of ensuring any necessary revisions and should be continued;

That the continued development of a Canadian text book literature was a wise and judicious policy and should be encouraged.

References

Ontario, *Text Book Committee*, 1897.

146 COMMISSION OF INQUIRY INTO THE MATTERS REFERRED TO IN A RESOLUTION OF THE SENATE OF THE UNIVERSITY OF TORONTO
(Judicial Commission)

<u>Appointed</u> February 2, 1905

<u>Reported</u> May 16, 1905

<u>Commission</u> Five members; W.R. Meredith (Chief Justice of Ontario) chairman

<u>Purpose</u> To investigate certain anonymous communications reflecting on the conduct of President Loudon and Professor McLennon in connection with the awarding of the 1851 Exhibition Scholarships in the years 1900 and 1904, and in other matters.

Conclusions/Recommendations

That although the Commissioners felt there had been no intentional deviousness in awarding the 1900 scholarship, they were of the opinion that under the circumstances the recommendation that the scholarship should be awarded to Mr. Patterson was irregular, and should not have been made;

That the general charges affecting the capacity, character and conduct of the President were not supported by the evidence and were unfounded, but that the evidence showed that the Presidency was heavily weighted with a multiplicity of duties not necessarily attaching to the office and of such a nature as in the judgment of the Commissioners to interfere seriously with the general oversight and careful co-ordination which were necessary to efficient and harmonious working in any large institution;

That the President be relieved of some of the duties which in their nature are less closely connected with his office;

That in respect of duties essential to his office, the President's hands be strengthened by a clear definition of his responsibilities and powers and by the increase thereof where necessary.

References

Ontario, *Report of the Commissioners Appointed to Inquire into and the Matters Referred to in a Resolution of the*

Ontario / 143

Senate of the University of Toronto Passed on the 20th Day of January, 1905.

147 ROYAL COMMISSION ON THE UNIVERSITY OF TORONTO (General Commission)

Appointed October 3, 1905

Reported April 4, 1906

Commission Seven members; Joseph W. Flavelle (Financier) chairman

Purpose To inquire into and report upon:

(a) A scheme for the management and government of the University of Toronto in the room and stead of the one under which the said University is now managed and governed.

(b) A scheme for the management and government of University College, including its relations to and connection with the said University of Toronto.

(c) The advisability of the incorporation of the School of Practical-Science with the University of Toronto.

(d) Such changes as in the opinion of the Commissioners should be brought about in the relations between the said University of Toronto and the several Colleges affiliated or federated therewith, having regard to the provisions of the Federation Act.

(e) Such suggestions and recommendations in connection with or arising out of any of the subjects thus indicated as in the opinion of the said Commissioners may be desirable.

Conclusions/Recommendations

That the administration of the University be divided between a Board of Governors (chosen by the Lieutenant-Governor-in-Council) which would possess the general oversight and financial control, and a Senate (representative of the federated and affiliated institutions and the faculties and graduates) and Faculty Councils which would direct the academic work and policy;

That the connecting bond between the Governors and the Senate be the President.

References

Ontario, *Report of the Royal Commission on the University of Toronto*, 1906.

148 COMMISSION OF INQUIRY INTO COST AND PRICES OF TEXT BOOKS (General Commission)

Appointed July 12, 1906

Reported January 31, 1907

Commission Two members; T.W. Crothers (St. Thomas Barrister) chairman

Purpose To enquire into and report upon the reasonableness of the present prices of School Text Books now on the authorized list, and to enquire into the prices of such publications elsewhere.

Conclusions/Recommendations

That it is clear that text book publishing in Ontario has fallen behind the times and that most of the books produced today are no better than those produced twenty years ago, whereas in the United States and Great Britain great progress has been made;

That if a satisfactory and modern set of readers cannot be secured one should be prepared by the Department, the copyright of all selections secured, the plates made, and the printing be given out by tender, under proper specifications to one firm;

That since the price of nearly all the high school books was too high, prices could be materially reduced without depriving the publishers of a fair profit;

That the Government investigate the free text book systems in vogue in Manitoba, the City of Toronto, and may cities of the United States.

References

Ontario, *Report of Text Book Committee*, 1907.

149 COMMISSION OF INQUIRY TO INVESTIGATE THE WORKINGS OF THE BLIND INSTITUTE AT BRANTFORD, AND THE DEAF AND DUMB INSTITUTE AT BELLEVILLE
(Judicial Commission)

Appointed October 5, 1906

Reported 1907 (?)

Commission One member; Alexander John Russell Snow (Toronto Barrister)

Purpose To investigate the workings of the Blind Institute at Brantford, and the Deaf and Dumb Institute at Belleville.

Conclusions/Recommendations

References

Ontario, Order-in-Council dated October 5, 1906, Executive Council files.

150 SURVEY OF TECHNICAL EDUCATION IN THE UNITED STATES AND EUROPE

(Departmental Committee)

Appointed 1909

Reported [ ]

Committee One member; John Seath (Superintendent of Education)

Purpose To visit Great Britain, France, Germany and Switzerland and examine the instruction given in the trade schools at certain centres in those countries.

Conclusions/Recommendations

References

Ontario, *Sessional Papers*, 1910, No. 16.

151 SPECIAL INQUIRY INTO THE ENGLISH-FRENCH SCHOOLS, PUBLIC AND SEPARATE, IN THE COUNTIES OF ESSEX AND KENT AND ELSEWHERE IN THE PROVINCE
(Departmental Committee)

Appointed November 4, 1910

Reported March 6, 1912

Committee One member; F.W. Merchant (Chief Inspector of Schools)

Purpose To investigate and report upon the English-French Schools, Public and Separate, of the Province.

Conclusions/Recommendations

References

Ontario, *Journals*, 1912.

152 SURVEY OF THE SYSTEMS OF INDUSTRIAL AND TECHNICAL INSTRUCTION IN EUROPE
(Departmental Committee)

Appointed 1913 (?)

Reported 1913

Committee One member; F.W. Merchant (Director of Industrial and Technical Education)

Purpose To investigate the systems of industrial and technical instruction in Europe.

Conclusions/Recommendations

References

Ontario, *Journals*, 1914.

153 COMMISSION OF INQUIRY INTO MEDICAL EDUCATION IN ONTARIO
(Related Commission)

Appointed September 29, 1915

Reported October 13, 1917

Commission One member; Frank E. Hodgins (Supreme Court Justice)

Purpose To investigate medical education in Ontario.

Conclusions/Recommendations

That the whole subject seemed to require a thorough inquiry into the standing, capacity, and numbers of those who desired to bring about any radical change, as well as into the educational record and constitution of the bodies advocating or resisting it, and a candid consideration of the results of all of those parties and to the interests of the public of the Province as well.

References

Ontario, *Report and Supporting Statements on Medical Education in Ontario*, 1917.

154 COMMISSION OF INQUIRY INTO CERTAIN COMPLAINTS AGAINST THE INTERNAL DISCIPLINE AND MANAGEMENT OF THE ONTARIO SCHOOL FOR THE BLIND, BRANTFORD
(Judicial Commission)

Appointed April 26, 1916

Reported February 12, 1917

Commission One member; N.B. Gash (King's Counsel)

Purpose To enquire into certain complaints made to the Department of Education of the Province against the internal discipline and management of the Ontario School for the Blind, Brantford, and the report upon the same, as well as the general administration, conduct and welfare thereof, and any other matters or questions arising thereout, or in the course of the inquiry.

Conclusions/Recommendations

(There were five pages of recommendations under the headings: Constitution, Management and Discipline; Literary Department; Gymnasium, Physical Exercises and Fire Drill; Physical, Social and Moral; Printing; School Premises; Extension of Manual or Vocational Training; Administration and Inspection; Prevention of Blindness and Conservation of Vision; The Adult Blind.)

That there be closer supervision by the principal and his assistants;

That the discipline of the institution be more strictly under the supervision of the superintendent, and where physical punishment is needed, only the strap be used;

That an open-air skating rink, as well as a slide for tobogganing or sleighing, be laid out on the grounds for use by the students during the winter months. The natural features of the grounds can be used for the latter.

References

Ontario, *Royal Commission to Inquire into the Administration, Management and Welfare of the Ontario School for the Blind,* 1917.

155 COMMISSION OF INQUIRY INTO THE CARE AND CONTROL OF THE MENTALLY DEFECTIVE AND FEEBLE-MINDED IN ONTARIO (Related Commission)

Appointed November 18, 1917

Reported October 18, 1919

Commission One member; Frank E. Hodgins (Supreme Court Justice)

Purpose To inquire into the care and control of the mentally defective and feeble-minded in Ontario.

Conclusions/Recommendations

That it is in the schools that the most useful work can be done in ascertaining the mental condition of the vast majority of children between the ages of 8 and 14 years, now increased to 18 years under the Adolescent School Attendance Act, 1919;

That special classes need trained teachers whose powers of observation have been quickened and informed by previous technical study;

That it is of great importance that these classes should be designated as for special training, as there is a distinct value to be got by avoiding the error of treating the children in them ostensibly as feeble-minded;

That it is comparatively easy to form these classes in urban centres where one school in a district can be equipped with a specially trained teacher and supplied with the necessary and appropriate aids to the teaching required;

That there should be thorough provision for physical, manual and vocational training and for physical development, as this saves very many from institutional life;

That the end to be aimed at is that when their schooling is done they may remain with their families and, under their care and supervision, progress in the direction of self-support in the community or pass into training schools specially fitted for their highest development in manual and industrial efficiency.

References

Ontario, *Report on the Care and Control of the Mentally Defective and Feeble-Minded in Ontario*, 1919.

156 COMMISSION OF INQUIRY INTO THE BUILDING DEPARTMENT OF THE BOARD OF EDUCATION OF THE CITY OF TORONTO
(Judicial Commission)

Appointed — January 9, 1918

Reported — [ ]

Commission — One member; Haughton I.S. Lennox (Supreme Court Justice)

Purpose — To inquire into and report upon the Building Department of the Board of Education of the City of Toronto as requested by said body.

Conclusions/Recommendations

References

Ontario, Order-in-Council, dated January 9, 1918,

Ontario / 151

Executive Council files.

157 COMMISSION OF INQUIRY INTO THE ADMINISTRATION, MANAGEMENT, CONDUCT, DISCIPLINE, EQUIPMENT, AND WELFARE OF THE VICTORIA INDUSTRIAL SCHOOL
(Judicial Commission)

Appointed January 29, 1920

Reported April 15, 1921

Commission Three members; John Waugh (Chief Inspector of Public and Separate Schools) chairman

Purpose To inquire into and report upon the administration, management, conduct, discipline, equipment and welfare of The Victoria Industrial School, and any other matters or questions arising thereout or in the course of the inquiry.

Conclusions/Recommendations

That the Victoria Industrial School at Mimico be replaced by: a Reception and Observation Home visited regularly by a psychiatrist, or physician, and an educational official; a Training School to provide for older boys with strongly marked anti-social tendencies; a Provincial Auxiliary School to take charge of normal unfortunates, retarded and physically defective boys;

That the organization be flexible enough to permit regrouping, or transfer from one school to another when found necessary or advisable;

That especial attention be given to making the lives of the boys as happy and homelike as possible if permanent improvement is to be accomplished.

References

Ontario, Order-in-Council dated January 29, 1920, Executive Council files.

158 ROYAL COMMISSION ON UNIVERSITY FINANCE
(General Commission)

<u>Appointed</u> October 27, 1920

<u>Reported</u> February 10, 1921

<u>Commission</u> Six members; Henry J. Cody (former Minister of Education) chairman

<u>Purpose</u> (a) to inquire into and report upon a basis for determining the financial obligations of the Province toward the University of Toronto, and the financial aid which the Province may give to Queen's University of Kingston and the Western University of London; (b) to recommend such permanent plan of public aid to the said Universities as shall bear a just and reasonable relation to the amount of the legislative grants to primary and secondary education, and (c) to make such suggestions on any of the above subjects as may seem, in the opinion of the Commission, to be desirable.

<u>Conclusions/Recommendations</u>

That there be substantially increased financial aid to higher education;

That for the maintenance of the Provincial University and of University College the basis of support in the 1906 Act be restored, that is, a yearly sum equal to 50 percent of the average of the succession duties for the preceding three years;

That annual maintenance grants, to be adjusted every five years, be paid to Queen's and Western Universities;

That for urgently needed buildings, capital grants of $1,500,000 to the University of Toronto, $800,000 to Western, and $340,000 to Queen's be awarded;

That if future enrollment made it necessary, the transfer of present first-year university work to collegiate institutes and high schools be considered;

That a Department of Graduate Studies and Research be organized in the Provincial University as soon as practicable.

References

Ontario, *Report of Royal Commission on University Finance*, 1921.

159 COMMISSION ON INQUIRY INTO EXAMINATION IRREGULARITIES (Judicial Commission)

Appointed 1921

Reported [ ]

Commission One member; J.H. Putman (Inspector of Public Schools)

Purpose To investigate the theft of examination papers during the 1921 examinations.

Conclusions/Recommendations

References

Minutes of University Matriculation Board, November 27, 1922.

Ontario, *Journals*, 1923.

160 SPECIAL COMMITTEE TO INVESTIGATE THE ORGANIZATION AND ADMINISTRATION OF THE UNIVERSITY OF TORONTO (Legislative Committee)

Appointed June 8, 1922

Reported May 2, 1923

Committee Nine members; E.C. Drury (Member for Halton)

chairman

Purpose — To investigate the organization and administration of the University of Toronto, including its relation with Federated Colleges and with the Toronto General Hospital and to make any recommendations which the committee desire in the public's interest.

Conclusions/Recommendations

References

Ontario, *Journals*, 1922.

Ontario, *Report of Special Committee Appointed by the Legislature to Inquire into the Organization and Administration of the University of Toronto*, 1923.

161 COMMISSION OF INQUIRY INTO THE BUILDING DEPARTMENT OF THE OTTAWA SCHOOL BOARD
(Judicial Commission)

Appointed — March 21, 1924

Reported — [ ]

Commission — One member; John A. McDonald (Ottawa Public School Board Trustee)

Purpose — To inquire into and report on the Building Department of the Ottawa Public School Board.

Conclusions/Recommendations

References

Ontario, Order-in-Council dated March 21, 1924, Executive Council files.

162 COMMISSION OF INQUIRY INTO AFFAIRS OF THE OSHAWA BOARD OF EDUCATION
(Judicial Commission)

Appointed September 1, 1925

Reported [ ]

Commission One commissioner; Judge Ruddy (Ontario County Judge) [Judge Ruddy declined, and information is not available as to whether a replacement was named.]

Purpose The Oshawa Board of Education desired an investigation into the affairs of the Board for the past three years.

Conclusions/Recommendations

References

Ontario, Order-in-Council dated September 1, 1925, Executive Council files.

163 SPECIAL INQUIRY INTO THOSE SCHOOLS IN THE PROVINCE ATTENDED BY PUPILS WHO SPEAK THE FRENCH LANGUAGE
(Departmental Committee)

Appointed October 21, 1925

Reported August 26, 1927

Committee Three members; F.W. Merchant (Chief Director of Education) chairman

Purpose To investigate those schools in the Province attended by pupils who speak the French language with a view of determining the efficiency of the schools, means for improving the instruction, and plans for securing a more constant supply of qualified teachers for the schools.

Conclusions/Recommendations

That the necessity for securing better instruction in English and in French and of improving the general status of the schools is so urgent it be made the responsibility of two special officers to be appointed by the Department of Education, a Director of English Instruction and a Director of French Instruction; and that the duty of these officers be to keep themselves constantly in touch with the schools in all parts of the Province, to study all phases of the problems presented, and to cooperate with inspectors and teachers in setting up standards and in devising ways and means to make instruction effective.

References

Ontario, *Report of the Committee Appointed to Enquire into the Conditions of the Schools Attended by French-Speaking Pupils*, 1927, App.A.

164 COMMISSION OF INQUIRY INTO OTTAWA COLLEGIATE CONDITIONS (Judicial Commission)

Appointed October 26, 1926

Reported January 6, 1927

Commission One member; John Fosbery Orde (Supreme Court Justice)

Purpose To enquire into and report upon the conditions alleged by Rev. E.B. Wyllie to exist in the Ottawa Collegiate Institute.

Conclusions/Recommendations

That there was not a tittle of evidence to indicate that at any of these school dances had there ever been any immoral or improper or objectional conduct or drinking;

That Dr. Wyllie has failed completely to justify his statements, and that, so far as the evidence discloses, there is no reason to believe that any of the conditions which he alleged as rendering it unsafe for parents to send their children to the Ottawa Collegiate Institute exist at all, or that the management and supervision of the schools and of the social activities of the pupils are not as efficient and perfect as is reasonably possible.

References

Ontario, Order-in-Council dated October 26, 1926, Executive Council files.

Ontario, *Royal Commission on Ottawa Collegiate Conditions*, 1927.

165 COMMITTEE TO INVESTIGATE THE COSTS OF EDUCATION IN ONTARIO
(Departmental Committee)

Appointed May, 1935

Reported March 25, 1938

Committee Eight members; D. McArthur (Deputy Minister of Education) chairman

Purpose To investigate the costs of education in Ontario.

Conclusions/Recommendations

That the total cost of education as well as the cost per pupil in elementary and secondary schools increased steadily from 1910 to 1930, but since that year has declined gradually;

That the increase in the cost of education was due (a) to the demand on the part of parents and employers for a longer period of training for youth in secondary schools and for a type of training which involved relatively large capital expenditures for buildings and equipment and (b) to the necessity for employing a larger number of teachers and to an increase in the salaries of teachers, due largely to the post-war increase in the cost of living;

That the decline in the cost of education since 1930 has been due chiefly to a reduction in teachers' salaries; that during the next ten years there should be a reduction in the amounts required annually for the retirement of debentures; and that during this period teachers' salaries are likely to be increased rather than reduced, because of a decline in the supply of teachers;

That the attendance at secondary schools is not likely to decline until there is an extension of opportunities for the employment of adolescents, and, consequently, that the number of teachers required is not likely to be reduced;

That criticism of the cost of education has been directed chiefly to the incidence of the taxes required for its payment, and, particularly, to the unequal distribution of the burden of taxation between real estate and other forms of property, between different municipalities, and between different groups in the same municipality;

That it is desirable that the burden of taxation on real estate should be reduced, and that, as a means to that end, consideration should be given to the taxation by the Province of other forms of wealth and to the distribution of the proceeds of such taxation to the municipalities in the form of increased grants in aid of education;

That there is great inequality in the assessed value of the taxable property of secondary school districts and of public school and separate school sections throughout the Province, and, consequently, in the mill rates of the taxation which must be imposed for the support of education.

References

Ontario, *Report of the Committee of Enquiry into the Cost of Education in the Province of Ontario*, 1938.

166 ROYAL COMMISSION ON EDUCATION
(General Commission)

Appointed March 21, 1945

Ontario / 159

Reported — December 15, 1950

Commission — Twenty-one members; John Andrew Hope (Supreme Court Justice) chairman

Purpose — To inquire into and report upon the provincial education system, and without derogating from the generality thereof, including courses of study, text books, examinations, financing, and the general system and scheme of elementary and secondary schools involving public schools, separate schools, continuation schools, high schools, collegiate institutes, vocational schools, schools for the training of teachers and all other schools under the jurisdiction of the Department of Education, as well as the selection and training of teachers, inspectors, and other officials of such schools, and the system of provincial and local school administration.

Conclusions/Recommendations

(Major recommendations included:)

That the province's school system be reorganized into a three phase 6-4-3 programme;

That publicly supported Roman Catholic separate schools terminate at grade 6;

That the official language of instruction and communication in all publicly supported schools of Ontario be English;

That school districts throughout the province be totally reorganized in order to create larger units of administration;

That a new system of grants and educational financing be created;

('Non-disagreement' recommendations included:)

That there be expanded research and experimentation in education;

That there be province-wide improvement in library facilities;

That there be multiple authorization of textbooks;

That education keep abreast of audio-visual and other teaching techniques;

That there be closer medical and dental supervision of students;

That there be a gradated counselling service;

That there be less stress on external examinations;

That there be more diversified technical training;

That there be closer concern for exceptional children.

References

Ontario, *Report of the Royal Commission on Education in Ontario,* 1950.

167 MINISTER'S COMMITTEE ON THE TRAINING OF SECONDARY SCHOOL TEACHERS
(Departmental Committee)

Appointed February 23, 1961

Reported 1962

Committee Twelve members; F.G. Patten (Superintendent of Secondary Schools) chairman

Purpose To investigate:

1. Admission requirements of colleges of education and the courses at universities leading thereto.

2. The curriculum in special subjects and summer courses therein.

3. Practice teaching in all its aspects.

4. Diplomas, certificates, and degrees.

5. The relationship of the colleges to the universities and to the Department of Education in matters both academic and non-academic.

6. The relationship of the academic and the professional education of teachers, in both time and arrangement.

Conclusions/Recommendations

(There were 148 recommendations under the headings of Staff, Admission Requirements, Courses, Theoretical Instruction, Practice Teaching, Evaluation, Extra Responsibilities, The Student, Summer Courses, Finances, Location and Structure.)

That at least two new colleges of education be established in different parts of the province, and that such new colleges follow the pattern of graduate school attached to a university;

That modern facilities be provided for the Ontario College of Education which would continue as a graduate school;

That secondary teacher training be a post-graduate year at a college of education rather than any scheme of concurrent training in academic and professional subjects.

References

Ontario, *Report of the Minister's Committee on the Training of Secondary School Teachers*, 1962.

168 SELECT COMMITTEE ON MANPOWER TRAINING
(Legislative Committee)

Appointed April 18, 1962

Reported March 27, 1963

Committee Eleven members; J.R. Simonett (Member for Frontenac-Addington) chairman

Purpose To investigate the entire range of manpower training and development programs in Ontario: full-time courses in secondary schools, trade schools, and technical institutes as well as part-time extension programs therein; training for employable unemployed as well as measures designed to upgrade those already employed; and formal apprenticeship programs as well as less formalized methods for occupational betterment and advancement.

Conclusions/Recommendations

That although many of the attributes of the whole man can be imparted to the student or worker at the same time he receives his vocational preparation, the time which can be devoted to such matters will leave much to be desired;

That for this reason the tremendous variety of academic and cultural enrichment courses which are being offered in night classes in many centres across the Province is very welcome;

That it does seem reasonable to assert that unless we turn out employable men we cannot hope to develop whole men;

That historically, Ontario has tended to emphasize academic preparation, often at the expense of vocational education and training; and that it is vital that this imbalance be corrected as quickly as possible.

References

Ontario, *Report of the Select Committee on Manpower Training*, 1963.

169 ONTARIO COMMITTEE ON TAXATION
(Related Commission)

Ontario / 163

Appointed February 26, 1963

Reported August 30, 1967

Commission Five members; Lancelot J. Smith (Chartered Accountant, Toronto) chairman

Purpose To inquire into and report upon the taxation and revenue system of Ontario and its municipalities and school boards in relation to their expenditures, the tax and revenue sources available to them, their debts and other financial obligations, with a view of determining whether, within the constitutional limitations existing and having regard to present and potential financial requirements, such tax and revenue system is as simple, clear, equitable, efficient, adequate and as conducive to the sound growth of the Province as can be devised.

Conclusions/Recommendations

That public education is peculiarly well suited to local government, and whether the criterion is a reasonably open market for teacher's services, diversity and experimentation in education, or the need for school programs that are accommodated to regional peculiarities, local authority over education hold out greater promise than central administration;

That if it is to be more than an illusion, such local authority must be marked by a genuine degree of autonomy, and to be genuine, governmental autonomy must have a basis in the revenue system;

That the requisitioning powers of public school boards, separate school boards and boards of education be terminated, and that these boards levy their own taxes to be collected through bills issued for the purpose by municipalities and payable at times distinct from those at which municipal tax bills are payable.

References

Ontario / 164

Ontario, *The Ontario Committee on Taxation: Report*, 1967.

170 ROYAL COMMISSION ON METROPOLITAN TORONTO
(Related Commission)

Appointed June 20, 1963

Reported June 10, 1965

Commission One member; H. Carl Goldenberg (Barrister of Montreal)

Purpose To inquire into and report upon

(a) the structure and organization of the Municipality of Metropolitan Toronto and, more particularly of the Metropolitan Council and the Metropolitan School Board, their functions and responsibilities and the relations with the area municipalities and the local school boards respectively and with municipalities and planning boards within the Metropolitan Toronto planning area,

(b) the purposes and objectives of the establishment of the Metropolitan Corporation and the Metropolitan School Board, the extent of the accomplishment of such objectives and whether such objectives can be better achieved under a new or revised system of local government, having regard to the past and future development and needs,

(c) the boundaries of the metropolitan area and of the area municipalities and their suitability in the light of the experience gained through the operations of the metropolitan government, with due regard to probable future urban growth within or beyond the present metropolitan limits and future service requirements,

(d) any related matters affecting the government

of the Toronto metropolitan region.

Conclusions/Recommendations

That the Metropolitan Toronto Board of Education be responsible for developing an acceptable and uniformly high standard consistent with area-wide formulae for most major items of expense, while the local districts be allowed some discretionary fiscal powers for special purposes, such as experimentation;

That the varying school rates in the area be replaced by a uniform tax rate for public schools.

References

Ontario, *Report of the Royal Commission on Metropolitan Toronto*, 1965.

171 GRADE 13 STUDY COMMITTEE
(Departmental Committee)

Appointed February, 1964

Reported June 26, 1964

Committee Seventeen members; Fred A. Hamilton (Director of Education, Guelph) chairman

Purpose To inquire into the nature and function of Grade 13.

Conclusions/Recommendations

That the secondary school proper conclude at Grade 12;

That beyond this, two-year community colleges be provided in addition to the existing pattern of universities, teachers' colleges, and polytechnical institutes;

That the university-preparatory courses be offered not in Grade 13 but in Grade 12, and (as the Matriculation Year) be but one of a number of programmes offered in that grade;

That the preparatory programme include studies in breadth and in depth;

That until this ideal situation was accomplished, course content in Grade 13 be somewhat lightened, some credit be given for a student's term work, and Departmental examinations be shorter with more options.

References

Ontario, *Report of the Grade 13 Study Committee*, 1964.

172 SELECT COMMITTEE ON YOUTH
(Legislative Committee)

Appointed May 8, 1964

Reported April 6, 1967

Committee Fourteen members; Sylvanus Apps (Member for Kingston) chairman

Purpose To conduct a comprehensive inquiry into and report upon the special needs of youth, with particular reference to educational, cultural, recreational, and employment opportunities, as well as the health, welfare and sports facilities now available to youth, and the steps to be taken which in the opinion of the Committee would ensure a wider participation by youth in the life of the community.

Conclusions/Recommendations

That a separate Provincial Department of Youth, with its own Cabinet Minister be formed at the earliest convenience of the Legislature;

That sex education be undertaken by the schools as part of a core of social subject matter that would include family living, alcohol, drugs, and smoking;

That a course in civics compiled and supervised by the

Department of Education be given in elementary and secondary schools;

That physical education and physical fitness be encouraged;

That guidance facilities be improved;

That teachers be given more training in the behavioural sciences of applied psychology, child development and sociology at the Teachers' Colleges;

That school facilities be made available to responsible groups within the community at token rates;

That equality of opportunity in education, recreation and job opportunities be provided for Indian citizens;

That the Ontario Government request the Federal Government to establish an Office of Education.

References

Ontario, *Votes and Proceedings of the Legislative Assembly of the Province of Ontario*, No. 69.

Ontario, *Report of the Ontario Legislative's Select Committee on Youth*, 1967.

73 MINISTER'S COMMITTEE ON THE TRAINING OF ELEMENTARY SCHOOL TEACHERS
(Departmental Committee)

Appointed September 28, 1964

Reported March 29, 1966

Committee Eighteen members; C.R. MacLeod (Superintendent of Public Schools) chairman

Purpose 1. to examine the teacher training programme now being followed at the Ontario Teachers' Colleges;

2. to examine other selected teacher training programmes;

3. to recommend changes that might be made immediately to improve the present One-year Course;

4. to develop, in some detail, what the committee considers to be an ideal programme for the training of teachers for the elementary schools of Ontario;

5. to suggest the successive steps that might be taken, over a period of time, to achieve the implementation of this ideal programme.

Conclusions/Recommendations

(Included in the 47 recommendations were the following:)

That responsibility for certification of teachers continue to rest with the Minister of Education;

That the program for teacher education be provided by the university; and that it be of four years' duration leading to a baccalaureate degree and professional certification, and elementary and secondary teacher education be offered within the same university faculty or college where feasible;

That all candidates for teacher education comply with regular university admission requirements and share the privileges and responsibilities of the students in other faculties;

That liberal arts professors and professors of education cooperate closely in preparing and carrying out the program of teacher education;

That approximately 75% of the four-year program be devoted to academic studies and approximately 25% to professional preparation;

That the four main components in teacher education be a liberal or academic education, foundations of education, curriculum and instruction, practice teaching;

That alternate routes of preparation include a concurrent plan, a consecutive plan, and an internship plan;

That programs be challenging, and there be opportunity for specialization;

That carefully chosen committees of selection appraise candidates' suitability for the teaching profession and recommend acceptance or rejection;

That the recruitment of capable students be undertaken cooperatively by the Department of Education, the Ontario Teachers' Federation, Colleges of Education, and local boards of trustees;

That every effort be made to attract to the staffs of the colleges competent scholars and distinguished and successful teachers;

That post-graduate study for teachers be encouraged.

References

Ontario, Department of Education memorandum dated September 28, 1964.

Ontario, *Report of Minister's Committee on the Training of Elementary School Teachers*, 1966.

174 COMMITTEE ON AIMS AND OBJECTIVES OF EDUCATION (Departmental Committee)

Appointed June 10, 1965

Reported June 12, 1968

Committee Twenty-two members; E.M. Hall (Supreme Court Justice) and L.A. Dennis (Secretary, Provincial Committee on Aims and Objectives) co-chairmen

<u>Purpose</u>

1. to identify the needs of the child as a member of society;

2. to set forth the aims of education for the educational system of the Province;

3. to outline objectives of the curriculum for children in the age groups presently designated as Kindergarten, Primary, and Junior Divisions;

4. to propose means by which these aims and objectives may be achieved;

5. to submit a report for the consideration of the Minister of Education.

<u>Conclusions/Recommendations</u>

(Among the 258 recommendations grouped under the headings of The Learning Program, Special Learning Situations, The World of Teaching, and Organizing for Learning, were the following.)

That a continuum for public education consisting of a minimum of kindergarten and 12 additional years be established;

That the Grade 13 year be phased out as soon as possible and its curriculum areas absorbed within the 12-year continuum;

That the lock-step system of organizing pupils, such as grades, streams, programs, etc., be eliminated, and learners be permitted to move through the school in a manner which will ensure continuous progress;

That horizontal and vertical divisions of pupils, such as elementary, secondary, academic, vocational and commercial be removed;

That learning experiences be organized around general areas such as Communications, Environmental Studies, and the Humanities;

That French or English be designated as the second language to be offered for study;

That student learning profiles that reveal the individual progress and experience of each student throughout the learning continuum be developed;

That the use of class standing, percentage marks, and letter grades be abandoned in favor of parent and pupil counselling as a method of reporting individual progress;

That the use of formal examinations be abandoned except where the experience would be of value to students planning to attend universities where formal examinations may still be in use;

That schools and school districts as demonstration schools and areas for particular projects and investigations be selected;

That decision-making related to curriculum design and implementation be located at the school board level and in particular at the individual school level;

That, where the membership in the Indian community agrees, the transfer of all federal schools on Indian reserves to school boards be negotiated with the Federal Government, the continuing costs of this program to remain a federal responsibility;

That a Teaching Profession Act be enacted which will make teaching a self-governing profession with powers to license and to discipline its members, these powers to be exercised through an organization to be known as the College of Teachers of Ontario;

That all teachers' organizations be consolidated into one association to be known as the Ontario Teachers Association;

That each faculty of education be allowed to develop its curriculum and its operations freely;

That the focus be upon the processes of learning rather than upon the acquisition of a methodology of teaching;

That professional and academic studies be included which will stress child development and psychology;

That, within the faculties, methods be employed, such as co-operative teaching, programmed instruction, field trips, group research, etc., in order to stimulate the student to accept them as a regular part of teaching practice.

References

Ontario, *Curriculum Bulletin*, Vol. 1 No. 2, May, 1965.

Ontario, *Living and Learning: The Report of the Provincial Committee on Aims and Objectives of Education in the Schools of Ontario*, 1968.

175 COMMISSION TO STUDY THE DEVELOPMENT OF GRADUATE PROGRAMS IN ONTARIO UNIVERSITIES
(Special Committee)

Appointed August, 1965

Reported November, 1966

Committee Three members; John W.T. Spinks (President, University of Saskatchewan) chairman

Purpose To study matters concerning the quality, need, introduction and expansion of graduate education and research in Ontario and the financial support for these programmes.

Conclusions/Recommendations

That the Provincial Government adopt a method of determining university operating and capital grants such as will permit rational forward planning with respect to graduate studies and research;

That the Province take appropriate steps to ensure co-operation and co-ordination between the universities in the field of graduate studies and research, with a view both to develop excellence and to economize resources;

That steps be taken to develop a number of centres of excellence in the universities of Ontario, which might achieve an international respect and renown;

That an Ontario Universities Research Council be established;

That the Ontario Universities Research Council be asked to assume responsibility for the Ontario Graduate Fellowship Program;

That the Provincial Government adopt a plan of adequate support for those graduate students not supported by Federal and private plans;

That the Provincial Government make provision for adequate research facilities;

That an Ontario Provincial Universities Library be established;

That a provincial University of Ontario be established to co-ordinate Ontario universities.

References

Ontario, *Report of the Commission to Study the Development of Graduate Programmes in Ontario Universities*, 1966. (Submitted to the Committee on University Affairs and the Committee of Presidents of provincially-assisted universities).

176 MINISTER'S COMMITTEE ON RELIGIOUS EDUCATION (Departmental Committee)

Appointed — January 27, 1966

Reported — February 2, 1969

Committee — Seven members; J. Keiller MacKay (former Lieutenant-Governor of Ontario) chairman

Purpose — To examine and evaluate the present program;

> to receive representations from all interested bodies about the effectiveness and desirability of the program; to consider suggestions for changes and improvement; to study means by which character building, ethics, social attitudes and moral values and principles may best be instilled in the young; to consider the responsibility of the Public Schools in these matters; and to make recommendations thereon for the information and consideration of the Minister.

Conclusions/Recommendations

That the present course of study in religious education in the elementary schools of Ontario be discontinued, and that its aims as set out in related legislation, programs of studies, regulations, and guide books, be abandoned;

That in the elementary schools of Ontario opening exercises consisting of the National Anthem and a prayer, either of universal character appealing to God for help in the day's activities, or the Lord's Prayer, be held in the home rooms each morning;

That in the secondary schools of the province opening exercises consisting of the National Anthem and either a prayer of universal character or the Lord's Prayer, be held at the beginning of any student assembly but not daily in the classroom;

That the high duty of public education to foster character building be discharged through a clearly understood, continuously pursued, universal program pervading every curricular and extracurricular activity in the public school system from the beginning of elementary to the close of secondary education;

That the acquisition of information about and respect for all religions be recognized as an essential objective of the educational system from kindergarten to grade 13. This should be achieved by a program of incidental teaching and study, not through a formal syllabus;

That a formal course of study dealing with the principal

religions of the world be offered as one of the optional courses in grades 11 and 12 in the secondary schools; instruction in these courses to be given by members of the history department;

That in addition to the assumption by the teachers' colleges, future faculties of education, and colleges of education, of the teacher-training responsibilities in relation to the new program as outlined in the body of this report, the Department of Education should provide for the professional development of the present teaching body through the planning and encouragement of workshops, summer courses, and other appropriate in-service activities.

References

Ontario, *Report of Committee on Religious Education in the Public Schools of the Province of Ontario*, 1969.

177 TASK FORCE ON SCHOOL HEALTH SERVICES
(Departmental Committee)

Appointed April, 1967

Reported December, 1972 [to Minister of Health]

Committee Ten members; Jean F. Webb (Chief, Maternal and Child Health Service) chairman

Purpose To examine school health programs and services in order to develop guidelines for the organization and delivery of health services in schools in Ontario.

Conclusions/Recommendations

That School Health Services be administered as an integral part of the community health program;

That the Chairman of the School Health Coordinating Committee be a member of the School Board staff;

That a health assessment of each student be carried out on

or before entry into the school system;

That vision screening be carried out three times and hearing screening twice during schooling;

That tuberculin testing be done on all school entrants and at age 15;

That health information gathered in a uniform manner through School Health Services be tabulated at regular intervals and used to evaluate current health needs and the effectiveness of programs in meeting these needs.

References

Ontario, *Report of the Task Force on School Health Services*, December 1972.

178 COMMITTEE ON FRENCH LANGUAGE SCHOOLS IN ONTARIO (Departmental Committee)

Appointed	November 24, 1967
Reported	November 28, 1968
Committee	Eleven members; R.R. Bériault (Department of Education Policy and Development Council) chairman
Purpose	To look at the broad spectrum of French language education in Ontario and to advise the Government as to the procedures required to provide adequate opportunities in the public education system for those who are French-speaking.

Conclusions/Recommendations

That a special committee (the French Language Committee) be created to represent the views of the Franco-Ontarians to the school boards;

That steps be taken at the departmental level to establish

special elementary schools for English-speaking pupils whose parents wish to have them achieve proficiency in the two official languages of this country;

That teachers in French-language schools follow the same pedagogical principles and basic instructional guidelines as teachers in other Ontario schools;

That the French-language secondary schools be given the opportunity of coming into contact with educational and cultural developments of the French-speaking society at large, either in Canada or in other French-speaking countries;

That wherever possible, French be the language of instruction in all subjects of the curriculum, with the exception of English;

That an effort be made to recruit teachers for French-language schools from other provinces of Canada and from French-speaking countries;

That staffs of French-language schools and universities encourage young French-speaking students to enter the teacher profession.

References

Ontario, *Report of the Committee on French Language Schools in Ontario*, 1968.

179 COMMISSION ON THE GOVERNMENT OF THE UNIVERSITY OF TORONTO (Special Committee)

Appointed December 1968

Reported October 16, 1969

Committee Nine members; L.E. Lynch (Chairman of Philosophy, St. Michael's College) and A.J. Webster (Graduate Student in Political Economy) co-chairmen

<u>Purpose</u> To examine the whole structure of the University of Toronto.

Conclusions/Recommendations

That meetings of all university councils and committees be open to members of the university community, university media, the mass media, and members of the general community;

That appropriate standard rating questionnaires be developed and administered routinely every year for all courses and teachers, so that broadly-based objective information is generated;

That promotions not involving tenure and below the rank of full professor be made by the chairman of the department on the advice of the departmental personnel committee;

That promotions to full professor and the award of tenure be made by the dean on the advice of an ad hoc personnel committee of the faculty council;

That faculty, college and departmental councils take responsibility for defining their long-term objectives, and relating those needs to developments in the university as a whole;

That the students in every department form a department students' union or club, and that this body be recognized as the legitimate representative voice of the students in any given department;

That any part of the university which administers its own degree or diploma programme be known as a faculty, and that the term 'division' be reserved for a section of a faculty.

References

Toward Community in University Government, University of Toronto Press, 1970. [Described as 'an independent commission of the university community as a whole']

180 COMMISSION ON POST-SECONDARY EDUCATION IN ONTARIO (Departmental Committee)

Appointed April 15, 1969

Reported December 20, 1972 [to Minister of University Affairs]

Committee Thirteen members; Douglas T. Wright (Chairman, Committee on University Affairs) first chairman; D.O. Davis (Council of Regents, Colleges of Applied Arts and Technology) final chairman

Purpose To consider, in the light of present provisions for university and other post-secondary education in Ontario, the pattern necessary to ensure the further effective development of post-secondary education in the Province during the period to 1980, and in general terms to 1990, and make recommendations thereon.

Conclusions/Recommendations

That socially useful alternatives to post-secondary education be provided;

That community involvement in manpower programs be established;

That legislation, structures and programs be devised to facilitate the return to learning opportunities for professionals, salaried employees, wage earners, and all other persons residing in Ontario;

That, where possible, institutions of post-secondary education provide part-time students with a range and quality of learning opportunities equal to those available to full-time students;

That provision be made for employees to have the right to time off for study;

That the present grade 13 standard of education be

attainable in 12 years, allowing individuals entry to all forms of post-secondary education after 12 years of schooling;

That there be established within the open educational sector an Open Academy of Ontario;

That the Government of Ontario adopt policies that would permit the establishment of a number of small, limited charter colleges;

That discrimination on the basis of sex in all sectors and on all levels of post-secondary education in Ontario, with regard to pay, rank and advancement, be abolished;

That efforts be made in the field of continuing education to provide appropriate educational and cultural services to adults among the native peoples.

References

Ontario, *The Learning Society: Report of the Commission on Post-Secondary Education in Ontario*, 1972.

181 STUDY COMMITTEE ON RECREATION SERVICES IN ONTARIO (Departmental Committee)

Appointed June, 1969

Reported 1970

Committee Thirty members; R. Secord (Director of Youth and Recreation Branch) chairman

Purpose To make recommendations regarding the provision of recreation services designed to obtain maximum benefits for the people of Ontario.

Conclusions/Recommendations

That services related to community recreation presently divided among several provincial departments be consolidated within the jurisdiction of a single and, if necessary, new provincial administration;

That the Ontario educational system examine completely its philosophy in relation to community development and community leisure services;

That boards of education be encouraged to extend the use of their facilities and services for leisure and community use;

That consultative services for the formulation of educational curriculum in leisure be provided without delay by the Department of Education to the Ontario educational system;

That schools provide some recreation programs based on their special resources during non-school time;

That boards of education, the local community college and the university strive to achieve and maintain a high level of operative coordination.

References

Ontario, *Report of the Study Committee on Recreation Services in Ontario*, 1970.

182 TASK FORCE ON INDUSTRIAL TRAINING
(Departmental Committee)

Appointed October 1970

Reported 1973 [To Minister of Colleges and Universities]

Committee Six members; W.R. Dymond (Chairman, Department of Public Administration, University of Ottawa) chairman

Purpose To study existing industrial training programs and to make recommendations.

Conclusions/Recommendations

That a single branch to be known as the Employer-centered Training Branch in the Ministry of Colleges and Universities be constituted, to be responsible for the development and co-ordination of all employer-centred training programs, including apprenticeship, in the province;

That an Employer-centred Training Division be established in each College of Applied Arts and Technology;

That a Vocational Counselling Service be established as part of the Ministry of Colleges and Universities.

References

Ontario, *Training for Ontario's Future: Report of the Task Force on Industrial Training*, 1973.

183 COMMITTEE OF INQUIRY INTO NEGOTIATION PROCEDURES CONCERNING ELEMENTARY AND SECONDARY SCHOOLS OF ONTARIO
(Departmental Committee)

Appointed November 5, 1970

Reported June, 1972

Committee Three members; R.W. Reville (Judge of County of Brant) chairman

Purpose To inquire into the process of negotiation between teachers and school boards and the roles of the various professional and trustee organizations in the bargaining process.

Conclusions/Recommendations

That the concept of professionalism must, by necessity, imply a sense of obligation to one's work. The teacher concentrates on the efficiency of his technique and on constant improvement of his performance. Matters such as remuneration, or the race or religion of pupils are relegated to a position of secondary importance.

Notwithstanding, the desire to improve one's financial status is not necessarily incompatible with one's obligations to his profession, but may indeed be fundamental in maintaining the high degree of excellence expected of that profession. Nevertheless, society demands that any such attempt be carried out in a professionally irreproachable manner;

That the negotiating entities consist on the one side of the teachers employed by a local school board, and on the other side, of the local board of trustees;

That a persistent disagreement between the parties as to any of the items that are subject to negotiations be referred to an adjudicator who is a member of a permanent Adjudicative Tribunal consisting of a chairman, one or more vice-chairmen and a number of part-time members, appointed by the Lieutenant Governor-in-Council on the advice of the Minister of Education, and financed by the Government of the Province of Ontario through the budget of the Ministry of Education; and further that the decision of the adjudicator be final and binding on both parties.

References

Ontario, *Professional Consultation and the Determination of Compensation for Ontario Teachers*, 1972.

184 ROYAL COMMISSION ON BOOK PUBLISHING
(Related Commission)

Appointed December 23, 1970

Reported December 1, 1972

Commission Three members; Richard Rohmer (Queen's Counsel, Author) chairman

Purpose To examine the publishing industry in Ontario and throughout Canada with respect to its position within the business community, the functions of the publishing industry in terms of its contributions to the cultural life and education of the people of the Province of Ontario and Canada; and the economic, cultural, social or other consequences for the people of Ontario and of Canada, of the substantial ownership or control of publishing firms by foreign or foreign-owned or foreign-controlled corporations or by non-Canadians.

Conclusions/Recommendations

That a specialized agency, the Ontario Book Publishing Board, be appointed to act as an interface between the Canadian book industry and the public;

That the Board develop and administer a program of title grants to Ontario-based, Canadian-owned publishers to assist the publication of completed book manuscripts by Canadian authors;

That the Board develop a program of assistance to bring about the re-issue of out-of-print Canadian works;

That the Board devise and introduce a program of annual Ontario Literary awards;

That the Ontario Institute for Studies in Education set as one of its important program objectives the development and evaluation of Canadian learning materials;

That teacher-training institutions provide special training in the evaluation of learning materials;

That the principle underlying the former book stimulation grants be re-introduced into the special book listings (Circulars 14 and 15) of the Ministry of Education.

References

Ontario, *Canadian Publishers and Canadian Publishing*, 1972.

185 COMMITTEE ON YEAR-ROUND USE OF SCHOOLS
(Departmental Committee)

Appointed April 5, 1971

Reported November 8, 1972

Committee Eight members; first G.H. Waldrum (Director, Supervision Branch, Ministry of Education) and then Gladys R. Mannings (Assistant Superintendent, Supervision Branch) chairman

Purpose To consider the overall feasibility and wisdom of a year-round use of schools, or of an extended school year, and patterns of 'semestering'.

Conclusions/Recommendations

That boards may submit to the Minister of Education for approval, plans for an experimental, innovative re-scheduling of the school year for its elementary or secondary schools, or for both;

That experimental schedules may provide for the establishment of summer school programs and vacations during June, July and August;

That school boards should carefully explore alternatives before any re-scheduling of the school year is undertaken and should inform the public they serve through an organized program of communication with teachers, parents, students, and the business community.

References

Ontario, *Report of Committee on Year-Round Use of Schools*, November, 1972.

186 COMMITTEE ON THE COSTS OF EDUCATION
(Departmental Committee)

Appointed April 21, 1971

Reported 1972 to 1977

Ontario / 186

Committee Seven members; T.A. McEwan (President, Beckton, Dickinson and Co.) chairman

Purpose To examine the costs of education for the elementary and secondary schools of Ontario in relation to the aims and objectives, programs, priorities, and the like, of the educational system and to evaluate the programs in the light of the experience with them, the requirements of the present day, and in terms of the expenditures of money for them.

Conclusions/Recommendations

That Stratford Teachers' College, Peterborough Teachers' College, Ottawa Teachers' College, and Hamilton Teachers' College be closed; that other designated Teachers' Colleges be integrated with university Faculties of Education; and that they train, as specified, elementary or elementary and secondary teachers;

That the Ministry of Education and local school boards make careful analyses of expected enrolments and accommodation needs;

That the Ministry of Education take a leadership role in the development of transportation policy and assist school boards in their efforts to achieve efficient and economical transportation services;

That the Ministry of Education establish a Planning unit responsible for the development on a continuing basis of an integrated, comprehensive plan for quality education in Ontario in accordance with accepted goals and expectations determined by concensus of those concerned; and that each school board give first priority to the development of a 'plan for planning';

That the Ministry of Education reaffirm its earlier commitment to the principle of decentralization of decision-making in education to the maximum extent possible;

That changes be made in the financing of education.

References

Ontario / 187

Ontario, *Committee on the Costs of Education*, Interim Reports, 1972 through 1977.

187 MINISTERIAL COMMISSION ON FRENCH LANGUAGE SECONDARY EDUCATION
(Departmental Committee)

Appointed October 1, 1971

Reported February 17, 1972

Committee One member; T.H.B. Symons (Vice-Chancellor of Trent University)

Purpose To inquire into the effectiveness of the legislation to implement a program of French language education in the schools in Ontario; and to direct particular attention to the establishment, operation, and progress of French language secondary schools and French language classes in secondary schools.

Conclusions/Recommendations

That the legislative provisions for the French Language Committee be retained, but that the functions of this committee be clarified and strengthened;

That the board consult with the French Language Committee on all matters affecting the establishment, program, and administration of French language schools, wings, or classes before any final decisions regarding such matters are taken by the board;

That a Linguistic Rights Commission in Education for Ontario be created;

That the Department of Education deal in French with the French language schools of the province;

That the Standing Committee on French Language Schools review procedures and set new criteria for the approval of texts for French-speaking students;

That admission requirements to French language Teachers' Colleges and Colleges of Education be progressively brought into line with those for English-speaking candidates.

References

Ontario, *Ministerial Commission on French Language Secondary Education*, 1972.

188 EDUCATIONAL RESOURCES ALLOCATION SYSTEM TASK FORCE (Departmental Committee)

Appointed November, 1971

Reported 1973 to 1975

Committee Sixteen members; J.S. Stephen (Assistant Deputy Minister) chairman

Purpose To develop, in co-operation with local school systems in Ontario, a resource allocation system that will emphasize planning for effective decision-making by educational authorities.

Conclusions/Recommendations

That Boards be requested to prepare annually, for the communities they serve, a three-year plan describing and forecasting all proposed changes in programs and services;

That the Ministry of Education utilize the Educational Resources Allocation System as a comprehensive decision-making approach in all its internal programs.

References

Ontario, *Report of the Educational Resources Allocation System Task Force to the Minister of Education*, 1975.

189 SELECT COMMITTEE ON ECONOMIC AND CULTURAL NATIONALISM

Ontario / 189

(Legislative Committee)

Appointed	December 17, 1971
Reported	1973
Committee	Eleven members; Russell D. Rowe (M.P.P. for Northumberland) chairman
Purpose	To review the Report of the Interdepartmental Task Force on Foreign Investment and the current status of opinion and information on economic and cultural nationalism in Canada.

Conclusions/Recommendations

That legislation be introduced to provide that within five years all chancellors, boards of governors or equivalent, presidents, vice-presidents, deans and chairmen of departments at universities in Ontario be Canadians;

That universities be directed to advertise all academic vacancies well in advance of the date on which it is intended offers will be made, in at least the two periodicals which are likely to reach the widest audience among prospective Canadian candidates in the discipline for which applicants are sought;

That plans be established to develop graduate programs likely to attract the highest international reputation and the ablest degree candidates from both Canada and abroad;

That each university in Ontario establish machinery to assure that very substantially higher percentages of its new faculty appointments are Canadian citizens on appointment, and that a similar high proportion have obtained most or all of their graduate training at Canadian universities;

That all universities be required to submit, on an annual basis, and by department, the citizenship and countries of undergraduate and graduate training of all new appointees, tenured faculty, department heads and other academic ranks, departures from strength, and persons on limited term appointments;

That the Ontario Human Rights Code be amended to enable universities to ask for citizenship of applicants for teaching positions, and to permit discrimination in favour of Canadian citizens in faculty appointments to universities in Ontario.

References

Ontario, *Interim Report of the Select Committee on Economic and Cultural Nationalism*, 1973.

190 SELECT COMMITTEE ON THE UTILIZATION OF EDUCATIONAL FACILITIES
(Legislative Committee)

Appointed December 17, 1971

Reported June, 1973; December, 1973; July, 1974; February, 1975

Committee Eleven members; Charles E. McIlvene (M.P.P. for Oshawa) chairman

Purpose To inquire into the potentialities and possibilities for the increased use of educational facilities throughout Ontario at all levels, including post-secondary facilities.

Conclusions/Recommendations

That the Government of Ontario, through the Provincial Secretary for Social Development, adopt, as the basis for the development of general policy guidelines, a system of community education which will emphasize the need for integration and coordination of educational and other community resources, services and facilities; equality of opportunity and access; and frameworks for local community involvement in decision-making;

That the Ministers of Education, Health, Community and Social Services, and Colleges and Universities work together with the Provincial Secretary for Social Development;

That general policy guidelines be adopted to encourage the development of programs that recognize the growth of leisure as an important and positive element in the life of the individual and of the community;

That community education be stressed in the teacher training curricula of the province's teacher colleges and faculties of education;

That arts, sports and other recreational activities be totally integrated into the school process;

That a Council on Open Education be established.

References

Ontario, *'What happens next is up to you': Final Report: Select Committee on the Utilization of Educational Facilities*, February, 1975.

191 TASK FORCE ON THE SCHOOL YEAR (Departmental Committee)

Appointed June, 1972

Reported September 1, 1972

Committee Eleven members; H.K. Fisher (Director, Supervisory Services Branch, Ministry of Education) chairman

Purpose To study the question of school closing dates and the length of the school year.

Conclusions/Recommendations

That for all schools operated by a board, the school year shall be defined within the calendar year as being 200 school days of which a minimum of 185 school days shall be designated as instructional days;

That each school board shall establish a pattern of attendance for students and staff within the defined school year which will reflect the particular needs of the schools and which may re-define the school year for the board as being more than 200 days;

That such patterns be subject to the annual approval of the Ministry of Education.

References

Ontario, *Report: Task Force: The School Year*, September, 1972.

192 STUDY TEAM ON THE SHARING OR TRANSFERRING OF SCHOOL FACILITIES
(Departmental Committee)

Appointed November, 1972

Reported February 1, 1973

Committee Six members; R.J. Christie (Former Chairman, Borough of York, Board of Education) and J.A. Marrese (Chairman, Metropolitan Separate School Board) co-chairmen

Purpose To study the sharing or transferring of school facilities.

Conclusions/Recommendations

That the Minister of Education provide for the mandatory establishment of a joint planning council of public and separate school boards, wherever such boards share common or overlapping attendance areas;

That the Minister of Education strongly recommend to school boards who may be experiencing problems with large-scale transferrals that the pairs of boards concerned agree upon dates for the determination of the final number of transfers for the following year;

That legislation be established to ensure that school boards, both public and separate, have representatives on local planning boards and access to complete information on the development of new areas.

References

Ontario, *Report of the Study Team on the Sharing or Transferring of School Facilities*, February, 1973.

193 MINISTERIAL COMMITTEE ON THE TEACHING OF FRENCH (Departmental Committee)

Appointed June 12, 1973

Reported September, 1974

Committee Twelve members; Robert Gillin (Curriculum Services Officer, Ministry of Education) chairman

Purpose To develop improved curriculum and techniques for teaching French to the English-speaking students of Ontario, and at the same time to review the aims and objectives of French language courses in our schools.

Conclusions/Recommendations

That French be introduced at the Kindergarten, Primary, or at the latest, the Junior level, and that from whatever level it is introduced, a carefully articulated program be provided to the end of the secondary level;

That, at whatever grade French is introduced, a daily class be offered to the end of the Junior Division;

That, beginning at Grade 7, each individual Board declare French to be either a compulsory or an optional subject;

That French teachers take the initiative in developing Canadian Studies courses;

That the Ministry of Education encourage the production of materials with Canadian content for all levels of the

French program;

That immediate steps be taken to ensure that there is an adequate supply of teachers capable of teaching French immersion classes and of teaching in French in other areas of the curriculum both in elementary and secondary schools to meet current needs.

References

Ontario, *Report of the Ministerial Committee on the Teaching of French*, 1974.

194 MINISTERIAL COMMISSION ON THE ORGANIZATION AND FINANCING OF THE PUBLIC AND SECONDARY SCHOOL SYSTEMS IN METROPOLITAN TORONTO
(Departmental Committee)

Appointed June 13, 1973

Reported June, 1974

Committee Four members; Barry Lowes (former Chairman of Metropolitan Toronto School Board) chairman

Purpose To inquire into the structure, operation and financing of the public and secondary school systems in Metropolitan Toronto.

Conclusions/Recommendations

That Area Boards of Education move to establish families of schools as their primary unit of educational administration;

That the two-tier structure of educational governance be retained;

That the powers of the Metropolitan Toronto School Board be modified, that these powers be designated, and that all residual powers and responsibilities remain with the Area Boards;

That Metropolitan Toronto be considered a region of the Province by the Ministry of Education.

References

Ontario, *Report of the Ministerial Commission on the Organization and Financing of the Public and Secondary School Systems in Metropolitan Toronto*, [1973]

195 ROYAL COMMISSION ON METROPOLITAN TORONTO
(Related Commission)

Appointed September 10, 1974

Reported June 15, 1977

Commission One member; John P. Robarts (former Premier of Ontario)

Purpose To examine, evaluate and make appropriate recommendations on the structure, organization and operations of local government within the Metropolitan Toronto area, including all municipal governments, boards and commissions.

Conclusions/Recommendations

That the boundaries of area municipalities and area boards of education in Metropolitan Toronto continue to coincide;

That the direct educational responsibilities of the Metropolitan Toronto School Board be transferred to the area boards of education, with provision to ensure that no child is thereby denied access to appropriate educational services;

That health-related costs and services of the school system, including those for special education, be paid from municipal public health budgets;

That the collection of education taxes in Metropolitan Toronto continue to be the responsibility of the area municipalities.

References

Ontario, *Report of the Royal Commission on Metropolitan Toronto*, 1977.

196 TASK FORCE ON THE EDUCATIONAL NEEDS OF NATIVE PEOPLES OF ONTARIO
(Departmental Committee)

Appointed October 23, 1974

Reported June 30, 1976 [to Minister of Colleges and Universities, Minister of Culture and Recreation, and the Minister of Education]

Committee Nine members; [no chairman designated]

Purpose To study the educational needs of the native peoples.

Conclusions/Recommendations

That a teacher-training programme be developed with the aid of Indian education specialists, so as to make it more appropriate to the educational background, heritage, and needs of the people of native ancestry;

That all teaching staff employed in schools serving native students be required to participate in cross-cultural sensitivity and awareness sessions, as well as workshops in up-to-date teaching techniques;

That native counsellor training programmes provide immersion courses in native culture and history, together with sound counselling techniques;

That native peoples be involved in the development of curriculum and programmes of study, text design, the writing of resource materials, the evaluation of present curriculum as it relates to native peoples, and that they be consulted before any new native studies material is introduced into the schools;

That governments (both federal and provincial) adjust their policies and practices so that native peoples are involved in all phases of the education of their children and are in a position to assume more responsibility for the provision of that education.

References

Ontario, *Summary Report of the Task Force on the Educational Needs of Native Peoples of Ontario*, June, 1976.

197 INTERIM COMMITTEE ON FINANCIAL ASSISTANCE FOR STUDENTS (Departmental Committee)

Appointed January, 1975

Reported January 31, 1977

Committee Nine members; J. Stefan Dupré (Chairman of Ontario Council on University Affairs) and Norman A. Sisco (Chairman of Council of Regents for the Colleges of Applied Arts and Technology) co-chairmen

Purpose To advise the Minister of Colleges and Universities of the financial arrangements required, in the long run, to assist students pursuing their post-secondary studies or training and to recommend the administrative steps and procedures considered most desirable for implementing these arrangements.

Conclusions/Recommendations

That a new program of student assistance to be called the Optional Loan and Need-Tested Grant Program (OLANG) be instituted which is designed to increase the accessibility of post-secondary education to students from low-income backgrounds; to foster accessibility for all students; to be simple to administer; to encourage individual responsibility and broaden the effective range of individual choice; and to operate entirely under the jurisdiction of the Government of Ontario.

References

Ontario, *Report of the Interim Committee on Financial Assistance for Students*, January, 1977.

198 STUDY OF WOMEN AND ONTARIO UNIVERSITIES
(Departmental Committee)

Appointed March, 1975

Reported October, 1975 [to Minister of Colleges and Universities]

Committee Gail McIntyre (independent consultant)

Purpose To investigate the current status of women in Ontario universities; to identify issues of concern to women students, faculty and support staff; and to recommend an action plan to eliminate inequalities between women and men.

Conclusions/Recommendations

That each institution issue a policy statement affirming its commitment to positive action to achieve equal opportunity for women;

That each institution assign responsibility at a senior level for the coordination, design, and implementation of measures for achieving equal opportunity for all women in the university community;

That each institution which has not already done so, conduct a formal study of the status of women students, faculty and staff;

That each university design and implement a program to increase the participation of women in graduate schools;

That, when recruiting faculty and staff, each institution conduct an active search for women candidates;

That the Ministry of Colleges and Universities review

annually the enrolment patterns of male and female students at the under-graduate and graduate levels, degrees granted by sex and field, representation of faculty by sex, rank and field, new faculty by sex, rank and field, faculty salaries by sex, rank and field, and senior administrative appointments in order to determine progress on a province-wide basis; and that this data be made public.

References

Ontario, *Women and Ontario Universities*, October, 1975.

199 ROYAL COMMISSION ON VIOLENCE IN THE COMMUNICATIONS INDUSTRY
(Related Commission)

Appointed May 7, 1975

Reported June, 1977

Commission Three members; Julia Verlyn La Marsh (Privy Councillor) chairman

Purpose To study the effect on society of the increasing exhibition of violence in the communications industry and to determine if there is any connection or a cause and effect relationship between this phenomenon and the incidence of violent crime in society.

Conclusions/Recommendations

That the great weight of research into the effects of violent media content indicates potential harm to society;

That we find a constantly increasing flow of television violence at all hours, including those when children are watching, in a cynical attempt to maximize audiences;

That television's escalation of violence is drawing other sections of the media along like the tail of a comet;

That we do not believe in censorship but we do believe in

providing more and better alternatives for public entertainment, information and education, and we believe that it is only just to demand accountability beyond the balance sheet from those who take a profit from communications;

That wide-scale changes in present procedures should be initiated to the end that the communications industry, by diminishing the exploitation of violence, will reflect more accurately the quality of life to which most Canadians aspire.

References

Ontario, *Report of the Royal Commission on Violence in the Communications Industry,* [1977].

200 ROYAL COMMISSION OF INQUIRY ON ALGOMA UNIVERSITY COLLEGE (Judicial Commission)

Appointed March 10, 1976

Reported June 30, 1976; July 30, 1977; November 15, 1977

Commission One member; John W. Whiteside (Faculty of Law, University of Windsor)

Purpose To inquire into, study and report upon all aspects of the management of Algoma University College bearing upon its effective operation.

Conclusions/Recommendations

That the existing major elements of the corporation and the college, namely, the Board of Directors, the Academic Council and the Membership of the corporation be disbanded for a period which should not exceed one year; and that an interim trusteeship be appointed in order that it may take immediate action to assure recovery of the college from its present problems and to institute appropriate proceedings to plan for the future;

That the undergraduate programme of Algoma University

College be terminated at June 30, 1978; that the Algoma College Association corporation be reorganized to assume the role of a regional education planning council at the earliest date; and that a substructure be created within the corporation to be known as Outreach Algoma to establish, finance and administer such educational and cultural programs, particularly in the areas of outreach, continuing education, research and development, as may be recommended by the planning council, within the means and resources available to the corporation.

References

Ontario, *Reports of the Royal Commission of Inquiry: Algoma University College: June 30, 1976 - November 15, 1977.*

201 COMMISSION ON THE REFORM OF PROPERTY TAXATION IN ONTARIO (Related Commission)

Appointed	May 5, 1976
Reported	March, 1977
Commission	Ten members; Willis L. Blair (Ontario Municipal Board, Toronto) chairman
Purpose	To review proposals with respect to property taxation in Ontario.

Conclusions/Recommendations

That assessment of all government property be pooled and assigned between the public and separate elementary schools in the same proportion as the taxable assessment assigned by the owners and occupants of residences; and that the pooling of taxable assessment be extended to incorporate all taxable assessment in respect of which a senior government will make payment in lieu of taxes;

That public school boards and separate school boards each be permitted to assign the taxable assessment of their own real property to the support of their respective school systems.

References

Ontario, *Report of the Commission on the Reform of Property Taxation in Ontario*, 1977.

202 WORK GROUP ON EVALUATION AND REPORTING
(Departmental Committee)

Appointed November 26, 1976

Reported April 15, 1977

Committee Seven members; Claudette Foisy-Moon (Executive Assistant, Ontario Teachers' Federation) chairman

Purpose To study how best to improve testing and evaluation in the classroom and how best to give teachers and parents a clear understanding of how their children are progressing.

Conclusions/Recommendations

That, in conjunction with teachers, trustees, and administrative officials, the Ministry develop, publish, and distribute to teachers, manuals, resource guides, handbooks, and information kits on evaluation, testing and reporting, which describe as comprehensively as possible how each function can be carried out effectively;

That the Ministry and the Ontario Teachers' Federation jointly fund, organize, and conduct in-service professional development for teachers in the areas of evaluation, testing, and reporting;

That the Ministry make every effort to develop programs and resources in the areas of evaluation, testing, and reporting that would take into account the needs of the Francophone students of the province;

That an advisory committee on evaluation and reporting be

established, and which would include evaluation in the broader context of curriculum design.

References

Ontario, *Report of the Work Group on Evaluation and Reporting*, April, 1977.

203 COMMISSION ON DECLINING SCHOOL ENROLMENTS IN ONTARIO (Departmental Committee)

Appointed August 24, 1977

Reported October 31, 1978

Committee One member; R.W.B. Jackson (former Director, Ontario Institute for Studies in Education) chairman

Purpose To study the implications of declining school enrolments in Ontario.

Conclusions/Recommendations

That since there is nothing we can do to stop the steady decline in enrolment of children and youth in our schools, we must learn to live with this phenomenon and strive to maintain the quality of education we provide in light of the unfavourable economic, social and financial conditions which prevail at present and which promise to remain our lot for many years to come;

That school boards increase their cooperation with each other in the design of programs and development of curriculum materials;

That the Ministry of Education play an active role in cooperation with the boards in providing empathetic guidance personnel able to increase the awareness of students of the range of options open to them;

That the Ministry of Education and the boards encourage the Native Peoples to exercise their rights of involvement in board and school affairs, including by seeking board membership;

That all teachers be prepared for teaching in a multicultural society;

That the teaching profession begin work together on: (a) early retirement plans; (b) job sharing plans, including night school and summer school jobs; (c) elimination of large classes; (d) encouragement of most kinds of part-time continuing employment; (e) encouragement or transfers, exchanges, and leaves of absence; (f) encouragement of in-service training, including retraining for teaching, as well as for related or even unrelated jobs in business and industry.

References

Ontario, *Implications of Declining Enrolment for the Schools of Ontario: A Statement of Effects and Solutions*, October, 1978.

MANITOBA

204 COMMISSION OF INQUIRY INTO THE WISDOM AND ADVISABILITY OF ESTABLISHING AND MAINTAINING AN AGRICULTURAL COLLEGE (General Commission)

Appointed	August 1, 1901
Reported	February 26, 1903
Commission	Seven members; William Patrick (Principal, Manitoba College) chairman
Purpose	To investigate agricultural education in the province and to inquire into the wisdom and advisability of establishing and maintaining an agricultural college.

Conclusions/Recommendations

That an agricultural college be established as soon as possible;

That the foundation for the work of the agricultural college be laid in the rural public schools of the Province;

That attendance at these schools be made compulsory;

That rural schools be combined in districts sparsely settled;

That greater attention be paid to English composition, arithmetic, and handwriting.

References

Manitoba, *Sessional Papers*, 1903, No. 17.

205 ROYAL COMMISSION ON THE UNIVERSITY OF MANITOBA (General Commission)

Appointed September 26, 1907

Reported November 30, 1909

Commission Seven members; J.A.M. Aikins (King's Counsel) chairman

Purpose To enquire into the government and management of the University of Manitoba; its financial status; relations with the several affiliated colleges; the nature, scope and method of teaching at the University; the suitability and sufficiency of the present building and premises; and other related matters.

Conclusions/Recommendations

That there be more monetary aid;

That there be a larger site;

That the office of president be created.

(Three separate reports were submitted with two commissioners supporting the *status quo*, two presenting a strong plea for an unfettered state university, and the other three proposing a sort of compromise whereby the provincial government would appoint a controlling board of twelve members to handle general administration, but the autonomy of the affiliated colleges would be respected in academic matters.)

References

Manitoba, *Sessional Papers*, 1910, No. 9.

206 COMMISSION OF INQUIRY INTO AIMS AND METHODS IN INDUSTRIAL EDUCATION
(General Commission)

Appointed August 26, 1910

Reported February 26, 1912

Commission Twenty-five members; G.R. Coldwell (King's Counsel) chairman

Purpose To enquire into aims and methods in industrial education.

Conclusions/Recommendations

That vocational training be supported as a means of discovering special aptitudes and fulfilling broader potentials, of raising the status of the worker, and of contributing to the industrial progress of the community;

That the foundation for such training be laid in the elementary school with regularly-organized industrial work in the higher grades;

That vocational and general education supplement one another;

That evening classes for adult education be provided;

That teachers be specially trained;

That at some future date a technical college be established.

References

Manitoba, *Sessional Papers*, 1912, No. 3.

207 SPECIAL REPORT ON BILINGUAL SCHOOLS IN MANITOBA
(Departmental Committee)

Appointed 1915 (?)

Reported January 15 and March 1, 1916

Committee One member; Charles K. Newcombe (Superintendent of Education)

Purpose To investigate bilingual schools in Manitoba.

Conclusions/Recommendations

That of all the children enrolled in Manitoba, one out of every six received his education in a bilingual school (16,720 out of a total enrolment of 100,963). There were 126 French bilingual schools in operation, employing 234 teachers, with an enrolment of 7,393 pupils and an average attendance of 3,465.27; there were 111 Ruthenian or Polish bilingual schools, employing 114 teachers, with an enrolment of 6,513 pupils and an average attendance of 3,884.96; there were 61 German bilingual schools, employing 73 teachers, with an enrolment of 2,814 and an average attendance of 1,840.61.

References

Manitoba, *Special Report on Bilingual Schools in Manitoba*, 1916.

208 COMMISSION OF INQUIRY INTO ALL MATTERS PERTAINING TO THE MANITOBA AGRICULTURAL COLLEGE
(Judicial Commission)

Appointed July 14, 1916

Reported January 30, 1917

Commission One member; Alexander C. Galt (Court of King's Bench Judge)

Purpose To investigate and inquire into all matters pertaining to the said Manitoba Agricultural College, and the contracts entered into therefor, and the expenditure of public money in respect thereof, and the sub-contracts let therefor, the persons interested in such sub-contracts, and the amounts paid to the sub-contractors.

Conclusions/Recommendations

References

Manitoba, *Sessional Papers*, 1917, No. 17.

209 COMMISSION ON STATUS AND SALARIES OF TEACHERS (Departmental Committee)

Appointed September 25, 1919

Reported [ ]

Committee Five members; Alfred A. Hill (Education Advising Board) chairman

Purpose To enquire into the serious situation of the Province arising from the shortage of teachers, the inequality of qualifications and the uncertainty as to salaries.

Conclusions/Recommendations

That teacher qualifications be upgraded;

That experience be recognized for salary purposes;

That a larger unit for the administration of school affairs be adopted;

That salary schedules have sufficient elasticity to permit revision;

That, since the work in public schools was at least equally important with that in high schools and collegiates, the pay, therefore, be equally high;

That more young men and women of superior qualifications and character be sought to give leadership to the future.

References

Manitoba, *Report of Committee on Status and Salaries of Teachers*, 1919.

210 SPECIAL COMMISSION ON THE POSSIBILITY OF READJUSTING THE RELATIONS OF THE HIGHER INSTITUTIONS OF LEARNING
(Special Committee)

Appointed 1923

Reported 1923

Committee One member; William S. Learned (Carnegie Foundation)

Purpose To investigate the possibility of readjusting the relations of the higher institutions of learning.

Conclusions/Recommendations

That the university be transferred to the fine and extensive St. Vital property of the Manitoba Agricultural College;

That the affiliated colleges build residences at the new location.

References

Manitoba, *Report of the Commission on the Possibility of Readjusting the Relations of the Higher Institutions of Learning*, [1923].

[Sponsored by The Carnegie Foundation]

211 ROYAL COMMISSION ON EDUCATION
(General Commission)

Appointed June 13, 1923

Manitoba / 211

<u>Reported</u> January, 1924 and January, 1925

<u>Commission</u> Five members; Walter C. Murray (President, University of Saskatchewan) chairman

<u>Purpose</u> To enquire into (a) the needs of the more recently settled and less developed districts of the province for better educational facilities (b) the better adaptation of the elementary and secondary schools to the needs of the communities they serve (c) the possibility of readjusting the relations of the higher institutions of learning so as to provide for their extension in the future, lessen the burden of their support, and increase their service to the province.

<u>Conclusions/Recommendations</u>

That legislative grants and special grants be given to equalize school support;

That a curriculum committee be formed with representation from the agricultural, industrial, commercial and professional life of the province;

That all normal school students be required to take a full course of one year;

That the teachers' pension fund be established on a sound actuarial basis;

That rural schools be used for practice-teaching purposes;

That adequate inspectorial supervision of rural schools be provided.

<u>References</u>

Manitoba, *Report of the Educational Commission*, 1924 and 1925.

212 COMMISSION OF INQUIRY INTO IMPAIRMENT OR DEPLETION OF

UNIVERSITY OF MANITOBA FUNDS
(Judicial Commission)

<u>Appointed</u> September 24, 1932

<u>Reported</u> March 27, 1933

<u>Commission</u> Three members; W.F.A. Turgeon, (Court of Appeal Judge) chairman

<u>Purpose</u> To inquire into impairment or depletion of University of Manitoba funds.

<u>Conclusions/Recommendations</u>

That the Board of Governors be enlarged;

That no member of the Board have any financial interest in university administration;

That security regulations be tightened.

<u>References</u>

Manitoba, 'Royal Commission on Impairment of University of Manitoba Trust Fund', 1933.

213 SELECT COMMITTEE TO ENQUIRE INTO THE ADMINISTRATION AND THE FINANCING OF THE PUBLIC EDUCATIONAL SYSTEM OF THE PROVINCE
(Legislative Committee)

<u>Appointed</u> April 6, 1934

<u>Reported</u> February 26, 1935

<u>Committee</u> Ten members; R.A. Hoey (Member for St. Clements) chairman

<u>Purpose</u> To enquire into the administration and the financing of the public educational system of the province.

<u>Conclusions/Recommendations</u>

That an inquiry be made into the cost of text books;

That a Salary Adjustment Board be formed to alleviate the diversity of salaries being paid to teachers, often in adjacent districts, for similar services;

That obligatory regulations with regard to school board-teachers contracts be inserted into the Public Schools Act;

That taxes be increased to make possible larger contributions on the part of the central authority.

References

Manitoba, *Journals*, 1935.

214 SPECIAL REPORT ON EDUCATION IN MANITOBA
(Special Committee)

Appointed 1937

Reported February and March, 1938

Committee One member; D.S. Woods (Dean of Education, University of Manitoba)

Purpose To assess education in Manitoba as part of a survey of the economic and social life of the province.

Conclusions/Recommendations

That, for all types of community irrespective of racial characteristics, the people of Manitoba are elementary school conscious and are becoming, more and more secondary school conscious;

That the evidence of this investigation would indicate that elementary school facilities, in so far as they may be provided in one-room rural and small and large graded schools, have been made available to almost every home in the province;

That provision for secondary education, measured by numbers and nearness of schools, bears a direct relationship to one or more of the following factors: age of settlement, racial characteristics of the population, and the economic ability of the area;

That industrial changes and depressed economic conditions have produced a new problem for secondary education in that employment is not readily available for young people between the ages of fifteen and twenty who would normally leave school for gainful occupations;

That, as a result of the changes which have occurred in the population of the secondary school, that institution has been called upon to provide for many whose interests are included towards practical subjects, as well as for those looking toward professional pursuits.

References

Manitoba, *Education in Manitoba,* February, 1938, Part I, and March, 1938, Part II.

215 SPECIAL SELECT COMMITTEE ON EDUCATION
(Legislative Committee)

Appointed March 10, 1944

Reported March 9, 1945

Committee Fifteen members; Ivan Schultz (Member for Mountain) chairman

Purpose To enquire and report upon:

(a) The administration and financing of the public school system of the province;

(b) Equalization of educational opportunity throughout the province, with particular reference to elementary and technical education;

(c) Technical education in the light of the present-day and post-war needs;

(d) The provision for, and control of, admission of students to various faculties of the University of Manitoba;

(e) Any and all matters relating to the above, including curriculum, training of teachers and post-war education.

Conclusions/Recommendations

That larger units of school administration be instituted;

That local boards with certain specific and definite powers be kept, however, in order to retain local interest;

That educational standards for the whole province be set by departmental decree;

That the equalization of educational opportunity be further assured by financial stabilization which would include uniform assessment and provincial assumption of 50% of the basic operational costs of education;

That courses and programmes be provided to fit the varying needs of different pupils with different capabilities and interests;

That the teaching profession be upgraded;

That higher salaries be paid; more men be encouraged to enter this field; but that the period of Normal School training not be extended at this time;

That a survey of the situation with regard to adult education be made forthwith by the Department of Education and the University of Manitoba, with a view to close co-operation in this field.

References

Manitoba, *Journals*, 1944.

Manitoba / 216

Manitoba, *Report of the Special Select Committee of the Manitoba Legislative Assembly on Education*, 1945.

216 ROYAL COMMISSION ON ADULT EDUCATION
(General Commission)

Appointed August 21, 1945

Reported April 8, 1947

Commission Five members; A.W. Trueman (President, University of Manitoba) chairman

Purpose To investigate the work now being carried on in the whole field of adult education in the Province of Manitoba, to advise and make recommendations to the Government of Manitoba on the co-ordination of such work in order to eliminate all overlapping, duplication and conflict, to advise as to whether the whole field is now being adequately covered and, if not, as to what steps should be taken to cover that portion which is not.

Conclusions/Recommendations

That the role of the provincial government in adult education be three-fold: to secure the greatest and most effective use of federal government resources; to assure maximum efficiency in the educational participation of provincial departments concerned; and to provide financial support to voluntary agencies without interfering with their educational policies;

That the adult educational efforts of the three departments of Agriculture, Education, and Health and Welfare be better co-ordinated;

That the university, as an educational institution of major significance for adult education, assume the responsibility for deciding what part it would play;

That a department of extension replace the faculty

committees used heretofore;

That voluntary agencies be encouraged in their vital work but that some sort of broad administrative organization be provided to ease the complexities and ensure the maximum results;

That the Government take the initiative in calling a conference of representatives of all voluntary agencies in order to establish an effective Manitoba Adult Education Council;

That library facilities be improved, and greater use be made of educational films, particularly those provided by the National Film Board;

That educational facilities be widened for handicapped groups such as the blind and deaf so that they might be able to support themselves, educate themselves, and adjust themselves to other groups.

References

Manitoba, *Report of the Manitoba Royal Commission on Adult Education*, 1947.

217 SELECT SPECIAL COMMITTEE APPOINTED TO STUDY AND REPORT ON ALL PHASES OF THE PENSION SCHEME FOR TEACHERS (Legislative Committee)

Appointed March 11, 1946

Reported February 11, 1948

Committee Six members; John Cameron Dryden (Member for Morris) chairman

Purpose To study and report on all phases of the pension scheme then in operation and to make suggestions.

Conclusions/Recommendations

That a teacher retirement system of the joint-contributing type be instituted with contributions from the teachers and from public funds.

References

Manitoba, 'Report of the Select Special Committee appointed to study and report on all phases of the pension scheme for teachers established under The Teachers' Retirement Fund Act', 1948.

218 GREATER WINNIPEG INVESTIGATION COMMISSION
(Related Commission)

Appointed September 6, 1955

Reported 1959

Commission Five members; J.L. Bodie, (Mayor of East Kildonan) chairman

Purpose To study the metropolitan development of Greater Winnipeg.

Conclusions/Recommendations

That the establishment of a metropolitan school district would ensure that all pupils throughout the Greater Winnipeg area obtained the same educational opportunity and that the cost of education was borne equally by the metropolitan community;

That a metropolitan administration -- 'the Municipality of Metropolitan Winnipeg' -- be formed.

References

Manitoba, *Report and Recommendations: Greater Winnipeg Investigating Commission*, 1959.

219 SURVEY COVERING COSTS AND OTHER FACTORS IN CONNECTION WITH

THE ESTABLISHMENT OF A DENTAL COLLEGE IN THE PROVINCE OF MANITOBA
(Departmental Committee)

Appointed 1956

Reported August, 1956

Committee One member; K.J. Paynter (Chairman, Post Graduate Studies, University of Toronto)

Purpose To inquire into the costs and other factors in connection with the establishment of a Dental College in the Province of Manitoba.

Conclusions/Recommendations

References

Manitoba, *Concerning the Establishment of a School of Dentistry in Manitoba: A Report to the Government of the Province of Manitoba,* 1956.

220 STUDY COMMITTEE ON PHYSICAL EDUCATION AND RECREATION
(Departmental Committee)

Appointed March 19, 1957

Reported 1958

Committee Five members; F.W. Kennedy (Head of Physical Education, University of Manitoba) chairman

Purpose To investigate provincial needs in physical education and recreation.

Conclusions/Recommendations

That the Physical Education Branch be made an integral part of the Department of Education;

That physical education receive more emphasis in the school

curriculum;

That specialization in physical education be offered at the diploma or degree level in provincial teacher training institutions;

That a provincial director of recreation be provided;

That the Government assist in a programme for training recreational leaders and providing better facilities.

References

Manitoba, *Physical Education and Recreation in Manitoba*, 1958.

221 ROYAL COMMISSION ON EDUCATION
(General Commission)

Appointed May 15, 1957

Reported November 30, 1959

Commission Five members; Ronald Oliver MacFarlane (former Deputy Minister of Education, Manitoba) chairman

Purpose To study and report on all aspects of education in Manitoba, up to University level, and without limiting the generality of the foregoing, in particular to study and report on the following:

1. administration;
2. finance;
3. buildings and equipment;
4. curriculum and standards;
5. supply, training, certification and terms of employment of teachers;
6. inspection and field services;
7. special groups, such as blind, deaf, physically and mentally handicapped;
8. special services such as audio, visual,

library, correspondence;
9. scholarships and bursaries;
10. official trustee and special schools;
11. school attendance and its enforcement;
12. advisory and statutory boards and committees.

Conclusions/Recommendations

That, since Manitoba bears a far smaller share of the cost of education than in most other provinces, more financial aid be given;

That equalization of educational opportunity be sought;

That larger administrative units be adopted;

That entrance requirements into teacher training be upgraded;

That Manitoba Teachers' College be made an affiliated college of the University of Manitoba, or, if this were unfeasible, that it be transferred to the Faculty of Pedagogy;

That pedagogical courses be of such weight and content that they could be recognized for credit towards a pedagogical degree;

That standards for inspectors be raised (five years of academic training, plus two years of professional training, plus seven years of successful teaching in the province).

References

Manitoba, *Report of the Manitoba Royal Commission on Education*, 1959.

222 SURVEY OF READING
(Departmental Committee)

Appointed May 1, 1962

Reported January, 1967

Committee: Twenty-one members (Advisory Board); W.M. Sibley (Dean of Arts and Science, University of Manitoba) chairman

Purpose: To examine the programme for the teaching of reading in elementary grades with a view to its improvement.

Conclusions/Recommendations

That the Manitoba Reading Program remain under continuous evaluation and review in all its aspects to ensure a pattern of development that is sequential, continuous, flexible, and up-to-date;

That in-service training in reading be provided for teachers on a continuous basis and that courses in developmental reading, diagnostic and remedial techniques, and children's literature be incorporated into the program for teachers in training at the Faculties of Education;

That school districts and divisions be encouraged to establish a public relations program to acquaint parents with the reading teaching methods used in their schools.

References

Manitoba, *Reading: A Report of the Advisory Board to the Minister of Education*, January 1967.

223 ROYAL COMMISSION ON LOCAL GOVERNMENT ORGANIZATION AND FINANCE
(Related Commission)

Appointed: February 13, 1963

Reported: April 28, 1964

Commission: Five members; Roland Michener (former Speaker of House of Commons) chairman

Purpose: To inquire into local government organization and finance.

Manitoba / 223

Conclusions/Recommendations

That a solution to the problem of costs of education be found by broadening the base of taxation for the financial support of public schools so that the costs will be spread as generally as the benefits throughout the province, in contrast to the old system by which these costs were borne only by the real property taxpayers of the locality.

References

Manitoba, *Report of the Manitoba Royal Commission on Local Government Organization and Finance*, 1964.

224 STUDY OF THE EDUCATION OF HANDICAPPED CHILDREN IN MANITOBA (Special Committee)

Appointed: October, 1963

Reported: July 15, 1965 [to the Premier]

Committee: One member; John A. Christianson (former M.L.A. for Portage la Prairie)

Purpose: To conduct a comprehensive study to determine the kind and numbers as well as the geographical distribution of handicapped children within the province, to conduct a comprehensive survey of facilities and programs, and to make recommendations.

Conclusions/Recommendations

That local and provincial governments co-operate to develop programs to provide educational opportunities for children with mental or physical handicaps;

That the handicapped child be educated in regular schools and helped to remain in his own home wherever possible;

That the public school system be reorganized on a non-graded basis;

That greater emphasis in basic teacher training be placed on the fundamental principles of child development;

That the education of trainable retarded children be the responsibility of the various School Boards;

That legally blind children with some degree of residual vision be educated as partially sighted children and be given all educational opportunities recommended for partially sighted children;

That programs of auditory training for the very young deaf child be organized;

That placement in the Manitoba School for the Deaf be made only after complete assessment of the child's physical and mental ability;

That the Departments of Education and Health, working with the Manitoba Medical Association develop a positive screening policy to attempt to identify all physically handicapped children at as early an age as is practicable;

That all physically handicapped children be educated in regular classes as long as they are able to function successfully.

References

Manitoba, *A Study of the Education of the Handicapped Children in Manitoba,* 1965.

225 LOCAL GOVERNMENT BOUNDARIES COMMISSION
(Departmental Committee)

Appointed August 18, 1966

Reported September, 1970 [to Minister of Municipal Affairs]

Committee Eleven members; R.G. Smellie (former M.L.A. for Birtle-Russell) chairman

Purpose — To make such inquiries as are deemed necessary, so as to enable the Commission to recommend the territory to be included in and the boundaries of Local Government within the Province.

Conclusions/Recommendations

That it was very apparent that a major part of rural Manitoba was not yet ready to undertake such a massive reorganization of the education system [the Provisional Plan], particularly when such a reorganization to many of them seemed designed to hasten the end of the rural way of life;

That the goals and criteria were still valid but that a structure must be designed to allow a greater degree of local participation in the effort to reach these goals;

That the most immediate solution to this 'local planning' concept seemed to be to allow the individual existing school divisions to be the local planning authority;

That as the basic premise of the Final Education Plan the theory that a *regional system* built around existing school divisions offered the best combination of a pooling of resources and a retention of local planning control over the education system to be developed within the specific region.

References

Manitoba, *Final Plan for the Educational Structure in Manitoba outside of the Interlake Area and the Metropolitan Winnipeg Study Area,* September 1970.

226 CORE COMMITTEE ON THE REORGANIZATION OF THE SECONDARY SCHOOL
(Departmental Committee)

Appointed — July, 1969

Reported — 1973

Committee Thirty-five members; S.A.V. Bullock (Director of Curricula) chairman

Purpose To make recommendations concerning the revision of the entire process of secondary education in the province, including the aims, objectives, philosophy, structure, and curriculum.

Conclusions/Recommendations

That continuous progress and the individualization of student programs be adopted as the priorities of all secondary schools;

That a balance be maintained within the total school program between studies of a general nature and those that are of more immediate local interest and application;

That larger numbers of teachers be involved in curriculum development at the local level;

That there be greater utilization of group and individual counselling;

That a program of intensive in-service training focusing on this report be provided for trustees, divisional administrators, and secondary-school principals;

That the professional preparation of teachers, both pre-service and in-service, be modified to ensure that the knowledge, skills, and attitudes developed will be complementary to the requirements for successful development of the proposals in this report.

References

Manitoba, *The Secondary School: Report of The Core Committee on The Reorganization of The Secondary School*, 1973.

227 TASK FORCE ON TEXT BOOK EVALUATION
(Departmental Committee)

Manitoba / 227

Appointed 1972

Reported November, 1973

Committee Six members; Caroline B. Cramer (Manitoba Human Rights Commission) chairman

Purpose To explore ways and means of ensuring a reasonable limitation on bias in materials used for educative purposes.

Conclusions/Recommendations

That the Minister of Education approach the Council of Ministers to request the Canadian Publishers to develop mechanisms to carry out a content analysis of all basic texts; and request publishers and authors to incorporate into their works, contributions made by various groups of people in Canadian society;

That the Faculty of Education through pre-service studies and the Department of Education through in-service programs, provide training of all school personnel which will incorporate the study of bias and prejudice, the effects of discrimination and stereotyping, the legislation affecting rights and responsibilities, the declarations of human rights, and which will develop the skills to identify and cope with bias and prejudice in learning materials;

That the Minister of Education direct his department through its Curriculum Branch, to continue its present procedures for the evaluation of textual materials, and include evaluation for bias and discrimination as one of the criteria applied by the various curriculum and materials selection committees.

References

Manitoba, *Report of the Task Force on Text Book Evaluation*, 1973.

228 TASK FORCE ON POST-SECONDARY EDUCATION IN MANITOBA
(Departmental Committee)

Appointed February, 1972

Reported July, 1973 [to Minister of Colleges and Universities Affairs]

Committee Seven members; Michael Oliver (President of Carleton University) chairman

Purpose To survey the educational needs of Manitoba in relation to post-secondary education, to assess the adequacy of existing facilities and resources for fulfilling those needs, and to make recommendations for post-secondary development and the institutional arrangements by which this development may best be achieved.

Conclusions/Recommendations

That full-time enrolment at the University of Manitoba not exceed 15,000 students, graduate and undergraduate, by 1980-81;

That the Universities Division of the Commission on Post-Secondary Education work out with the three universities an acceptable plan for enrolment control;

That Brandon University concentrate exclusively on undergraduate education, following its liberal arts tradition;

That the University of Winnipeg continue to operate primarily as an undergraduate institution;

That each university establish a committee on the status of women;

That Keewatin Community College develop its program in mining technology and establish programs in forestry and conservation; and that it broaden its offerings to include practical nursing and social aid courses;

That Assiniboine Community College and Brandon University continue to develop close coordination;

That a regional organization for post-secondary education

be established to make learning opportunities accessible to all Manitoba citizens;

That a committee representing the public schools, the universities and colleges, and the community at large be set up to undertake a study of methods of evaluating student achievement at the shifting boundary between secondary and post-secondary education;

That a Commission on Post-Secondary Education be established.

References

Manitoba, *Report of the Task Force on Post-Secondary Education in Manitoba*, 1973.

229 TASK FORCE ON GOVERNMENT ORGANIZATION AND ECONOMY (Special Committee)

Appointed November 16, 1977

Reported March 31, 1978

Committee Four members; Sidney J. Spivak (Member for River Heights) and Conrad S. Riley (Winnipeg business executive) co-chairmen

Purpose To review and study the organization of the Executive Government of the province and the various departments thereof, the Crown agencies and the boards and commissions that perform duties and functions under various Acts of the Legislature to ascertain whether any improvement in the administration of government can be achieved.

Conclusions/Recommendations

That all curriculum development work should be centralized in the Program Development Branch (School Program Division) and not be dispersed as at present in Native Education, Small Schools, Frontier School Division and other branches;

That an attempt be made to consolidate some of the current operating grants;

That a study be conducted to determine what student and teacher records are needed in the Department;

That School Boards and funded agencies be encouraged to conform to the same restraints and economies as provincial government departments and agencies.

References

Manitoba, *Report on Government Organization and Economy*, Vol. I & II, April, 1978.

SASKATCHEWAN

230 ROYAL COMMISSION ON MUNICIPAL ORGANIZATION
(Related Commission)

Appointed October 3, 1906

Reported August 30, 1907

Commission Five members; J.W. Smith (Mayor of Regina) and P. Ferguson (Ex Councillor of Indian Head) co-chairmen

Purpose To inquire into municipal organization in the province.

Conclusions/Recommendations

That school district accounts be subject to government inspection;

That school taxes be collected by the municipalities on demand by the board of school trustees.

References

Saskatchewan, *Report of the Municipal Commission*, 1907.

231 COMMISSION OF INQUIRY INTO MORANG TEXT BOOK CONTRACT
(Judicial Commission)

Appointed January 13, 1909

Reported March 9, 1909

Commission Two members; E.L. Wetmore (Chief Justice of Saskatchewan) chairman

Purpose To investigate text book contracts.

Conclusions/Recommendations

That the evidence satisfied the Commissioners that there was no graft -- in any sense of the word -- in the deal, and that the Morang set was equal, if not superior, to any readers in use in Canada, and equal to any in the United States; that the prices paid for the Morang readers were less than the price paid by the Government of Manitoba for books of the same character, and which were shown to be inferior in manufacture.

References

Saskatchewan, 'Royal Commission on Morang Text Book Contract', 1909.

232 ROYAL COMMISSION ON AGRICULTURAL AND INDUSTRIAL EDUCATION, CONSOLIDATION OF SCHOOLS, TRAINING AND SUPPLY OF TEACHERS, COURSES OF STUDY, PHYSICAL AND MORAL EDUCATION (General Commission)

Appointed May 9, 1912

Reported November 15, 1913, and September 1, 1914

Commission Five members; Duncan P. McColl (Superintendent of Education) chairman

Purpose To enquire into agricultural education in public and high schools, technical education, consolidation of schools, training and supply of teachers, courses of study and text-books for public and high schools, physical education, and other related matters.

Conclusions/Recommendations

That systematic efforts be made to introduce more generally into the public schools the subjects of nature study and school gardening, manual training and elementary household science and to provide in the more advanced schools such instruction and training as will prepare teachers and leaders in these departments;

That young men and young women of Saskatchewan be encouraged to enter the teaching profession;

That teacher training be upgraded;

That consolidation of schools be encouraged and districts wishing to consolidate receive such guidance and assistance from the Department of Education as conditions seem to warrant.

References

Saskatchewan, *Report of the Saskatchewan Educational Commission on Agricultural and Industrial Education, Consolidation of Schools, Training and Supply of Teachers, Courses of Study, Physical and Moral Education, with Recommendations*, 1915.

233 GENERAL SURVEY AND INVESTIGATION OF THE INCIDENCE OF TAXATION IN THE URBAN MUNICIPALITIES OF SASKATCHEWAN (Special Committee)

Appointed 1917

Reported November 5, 1917

Committee One member; Robert Murray Haig (Department of Economics, Columbia University)

Purpose To investigate the incidence of taxation in the urban municipalities of Saskatchewan.

Conclusions/Recommendations

That high schools and collegiate institutes in Saskatchewan are municipally controlled institutions which receive their financial support primarily from taxes levied by the cities and towns, whereas the students are often drawn from a wide territory, and consequently the urban taxpayers are called upon to bear the total cost of high schools which serve both city and country.

References

Saskatchewan, *Taxation in the Urban Municipalities of the Province of Saskatchewan*, 1917.

234. SURVEY OF EDUCATION IN THE PROVINCE OF SASKATCHEWAN (Special Committee)

Appointed June 7, 1917

Reported January 20, 1918

Committee One member; Harold W. Foght (Bureau of Education, Washington)

Purpose To survey the system of education in Saskatchewan.

Conclusions/Recommendations

That everywhere on the North American Continent today and particularly in those sections where economic and civic life is most dynamic, there is a deepseated public feeling that educational institutions have not kept pace with the rapidly advancing life of modern civilization;

That Saskatchewan, in common with the other prairie provinces of Canada, is dominated by people of progressive type -- forward looking people, who have shown a striking determination to escape the hindering influence of back-eastern conservatism by taking action before their educational institutions shall become affected with inertness, resulting in failure to respond to the changing life of their democratic civilisation;

That the people of the Province have failed to use the schools as fully as they should have done;

That the prevailing system of school organization and administration in rural districts particularly, is no longer adequate for modern uses;

That abnormal opportunities in other occupations and other causes have conspired to make it difficult to train and keep in the profession an adequate number of well-prepared teachers;

That the courses of study in elementary and secondary schools do not in all respects meet the demands of a democratic people occupied with the conquest of a great agricultural country;

That the schools in their internal organization are planned less for the normal child than for the exceptional child, and offer slight opportunity for individual aptness and initiative;

That the system of examinations in use is a questionable norm of the average pupil's scholarship, ability, maturity and fitness for advancement;

That bodily health and hygenic conditions in the schools, so essential to effective study, have received little attention in the daily teaching and are largely disregarded in the physical equipment of the schools;

That the schools, while liberally maintained, must receive even larger support in order that commensurate returns may be obtained on the school investment.

References

Saskatchewan, *A Survey of Education in the Province of Saskatchewan*, 1918.

235 COMMISSION OF INQUIRY TO STUDY THE PUBLIC REVENUES TAX AND TO INQUIRE GENERALLY INTO THE MATTER OF EQUALIZATION OF ASSESSMENTS FOR PURPOSES OF PROVINCIAL TAXATION IN THE MUNICIPALITIES OF THE PROVINCE, URBAN AND RURAL
(Related Commission)

Appointed May 17, 1921

Reported January 10, 1922

Commission Five members; George Armstrong (Wildlands Tax Commissioner) chairman

Purpose To study the Public Revenues Tax and to inquire generally into the matter of equalization of assessments for purposes of provincial taxation in the municipalities of the Province, urban and rural.

Conclusions/Recommendations

That, if land values are to be taken as a basis, the system fails because different systems of valuation are adopted in the different classes of municipalities, and in municipalities of the same class. If ability to pay is taken as a basis, the system fails because the rural dweller is paying on a larger proportion of his wealth than the urban dweller, and again the city dweller pays more than the inhabitant of the town, who in turn pays more than the inhabitant of a village. The system also fails on account of the large percentage of businesses and individuals who pay none or a very small percentage of the tax.

References

Saskatchewan, *Sessional Papers*, 1921-22, No. 19.

236 SELECT COMMITTEE TO INVESTIGATE THE ADVISABILITY OF ESTABLISHING THE RURAL MUNICIPALITY AS THE UNIT OF ADMINISTRATION FOR RURAL SCHOOLS
(Legislative Committee)

Appointed February 9, 1923

Reported March 9, 1923

Committee Twenty-seven members; Donald Finlayson (Member of Jack Fish Lake) chairman

Purpose — To investigate the advisability of establishing the rural municipality as the unit of administration for rural schools.

Conclusions/Recommendations

That, in view of the many difficulties with which the subject of administration of rural schools is surrounded, further exhaustive consideration be given to this question.

References

Saskatchewan, *Journals*, 1923.

237 COMMITTEE ON SCHOOL FINANCE AND SCHOOL GRANTS (Departmental Committee)

Appointed — April, 1932

Reported — March 1, 1933

Committee — Five members; N.L. Reid (Assistant Deputy Minister) chairman

Purpose — To investigate school finance and school grants.

Conclusions/Recommendations

That, if education is a public responsibility, there is something unsatisfactory and even unfair about a system where, in the case of two adjoining districts providing similar educational facilities, one district with inferior taxable resources is called upon to levy a school rate four or five times as high as its neighbor;

That a system of taxation and a basis for payment of school grants be instituted that will make for equality of educational opportunity and equality of costs as well.

References

Saskatchewan, *Report of the Committee on School Finance and*

Saskatchewan / 238

School Grants, 1933.

238 DEBT SURVEY COMMITTEE
(Departmental Committee)

<u>Appointed</u> August 23, 1934

<u>Reported</u> February, 1935

<u>Committee</u> Three members; J.W. Estey (King's Counsel) chairman

<u>Purpose</u> To survey the debts of individuals, corporations, and municipal and other public bodies within the province.

<u>Conclusions/Recommendations</u>

That of 4509 school districts, 2894 owe no teachers' salaries, 203 could pay all salaries from cash on hand, 1389 could not pay salaries from cash on hand, 22 are not in operation, and one has no return in for 1933.

<u>References</u>

Saskatchewan, 'Report of the Debt Survey Committee', 1935.

239 COMMISSION OF INQUIRY INTO PROVINCIAL AND MUNICIPAL TAXATION
(Related Commission)

<u>Appointed</u> August 21, 1936

<u>Reported</u> December 19, 1936

<u>Commission</u> Five members; Neil Herman Jacoby (Illinois Department of Finance) chairman

<u>Purpose</u> To enquire into the whole subject of taxation within the Province of Saskatchewan.

Conclusions/Recommendations

That it is assumed that governmental services will be continued upon generally the same scale and with the same degree of completeness as at present;

That it is assumed that both the people of Saskatchewan and their provincial and local governments desire and intend to discharge past and present obligations in accordance with the terms of existing contracts or in accordance with terms voluntarily agreed upon by governmental or private creditors;

That it is assumed that the income of the people of the Province at large during the ensuing five years will be somewhat higher than the average income of the five-year period 1931-1935.

References

Saskatchewan, *Report of the Commission of Inquiry into Provincial and Municipal Taxation to the Government of the Province of Saskatchewan*, 1936.

240 COMMITTEE ON SCHOOL ADMINISTRATION
(Departmental Committee)

Appointed July 12, 1938

Reported December, 1939

Committee Five members; William M. Martin (Court of Appeal Judge) chairman

Purpose To inquire into and to report on the subject of school administration.

Conclusions/Recommendations

That, while the Committee is not prepared to recommend the formation and operation of experimental units without the approval of the ratepayers concerned, it is of the opinion that several areas of the Province should be selected and the ratepayers resident therein given an opportunity to decide whether or not the schools in the selected areas are to be subjected to a larger unit administration.

References

Saskatchewan, *Report of the Committee on School Administration*, 1939.

241 SASKATCHEWAN RECONSTRUCTION COUNCIL
(Departmental Committee)

Appointed — October, 1943

Reported — August, 1944

Committee — Seven members; F.C. Cronkite (Dean of Law, University of Saskatchewan) chairman

Purpose — To study and investigate conditions and problems likely to arise during or after the war and to consider, develop and recommend plans, policies and activities for the purpose of meeting such conditions and problems.

Conclusions/Recommendations

That education in Saskatchewan must develop on the following bases:

First, a sustained and increased attention to technical and vocational education so that our youth may be fitted for a part in a community and world of constantly changing technology;
Second, an increased attention to social studies, which seek an understanding of group relationships whether social, political or economic;
Third, a sustained attention to the humanities, to literature, art, language and philosophy, with a view to developing a maximum range of human interests. Constant care must be exercised that all studies are couched in terms of current experience while sacrificing nothing of permanent value;

and finally, constant care must be exercised to ensure that instruction, particularly in the field of social studies, shall not become indoctrination, and that the goal of teaching be development of the student's ability to make informed and reasoned judgements upon constantly emerging problems.

That the Council approves of the principle of larger units;

That the Department of Education should make a careful study of the problem of the larger administrative unit, and after such study, openly favour or oppose the establishment of these units and give guidance to districts, making known the advantages or disadvantages.

References

Saskatchewan, *Report of the Saskatchewan Reconstruction Council*, 1944.

242 COMMITTEE ON PROVINCIAL-MUNICIPAL RELATIONS (Departmental Committee)

Appointed 1948

Reported October 16, 1950

Committee Three members; G.E. Britnell (Head of Economics and Political Science, University of Saskatchewan) chairman

Purpose To make a complete examination of the financial history of the province from the time of its formation in order to throw light on the common assumptions that real property is being over-taxed and that the municipalities are over-burdened with obligations in relation to their fiscal strength.

Conclusions/Recommendations

That in its desire to provide the children of the province with an opportunity equal to those of other provinces the provincial government has undoubtedly assumed a burden out of proportion to the resources at its disposal, and, in order that educational opportunity may be equalized as far as may be possible throughout the Dominion, some equalization plan based on differences in provincial resources should be undertaken by the Dominion government.

References

Saskatchewan, *Report of the Committee on Provincial-Municipal Relations*, 1950.

243 ROYAL COMMISSION ON AGRICULTURE AND RURAL LIFE
(Related Commission)

Appointed October 31, 1952

Reported Fourteen reports from March 18, 1955 to April 10, 1957

Commission Six members; William Bernard Baker (School of Agriculture, University of Saskatchewan) chairman

Purpose To study and make recommendations regarding:

(1) the problems involved in present day trends in agricultural production, land use and farm costs;

(2) the need for farm capital and credit;

(3) the further adaptation of social services and educational facilities to meet changing rural conditions; and

(4) the further development of rural transportation, communication and community services; and for these purposes to consult with all organizations and individuals interested and to accept for consideration, articles, submissions or other representations made by or on behalf of interested persons or

organizations, and to include in their considerations any questions which they may hold to be relevant.

Conclusions/Recommendations

That, since education in rural Saskatchewan functions within the rural social system, the basic characteristics of agriculture and population have vital implications for the provision of rural education;

That regrouping into larger units of school administration be continued;

That balanced recourse to local, provincial, and federal financial resources is imperative if there is to be maintenance and expansion of educational programmes;

That the problems of staffing rural schools with adequate teaching personnel and of retaining students in schools be faced;

That vocational education and continuing education be expanded to meet the evergrowing demands of a technical world and a complex society.

References

Saskatchewan, *Royal Commission on Agriculture and Rural Life: The Scope and Character of the Investigation*, 1955.

Saskatchewan, *Royal Commission on Agriculture and Rural Life: Rural Education*, 1956.

244 CONTINUING COMMITTEE ON LOCAL GOVERNMENT
(Departmental Committee)

Appointed June 21, 1957

Reported March 1, 1961

Committee Fifteen members; John McAskill (Mayor of Saskatoon) chairman

Purpose To study reorganization and boundaries and reallocation of finances and responsibilities.

Conclusions/Recommendations

That the provincial government undertake general reorganization of local government in Saskatchewan through the following steps:

(a) Establish coterminous boundaries;

(b) As soon as practical, organize each coterminous area into a county or modified county, the choice between modified county or county to be made by a vote of the electors in each area;

(c) Reorganize school administration in each coterminous area as required by the selection made under (b).

References

Saskatchewan, *Local Government in Saskatchewan*, 1961.

245 COMMITTEE ON CONTINUING EDUCATION
(Departmental Committee)

Appointed September, 1962

Reported January, 1963

Committee Thirteen members; John H. Archer (Legislative Librarian and Provincial Archivist) chairman

Purpose To delineate a policy of continuing education for Saskatchewan and to determine roles and responsibilities of formal agencies and voluntary organizations active in this field.

Conclusions/Recommendations

That because continuing education is so closely linked to citizenship, government must treat it as a necessary part of the educational provision of the province, and must also achieve a sound balance between private and voluntary efforts and public resources.

References

Saskatchewan, 'Report of Saskatchewan Commission on Continuing Education', [1963].

246 ROYAL COMMISSION ON TAXATION
(Related Commission)

Appointed June 4, 1963

Reported May 1, 1965

Commission Three members; Thomas H. McLeod (Dean of Commerce, University of Saskatchewan) chairman

Purpose To consider and report upon the systems of taxation which comprise the total tax structure in effect in the Province.

Conclusions/Recommendations

That the idea of the foundation or basic programme in education reflects a social belief that all students should be guaranteed some adequate, uniform, minimum standard of educational opportunities, regardless of where they live.

References

Saskatchewan, *Report of the Royal Commission on Taxation*, 1965.

247 COMMITTEE ON INSTRUCTION IN LANGUAGES OTHER THAN ENGLISH
(Departmental Committee)

Appointed August 11, 1965

Reported June 29, 1966

Committee — Five members; J.W. Tait (Director of Teacher Training, Department of Education) chairman

Purpose — To conduct a study of present programs of instruction in languages other than English in the provincial school system.

Conclusions/Recommendations

That English remain the language of instruction in the schools of Saskatchewan except as specifically recommended;

That *The School Act* which reads: 'English shall be the sole language of instruction in all schools, and no language other than English shall be taught during school hours.' be amended to read: 'Except as hereafter provided, English shall be taught during school hours.'

References

Saskatchewan, *Report of the Saskatchewan Committee on Instruction in Languages other than English*, 29 June 1966.

248 JOINT COMMITTEE ON HIGHER EDUCATION
(Special Committee)

Appointed — November 5, 1965

Reported — July 31, 1967

Committee — Sixteen members; J.W.T. Spinks (President, University of Saskatchewan) chairman

Purpose — To examine all aspects of post school education; to examine the feasibility of regional decentralization of post school education; and to examine and evaluate the articulation of all formal and informal educational programs in a community and, by so doing, to develop instruments and methods of enquiry with which other communities can carry out self evaluations.

Conclusions/Recommendations

That a number of educational regions be defined to provide for development of effective 'middle-range' educational services;

That these services be developed under a Commission for Middle-Range Education, representative of the Government, the University, the Saskatchewan School Trustees' Association, the Saskatchewan Teachers' Federation and the regions;

That a Provincial Educational Advisory Council be established to act in an advisory capacity to the Minister of Education with respect to the overall coordination and articulation of provincial educational services.

References

Saskatchewan, *Second Interim Report: Joint Committee on Higher Education*, July, 1967.

249 COMMITTEE ON TEACHERS' SALARY NEGOTIATION: LEGISLATION AND PROCEDURES
(Departmental Committee)

Appointed December 21, 1965

Reported January 9, 1967

Committee Three members; Benjamin Moore (Judge, Swift Current) chairman

Purpose To inquire into the application of existing legislation to teachers' salary negotiation procedures.

Conclusions/Recommendations

That further study by a committee consisting of members of the Department of Education, the Saskatchewan School Trustees' Association and the Saskatchewan Teachers' Federation be made to determine the feasibility of a system of compulsory area bargaining under the present system of school administration;

That present legislation make provision for area bargaining on a voluntary basis;

That legislation provide a definite step by step time table for negotiations, and that January 1 would be a realistic anniversary date for agreements negotiated between boards and their teachers;

That in the event of the parties failing to reach a voluntary agreement, or if jointly requested at an earlier date by the board and its group of teachers, the Minister shall appoint a Conciliation Officer from the Department of Labour to mediate the dispute and assist the parties thereto in reaching a voluntary agreement.

References

Saskatchewan, *Report to the Minister of Education of the Committee on Teachers' Salary Negotiation: Legislation and Procedures*, 1967.

250 ADVISORY COMMITTEE ON DIVISIONS THREE AND FOUR (Departmental Committee)

Appointed — December, 1967

Reported — August 15, 1969

Committee — Two members; L.S. Nicks (Past President, Saskatchewan School Trustees Association) and F.J. Gathercole (Director of Education, Saskatoon Public Schools and Collegiates) co-chairmen

Purpose — To inquire into the general efficacy and suitability of the division system as an educational plan for the province of Saskatchewan.

Conclusions/Recommendations

That the Department of Education immediately reaffirm to teachers, to school boards, and to the general public its support of the plan for reorganizing elementary school education in keeping with the concepts of non-gradedness and continuous pupil progress, its belief in the need of a special educational program for young adolescents, and its conviction that the comprehensive high school program should be retained as the model for secondary school education;

That the basic educational program be planned by the Department of Education as a twelve-year continuum; leaving to local education authorities the decision as to what grades or students are to be grouped together in schools.

References

Saskatchewan, *Report of the Minister of Education's Advisory Committee on Divisions Three and Four in the Province of Saskatchewan*, 15 August 1969.

251 SPECIAL PROVISIONAL COMMITTEE ON HIGHER EDUCATION (Departmental Committee)

Appointed — October 20, 1969

Reported — June 15, 1970

Committee — Four members; L.A. Riederer (Director of Program Development) chairman

Purpose — To investigate adult educational needs of the Province of Saskatchewan in relation to existing programs and institutions, and to draft legislative proposals for 'middle-range' education.

Conclusions/Recommendations

That a decision be made as to whether all of post-secondary education (including the University) be placed under one provincial Board of Governors, or that there be a separate Board of Governors for Community Colleges.

References

Saskatchewan, *Interim Submission to the Minister of Education concerning Governance of 'Middle-Range' Education in Saskatchewan*, 15 June, 1970.

252 COMMITTEE ON KINDERGARTEN EDUCATION
(Departmental Committee)

Appointed October 13, 1971

Reported June 30, 1972

Committee Eight members; E.H. Fowlie (Director of Curriculum, Department of Education) chairman

Purpose To examine the need, feasibility and desirability of a province-wide, publicly-supported kindergarten program; to recommend suitable objectives for such a program; and to recommend appropriate means of achieving and implementing these objectives.

Conclusions/Recommendations

That publicly-supported kindergartens be established in Saskatchewan;

That the decision to establish kindergarten in any school jurisdiction be a school board decision, rather than a provincial one;

That kindergarten teachers be certificated on the same basis as other teachers;

That because specialization in early childhood education is highly desirable, teacher education programs in the field of early childhood education be expanded and made more accessible.

References

Saskatchewan, *Report of the Minister's Committee on*

Saskatchewan / 251

Kindergarten Education, 1972.

253 ADVISORY COMMITTEE ON COMMUNITY COLLEGES
(Departmental Committee)

Appointed February 15, 1972

Reported August 15, 1972

Committee Ten members; Ron Faris (Senior Advisor on Educational Community Development) chairman

Purpose To advise the Minister on the role of community colleges in Saskatchewan's educational system and the educational process throughout the province which would foster understanding of the philosophy and potential of community college development.

Conclusions/Recommendations

That the purpose of community colleges be to maximize opportunities for continuing education through a decentralization of formal learning opportunities and the organization of programs at community and regional levels to meet informal learning needs;

That colleges be developed on a regional basis with priority in development given to rural areas;

That community college programs be organized to meet identified needs and be disbanded when the need is met;

That community colleges grant no degree or diplomas, but that formal programs be contracted as required from existing educational institutions.

References

Saskatchewan, *Report of the Minister's Advisory Committee on Community Colleges*, August, 1972.

254 ADVISORY COMMITTEE ON DENTAL CARE FOR CHILDREN
(Departmental Committee)

Appointed November 30, 1972

Reported March 31, 1973

Committee Six members; K.J. Paynter (Dean of Dentistry, University of Saskatchewan) chairman

Purpose To advise the Minister on proposals for a dental care program for children in Saskatchewan.

Conclusions/Recommendations

That dental care benefits extend through the age of 17 for all children;

That children younger than three years of age be included in the plan on the basis of parental initiative;

That great care be taken in designing a system that will ensure that treatment service does not gain dominance over preventive service in terms of importance;

That in the interests of both dental health and economics, water supplies in all communities with a central water system be fluoridated and a constant promotional and educational campaign be mounted to bring this about.

References

Saskatchewan, *Saskatchewan Advisory Committee on Dental Care for Children Report*, 31 March 1973.

255 ADVISORY COMMITTEE ON PHYSICAL EDUCATION
(Departmental Committee)

Appointed March 5, 1973

Reported August, 1973

Committee — Eight members; John Campbell (Physical Education Consultant, Department of Education) chairman

Purpose — To make recommendations to the Minister with respect to Physical Education programs at the elementary and secondary level.

Conclusions/Recommendations

That a Saskatchewan Branch of Physical Education and Recreation be created within the Department of Education;

That the Department of Education investigate the possibility of a Liaison Committee between the Departments of Health, Culture & Youth and Education;

That a Physical Education Curriculum Steering Committee be established on a permanent and rotating basis;

That Physical Education be a required daily subject for all students from Kindergarten to 12;

That all students in Kindergarten through Grade 12 should participate in Physical Education according to physiological development, ability, interests, and individual needs;

That Physical Education must be required for promotion from all grades;

That certification standards for Physical Education personnel be established;

That the first responsibility of the Physical Education teacher is to the instructional programs, the second to the inter-house activity program and the third to the athletic program.

References

Saskatchewan, *Report of the Minister's Advisory Committee on Physical Education*, August, 1973.

256 TASK FORCE ON THE STATUS OF WOMEN IN SASKATCHEWAN (Departmental Committee)

Appointed April 17, 1973

Reported November, 1973 [to Minister responsible for Status of Women Matters]

Committee Two members; Arleen N. Hynd (Deputy Minister, Department of Consumer Affairs) and Mary Rocan (Women's Bureau, Department of Labour)

Purpose To study the recommendations of the Report of the Royal Commission on the Status of Women as they affect the government of the Province of Saskatchewan.

Conclusions/Recommendations

That consideration be given to promoting the production of and obtaining textbooks which do portray men and women in diversified roles;

That teacher training give greater emphasis to career counselling;

That the Department of Education give consideration to determining the adequacy of career counselling in Saskatchewan schools;

That consideration be given to determining the degree to which the Department of Education can exert pressure on local school boards to have Family Life Education taught in the schools; keeping in mind that the training of teachers in Family Life Education is crucial to the success of such a program;

That a study be made to determine whether or not girls have an equal opportunity with boys to participate in sports activities;

That the Department of Continuing Education ensure that the post-secondary education institutions develop programs to meet the special educational needs of women with family responsibilities;

That consideration be given to extending the Saskatchewan Student Aid Fund to include part-time students;

That continued attention be paid to providing facilities and encouraging native peoples to take upgrading and training courses, and to encouraging native persons to become trained to teach their own people.

References

Saskatchewan, *Saskatchewan Women '73: Task Force Report on the Status of Women in Saskatchewan,* 1973.

257 ROYAL COMMISSION ON UNIVERSITY ORGANIZATION AND STRUCTURE (General Commission)

Appointed May 3, 1973

Reported December 22, 1973

Commission Three members; Emmett Hall (former Supreme Court Justice) chairman

Purpose To inquire into and report on university organization and structure in the Province of Saskatchewan.

Conclusions/Recommendations

That the campuses at Saskatoon and Regina be established as independent universities;

That there be a body to be known as The Saskatchewan Universities Commission which shall be comprised of nine part-time members, including the chairperson, all of whom shall be appointed by the Lieutenant Governor-in-Council;

That, under The Saskatchewan Universities Commission, there be a twenty-one member Universities Coordinating Committee, an eight member Capital Planning and Development Committee, and an eleven member Graduate Studies and Research Committee;

That a degree program in Engineering be re-established at the University of Regina.

References

Saskatchewan, *Report of the Royal Commission on University Organization and Structure*, 1973.

258 ADVISORY COMMITTEE ON THE EDUCATION OF THE DEAF (Departmental Committee)

Appointed October 19, 1973

Reported July 8, 1974

Committee Fifteen members; D.G. Drozda (Chief, Guidance and Special Education, Department of Education) chairman

Purpose To study and make recommendations concerning communication and instructional policies at the Saskatchewan School for the Deaf, the development of community-based educational programs for the deaf, and the education of the deaf at the post-school level.

Conclusions/Recommendations

That preschool and kindergarten classes should follow an oral program, and that provision should be made to assist parents in learning Total Communication;

That Division 1 (Primary section) should provide two programs (oral and Total Communication) and that Divisions 2 and 3 should provide Total Communication;

That at all stages of the school program there should be ready mobility from the School for the Deaf to community-based classes and vice versa;

That the Education Act should be amended to provide for the education of hearing impaired children from the age of three up;

That the Saskatchewan Department of Education continue to place greater dependence on Canadian based technical-vocational and university program, rather than continuing the traditional dependence on United States programs such as those at St. Paul Technical Vocational Institute and Gallaudet College in Washington.

References

Saskatchewan, *Kernel Report of the Minister's Advisory Committee on the Education of the Deaf*, 1974.

259 ADVISORY COMMITTEE ON STUDENT EVALUATION
(Departmental Committee)

Appointed November 27, 1973

Reported October 20, 1975

Committee Thirteen members; F. Nakonechny (Chief, Student Evaluation, Department of Education) chairman

Purpose To inquire into and make recommendations regarding student evaluation.

Conclusions/Recommendations

That a major function of the preservice and inservice education of teachers in student evaluation should be to enhance the repertoire of evaluation strategies used by teachers;

That a review of the teacher training programs be undertaken to ensure that teachers display an understanding of the philosophy and procedures of student evaluation; that they display competence in the selection, development, application, and interpretation of a wide variety of evaluation procedures; and that they be able to construct, use and evaluate teacher-made tests.

That a provincial inservice education program in student evaluation be undertaken by the Department of Education, in collaboration with the Saskatchewan Teachers' Federation, the Saskatchewan School Trustees Association, and the two universities;

That teacher reports to parents be in terms of the intended learning outcomes of the courses of studies;

That parent-teacher interviews be encouraged as an appropriate and desirable reporting procedure to complement written reports on student progress;

That information kept by schools, school systems, and the Department of Education concerning student evaluation be such that it can be disclosed to students and their parents.

References

Saskatchewan, *Student Evaluation - Report of the Minister's Advisory Committee*, October, 1975.

260 ADVISORY COMMITTEE ON SCHOOL LAW
(Departmental Committee)

Appointed February 3, 1975

Reported January 31, 1976

Committee Five members; Clarence Amundrud (Chief, School Administration, Department of Education) chairman

Purpose To study all existing statutes which have reference to and effect upon the K-XII educational system of Saskatchewan, and to investigate and make recommendations regarding the consolidation and upgrading of existing statutes.

Conclusions/Recommendations

That fifteen separate statutes be consolidated and incorporated in a new statute, *The Education Act;*

That the existing high school districts be disorganized and their functions transferred to the school division in which they are incorporated;

That the role, powers and duties of boards of education be clearly defined in law;

That legislative provision be made for establishment of new school divisions, public and separate, in addition to those divisions which are created under this Act from existing administrative units;

That the basic rights of pupils be given specific definition in law;

That the duties and functions of teachers should be defined in general terms only;

That present provisions of *The Teacher Collective Bargaining Act*, 1973, be embodied in the new Education Act.

References

Saskatchewan, *Report of the School Law Review Committee*, January, 1976.

261 COLLEGE MATHIEU REVIEW COMMITTEE
(Departmental Committee)

Appointed March, 1976

Reported December 17, 1976

Committee Ten members; L.M. Ready (Associate Deputy Minister of Education) chairman

Purpose To review existing Department of Education policy with respect to the provision of French language opportunities in the elementary and secondary schools of the province, and to assess the situation at College Mathieu.

Conclusions/Recommendations

That secondary bilingual education opportunities be offered by fiscally-responsible school boards which have a designated French elementary program, provided that certain minimum requirements with respect to enrolments, time allotments, qualifications of teachers and instructional resource materials are met;

That the Department of Education establish a Designated High School Committee to make recommendations concerning provincial policy with respect to the provision of standards for secondary bilingual education;

That College Mathieu continue to offer a Roman Catholic secondary education to Saskatchewan Francophones;

That designated secondary French programs should be instituted in a location central to a region and financed in a manner similar to the present financing of College Mathieu.

References

Saskatchewan, *Report of the College Mathieu Review Committee*, December, 1976.

262 COMMITTEE ON SERVICE FUNDING OF THE COLLEGE OF MEDICINE, UNIVERSITY OF SASKATCHEWAN
(Departmental Committee)

Appointed January, 1977

Reported September 14, 1977 [to Minister of Health and Minister of Continuing Education]

Committee Five members; N. Duane Adams (Assistant Deputy Minister of Health) chairman

Purpose To review the funding of medical education and related service components and their relationship to cost-sharing agreements with the federal government.

Conclusions/Recommendations

That an Advisory Committee on Service Funding of the Saskatchewan Medical Education System be established;

That a Clinical Service Fund be established in the Department of Health;

That the financing of the University of Saskatchewan, College of Medicine Regina component be altered according to specific recommendations;

That the employment of part-time teachers by the College of Medicine be encouraged;

That the University of Saskatchewan review the education mandate assigned to the College of Medicine for the purpose of evaluating and monitoring the teaching load and ascertaining whether or not it is satisfied with the value received for education dollars.

References

Saskatchewan, *Report of the Committee on Service Funding of the College of Medicine, University of Saskatchewan*, September, 1977.

ALBERTA

263 COMMITTEE ON REVISION OF THE SCHOOL CURRICULUM FOR THE PROVINCE
(Legislative Committee)

Appointed 1911 (?)

Reported December 7, 1911

Committee

Purpose To investigate the need for revision of the school curriculum for the Province.

Conclusions/Recommendations

References

Alberta, *Journals*, 1911.

264 COMMISSION OF INQUIRY TO CONSIDER THE GRANTING OF DEGREE-CONFERRING POWERS TO CALGARY COLLEGE
(General Commission)

Appointed May 22, 1914

Reported February 25, 1915

Commission Three members; Robert Alexander Falconer (President, University of Toronto) chairman

Purpose To consider the granting of degree-conferring powers to Calgary College.

Conclusions/Recommendations

That there be no departure from the historic policy of Western Canada which was inaugurated by the Province of Manitoba, adopted by the North West Territories, and re-affirmed by the Province of Alberta, to establish one university and one only, to be supported and controlled by the Province for the purpose of giving instruction, granting degrees and controlling the requirements for admission to the professions;

That an Institute of Technology and Art be established in the City of Calgary to be supported and controlled jointly by the City and the Province.

References

Alberta, *Report of the Commission Appointed to Consider the Granting of Degree-conferring Powers to Calgary College*, Sessional Paper No. 1, 1915.

265 GENERAL COMMITTEE ON THE REVISION OF THE ELEMENTARY SCHOOL CURRICULUM
(Departmental Committee)

Appointed February, 1921

Reported [ ]

Committee Fifteen members; G. Fred McNally (Supervisor of Schools) chairman

Purpose To consider and recommend the subjects which are of most worth to Alberta boys and girls, and to plan a new course which will be flexible and easily adaptable to the varying needs of the children of all parts of the Province, but which will make any other than thorough work and the development of habits of industry impossible, no matter what subjects have to be sacrificed.

Conclusions/Recommendations

References

Alberta, *Journals*, 1921.

Alberta, 'General Committee on the Revision of the Elementary School Curriculum', 1921.

266 ADVISORY COMMITTEE ON TAXATION
(Departmental Committee)

Appointed April, 1926

Reported February 14, 1928

Committee Five members; H.M. Tory (President, University of Alberta) chairman

Purpose To enquire into the following subjects:

A. The equalization of the burden of taxation.

B. Improved methods of collecting revenue.

C. Methods of collecting revenue from the natural resources of the Province, having regard to their possible transfer to the Province, paying particular attention to the taxation of mineral resources by provincial and municipal authorities.

D. The extent to which any tax may be reduced or modified, or one form of taxation substituted for another, having particular regard to the Supplementary Revenue Tax and the Wild Lands Tax.

E. The division of responsibility for revenue and expenditure as between the Government and the municipalities, urban and rural, including the question of Mother's Allowance and the care of indigents.

F. Adequacy of Sinking Fund and provision for the retiral of provincial and local funded debts.

G. Systems of local government obtaining in the Province of Alberta and elsewhere.

Conclusions/Recommendations

References

Alberta, *Report on Taxation by Advisory Committee on Taxation*, 1928.

267 ALBERTA TAXATION INQUIRY BOARD ON PROVINCIAL AND MUNICIPAL TAXATION
(Departmental Committee)

Appointed December 1, 1933

Reported November 30, 1935

Committee Four members; J.F. Percival (Deputy Provincial Secretary) chairman

Purpose To make a survey of the sources and incidence of taxation in the province.

Conclusions/Recommendations

That the burden of educational costs in the cities of the Province has become so serious as to cause the gravest concern;

That the raising of the necessary revenue solely by the taxation of real property is discriminatory as between classes composing the community, and that the burden so placed cannot now be justified;

That the duty imposed by law upon the city to pay 100% of the demand of the School Board, whether it is collected or not, has a crippling effect on the finances of the city, and that the power now vested in School Boards to requisition large sums of money from the city irrespective of the latter's capacity to collect taxes, should be restricted;

That the Provincial Government is primarily responsible for education, and that its delegation of the financial burden to the Municipality to the extent of over 90% is an inequitable division of that burden;

That the Provincial Government, possessing as it does far wider powers of taxation than those enjoyed by the municipalities, should assume a much greater share of cost of education;

That due to the increasing cost of various social services which real property is now compelled to bear, land is being forfeited to the cities to an alarming extent, and the physical structure upon which the cities depend so largely for their revenue is steadily shrinking both as to area and revenue-producing capacity;

That the Federal Government should contribute substantially to the cost of technical education.

References

Alberta, *Report of the Alberta Taxation Inquiry Board on Provincial and Municipal Taxation*, 1935.

268 COMMISSION OF INQUIRY INTO REHABILITATION OF THE METIS (Related Commission)

Appointed December 12, 1933

Reported February 15, 1936

Commission Three members; Albert Freeman Ewing (Supreme Court Judge) chairman

Purpose To inquire into the problems of health,

education and the general welfare of the half-breed population of the Province.

Conclusions/Recommendations

That a farm colony plan of settlement be established that would keep groups of Metis families together for at least parts of the year. Schools could be built and the wives and families encouraged to remain in the colony. In any case, all the children could be able to attend during some portion of the year. The children should be taught reading and writing and elementary arithmetic. In addition, the boys should be taught stock raising and farming, while the girls should be taught the elements of sanitation, cleanliness, sewing, and knitting. The cost would not be great and the Province would be saved the stigma which attaches to any civilized country that permits a large number of children to grow up within its boundaries without the slightest elementary education.

References

Alberta, *Journals*, 1933.

Alberta, 'Royal Commission on Rehabilitation of the Metis', 1936.

269 LEGISLATIVE COMMITTEE APPOINTED TO MAKE A COMPREHENSIVE SURVEY AND STUDY OF EDUCATION IN THE RURAL DISTRICTS OF ALBERTA
(Legislative Committee)

Appointed April 3, 1934

Reported April 12, 1935

Committee Ten members; Perren E. Baker (Member for Cypress) chairman

Purpose To make a comprehensive survey and study of education in the rural districts of Alberta.

Conclusions/Recommendations

That residential schools be established for families on the fringe of settlement;

That secondary education in rural areas be provided;

That school library facilities be expanded;

That scholarships be available for deserving students;

That radio school broadcasts be provided;

That a Library Commission be instituted and adult education be encouraged;

That Grade 12 be required for normal school entrance, or a two-year training course for all teachers be instituted;

That refresher courses be provided for those returning to teaching;

That the curriculum for smaller schools be enriched;

That more supervision be provided for rural schools;

That equalization of educational costs and opportunities be sought;

That the larger unit of administration be given careful study.

References

Alberta, 'Report of the Legislative Committee Appointed to Make a Comprehensive Survey and Study of Education in the Rural Districts of Alberta', 1935.

270 UNIVERSITY OF ALBERTA SURVEY COMMITTEE
(Departmental Committee)

Appointed August 7, 1941

Reported February 25, 1942

Committee — Six members; H.H. Parlee (Chairman, Board of Governors, University of Alberta) chairman

Purpose — To conduct a survey of the affairs of the University in order to determine (a) the place of the university in the educational system of the Province, (b) whether the University can be made to serve more completely the cultural needs of all the people of the Province, and (c) whether it is possible to have the University function more effectively in the development of the agricultural and industrial resources of the Province.

Conclusions/Recommendations

That the College of Education be given faculty status;

That greater use be made of the existing University plant by extending the time it is in full operation;

That a more systematic effort be made to inspire students with loyalty and a sense of responsibility towards the University, as a basis for Alumni interest and support;

That the work of the University Department of Extension be expanded by at least one-third;

That junior college work be expanded;

That a small annual grant be earmarked for the encouragement of research;

That the Board of Governors be the controlling body in all University affairs;

That the Senate be reduced in size; that it be representative of the various elements of provincial society including students and alumni, and that it have the important function of acting as a bridge between the University and the life and activities of the Province;

That the General Faculty Council take over most of the purely academic functions presently discharged by the Senate;

That there be a long-term financial policy ensuring steady growth; and that new responsibilities not be accepted until capacity to finance has been fully explored;

That a satisfactory salary schedule be implemented;

That the Administration review frequently the aptitudes, progress, and teaching loads of the staff.

References

Alberta, Order in Council 1117/41, August 7, 1941.

Alberta, *University of Alberta Survey Committee Interim Report*, 1942.

271 SUBCOMMITTEE ON EDUCATION AND VOCATIONAL TRAINING (Departmental Committee)

Appointed — 1943 (Part of the Post-War Reconstruction Committee)

Reported — December 18, 1944

Committee — Five members; Robert Newton (President, University of Alberta) chairman

Purpose — To enquire into the functions, organization, and machinery of education and vocational training in the Province, and of recommending such measures as seem to be required to adapt, improve, or expand the system in whole or part, to meet the expected needs of the post-war period.

Conclusions/Recommendations

That in the interests of education the public be enlightened with respect to the highly unsatisfactory conditions surrounding the teaching profession;

That the Province expand its programme of educational reform, in order to promote improvements in teachers' salaries, training, legal status, pension provisions, and rural living conditions, in order that the profession may attract and hold the high calibre of personnel which its vital importance warrants;

That a minimum salary schedule be established, based on $1200 for the first year after certification, and recognizing the cost and professional value of successive years of training, also the value of increasing experience and the assumption of successive degrees of responsibility;

That the possibility of recruiting teacher material from returned men and women be explored;

That all teacher-training in Alberta be integrated;

(Other recommendations dealt with scholarships, school buildings and equipment, transportation, community schools and vocational institutes, home and school associations, adult education, and school finance.)

References

Alberta, *Report of the Subcommittee on Education*, 1944.

272 ROYAL COMMISSION ON TAXATION
(Related Commission)

Appointed July 22, 1947

Reported February 12, 1948

Commission One member; J.W. Judge (Deputy Minister of Municipal Affairs)

Purpose To inquire into the taxation imposed by the Province and by Municipalities, urban and rural.

Conclusions/Recommendations

That there is a place for inter-provincial equalization of educational opportunity. This would mean the creation by the Dominion Government of an inter-provincial equalization fund to be distributed among the Provinces according to need for the purpose of providing equal educational opportunity to all the children of all the people of all the Provinces;

That, in the opinion of the Commission, there is no legal hindrance to the Dominion in establishing such a fund, and further the Commission believes that no infringement of the rights of the Province need take place in the administration of such fund.

References

Alberta, *Report of the Royal Commission on Taxation*, Sessional Papers, No. 71, 1948.

273 ROYAL COMMISSION ON THE METROPOLITAN DEVELOPMENT OF CALGARY AND EDMONTON
(Related Commission)

Appointed July 19, 1954

Reported January 31, 1956

Commission Five members; George Frederick McNally (former Chancellor, University of Alberta) chairman

Purpose To enquire into the administration and financing of schools and municipal services in the City of Edmonton and surrounding areas, and the City of Calgary and surrounding areas.

Conclusions/Recommendations

That Edmonton and Calgary are especially liable to rising future costs because of their rapid growth and high proportion of children; and because a larger proportion of pupils tend to stay on in high school, special instruction for the handicapped increases, courses tend to proliferate, teachers' qualifications tend to rise and so forth;

Alberta / 273

That the need for the planning of capital and operational budgets to prepare for the expected rising costs is obvious, and has been to a great extent taken in hand by province and the city school boards.

References

Alberta, *Report of the Royal Commission on the Metropolitan Development of Calgary and Edmonton*, 1956.

274 ROYAL COMMISSION ON TEACHERS' SALARIES
(General Commission)

Appointed July 9, 1957

Reported January 31, 1958

Commission Three members; Gilbert McNeil Blackstock (Queen's Counsel) chairman

Purpose To consider:

(a) the feasibility of establishing a scale or scales of salaries for teachers in the Province;

(b) the form or forms which such salary scales might take;

(c) the manner by which such salary scales might be arrived at and altered from time to time;

(d) the effects of the establishment of teacher salary scales upon
 (i) the financing of education both in the Province generally and in particular areas within the Province, and
 (ii) the supply of teachers and upon the quality and morale of the teaching profession generally.

Conclusions/Recommendations

That, in the judgement of the Commission, the establishment of salary scales on a Provincial basis can have no other effect than to increase the supply of teachers available for service in Alberta's schools;

That, in view of these considerations, the Commission is convinced that the establishment of Provincial salary scales would improve the quality and morale of the teaching profession generally.

References

Alberta, *Report of the Royal Commission on the Feasibility of Establishing a Scale or Scales of Salaries for Teachers in the Province of Alberta and Allied Matters*, 1958.

275 ROYAL COMMISSION ON EDUCATION
(General Commission)

Appointed — December 31, 1957

Reported — November 9, 1959 (A minority report was included)

Commission — Six members; Donald Cameron (Senator) chairman

Purpose — To study and consider the aims and objectives essential to maintain a proper and adequate educational program for pupils of the elementary and secondary schools of the Province; and to inquire into the various aspects of elementary and secondary education, having special regard to the curricular programs of the several school levels, the attainment of school pupils and the procedures governing their classification and promotion, the extent to which various special services are desirable and necessary, types of school organization, physical facilities, the quality and supply of teachers, the relationship of the educational system to the requirements of industry and the modern community, and the economics of education insofar as finance is a factor.

Conclusions/Recommendations

(The 280 separate recommendations included the following:)

That a plan of accreditation for qualifying school systems be implemented;

That departmental examinations be continued at the Grade IX and Grade XII levels;

That course offerings be broadened; for example to include vocational areas;

That community colleges be developed;

That the curriculum be changed to permit more time and more depth in studies;

That entrance requirements to the Faculty of Education be raised;

That a Bachelor of Education degree or its equivalent be required for permanent certification of elementary and secondary teachers;

That working conditions for teachers be improved.

References

Alberta, *Report of the Royal Commission on Education*, 1959.

276 HUTTERITE INVESTIGATION COMMITTEE
(Departmental Committee)

Appointed September 8, 1958

Reported September, 1959

Committee Three members; W.E. Frame (Chief Superintendent of Schools) chairman
[Upon the death of Mr. Frame, C.P. Hayes

assumed the chairmanship]

Purpose — To inquire into and report on certain matters in connection with the acquisition of lands by members of the Hutterian Brethren Church and the establishment of Hutterite colonies and to determine whether or not the existing educational facilities established for Hutterite colonies are satisfactory, especially in the matter of instruction in the responsibilities of Canadian Citizenship.

Conclusions/Recommendations

That the extraordinary mental health and freedom from mental conflicts and tensions can be attributed to the lack of contradiction between religious beliefs and social-political economic practice developed in individuals from early childhood;

That the problem, as it appears to the Hutterites, is that if their children are compelled to attend public schools they will be subject to indoctrination of values of the world outside the colony, which they regard as sinful.

References

Alberta, *Report of the Hutterite Investigation Committee*, 1959, App. A.

277 COMMITTEE ON ALBERTA SCHOOL BUS OPERATIONS
(Departmental Committee)

Appointed — November 30, 1960

Reported — April 1, 1961

Committee — Three members; Paul Lawrence (   ) chairman

Purpose — To inquire into and report all phases of school bus operations in the Province of Alberta, including the fatal accident involving a school bus which occurred at a level crossing at or near Lamont in the Province of Alberta on the 29th day of November, 1960.

Conclusions/Recommendations

That school boards recognize the fact of their responsibility for the safe transportation of children to and from school and for the qualifications of bus drivers, even though they may delegate by contract specific duties in connection with the students' transportation;

That wherever possible school bus systems be operated as publicly or privately owned fleets of buses;

That school boards prepare and promulgate policies respecting bus discipline;

That an officer or member of each school board examine each bus driver's licence and report thereon to the Highway Traffic Board.

References

Alberta, *Report of the Committee on Alberta School Bus Operations*, 1961.

278 SURVEY COMMITTEE ON HIGHER EDUCATION IN ALBERTA
(Departmental Committee)

Appointed 1961

Reported (Four interim reports to 1966)

Committee Seven members; E.W. Hinman (Provincial Treasurer) chairman

Purpose To inquire into and report on all those problems and possibilities which bear on the future growth and development of the programs of higher education in Alberta with particular emphasis on the development of the best possible policies consistent with the greatest economy of operation.

Conclusions/Recommendations

That Junior College Programs be encouraged;

That, provided they can meet the standards approved by the University, private schools be permitted, and encouraged, to offer first and second year courses in University work;

That the semester system be adopted at the earliest possible time, and studies be made of year round use and the trimester system;

That planning for the future of higher education be continued by both the Provincial Government and the University;

That every step be taken to make as efficient and economic use as possible of the resources available to higher education;

That formulae be devised to be used as a basis for determining future Provincial Government grants to the University;

That a study be made of adult education programs in Alberta to determine where expansion, consolidation, and coordination is necessary and feasible.

References

Alberta, 'Survey Committee on Higher Education: Second Interim Report', [1963].

279 SPECIAL COMMITTEE ON COLLECTIVE BARGAINING BETWEEN SCHOOL TRUSTEES AND TEACHERS
(Legislative Committee)

Appointed April 28, 1964

Reported March 24, 1965

Committee — Five members; first R.H. McKinnon (Member for Strathcona West) and then A. Ludwig (Member for Calgary East) chairman

Purpose — To review procedures for collective bargaining between school trustees and teachers, including provisions of The School Act, The Alberta Labour Act, and The Teaching Profession Act.

Conclusions/Recommendations

That the Government enact no legislation which would deny the teachers the right to strike;

That teachers' collective bargaining procedure be incorporated into a new Act with the suggested name of Salary Negotiation Act, to be administered by the Department of Labour.

References

Alberta, *Report of the Special Committee on Collective Bargaining between School Trustees and Teachers*, 1965.

280 SCHOOL CONSTRUCTION INQUIRY
(Departmental Committee)

Appointed — July 20, 1964

Reported — January 26, 1965

Committee — One member; Walter R. Badun (Faculty of Commerce, University of Alberta)

Purpose — To examine, inquire into and report upon the methods and procedures followed in the construction of school buildings in the Province of Alberta, north of the Saskatchewan River.

Conclusions/Recommendations

That, in order to give school boards guidance and to ensure that future school buildings are able to provide for the requirements of education, the Department of Education provide leadership in addition to regulation; and that the School Buildings Board be discontinued and a new committee formed - a 'School Planning Committee'.

That, because of the condition of property, buildings and equipment, a general maintenance program directed by the Department of Education be undertaken.

References

Alberta, *Province of Alberta School Construction Inquiry*, 26 January 1965.

281 PUBLIC INQUIRY INTO THE APPOINTMENT BY THE MINISTER OF EDUCATION OF AN OFFICIAL TRUSTEE FOR FORT VERMILION SCHOOL DIVISION #52
(Judicial Commission)

Appointed April 1, 1965

Reported February, 1966

Commission One member; Nelles V. Buchanan (Retired Chief Judge)

Purpose To investigate and report upon the events and causes leading to the appointment of an Official Trustee for the Fort Vermilion School Division #52 and the consequent replacement of the School Division's elected Board of Trustees.

Conclusions/Recommendations

That the Minister, in appointing on November 20, 1964, an Official Trustee for Fort Vermilion School Division No. 52 - thereby replacing the Division's elected Board of Trustees, was completely justified in so doing and that to have delayed the appointment would have been detrimental to the welfare of the Division and therefore unwarranted;

That thought be given as to whether the time has not now

arrived for the amendment of the Act making the Superintendent the appointee and employee of the Division rather than of the Department, or in the alternative, to defining more definitely the relationship between superintendent and secretary-treasurer.

References

Alberta, *Public Inquiry into the appointment by the Minister of Education of an Official Trustee for Vermilion School District #52*, February 1966.

282 SPECIAL COMMITTEE ON CENTRALIZATION AND CONSOLIDATION OF SCHOOLS
(Legislative Committee)

Appointed May 31, 1966

Reported March 30, 1967

Committee Five members; Romeo B. Lamothe (Member for Bonnyville) chairman

Purpose To enquire into and make recommendations regarding the interest and concern of the public with respect to the centralization of schools; the educational opportunities presently being offered in elementary and secondary schools; and the problem of centralization and consolidation in the rural areas and smaller cities with particular reference to vocational high schools.

Conclusions/Recommendations

That divisional and county officials make ratepayers aware of the superiority of educational standards and facilities available in large centralized schools;

That there be advance planning before centralization so that adequate facilities may be provided;

That further centralization be carried out only with the

approval of the majority of ratepayers concerned, particularly at the elementary level;

That parents be made aware that modern, well supervised residences have nothing in common with the makeshift dormitories of the thirties and early forties;

That, to ensure the availability of teachers for small rural high schools, governments make loans available to local authorities, or make it possible for them to borrow to provide modern housing for teachers;

That additional funds be provided to compensate teachers for the higher work load in small rural high schools, and for the lack of amenities of small communities;

That legislation providing for government assistance to private schools be studied to determine its effect on high school instruction.

References

Alberta, *Report of the Special Committee on Centralization and Consolidation of Schools*, 1967.

283 ROYAL COMMISSION ON JUVENILE DELINQUENCY
(Related Commission)

Appointed September 27, 1966

Reported February 15, 1967

Commission Three members; Francis Hugh Quigley (Calgary Magistrate) chairman

Purpose To make an inquiry into the nature and scope of juvenile delinquency in Alberta, the basic causes, preventive measures, and steps that should be taken to aid in rehabilitation.

Conclusions/Recommendations

That inadequacy in school, and poor achievement, is often a

burden which many children find difficult to bear; that they become psychological dropouts, present in body but not in mind, early in their school life; and that later many become truants, and later still seek expulsion or dropout as a release from a situation of failure;

That the Department of Education, in co-operation with the Alberta Teachers Association and the Alberta School Trustees Association, devise a continuing academic course for the teaching of morals, ethics, citizenship and law;

That readiness centres or pre-school classes be set up, possibly through the Preventive Social Service Act in those areas where children are having difficulty adjusting to formal Grade 1 teaching;

That special training in child study at University level, as well as in-service training, be required for elementary grade teachers;

That counselling services be provided at junior and high school levels by pupil personnel trained in this technique;

That Juvenile Squads of police departments in large centres have an educational section to inform youth at the school and community level of the positive function of police work in the community and to seek the assistance of young persons in fostering recognition of the value of good law enforcement.

References

Alberta, *Report of the Alberta Royal Commission on Juvenile Delinquency*, 1967.

284 COMMISSION ON EDUCATIONAL PLANNING
(General Commission)

Appointed June, 1967

Reported June 16, 1972

Commission Nine members; Walter H. Worth (former Vice-

President, University of Alberta) chairman

Purpose To enquire into current social and economic trends within the Province to determine the nature of Alberta society during the next two decades; to examine the needs of individuals within that society; to study the total educational organization inclusive of elementary and secondary schools, colleges, technical institutes, universities and adult educational programs to decide the necessary adaptations of these institutions to the trends and needs; to establish bases for the priority judgements of Government with respect to the course of public education in Alberta for the next decade; and to give consideration to financing.

Conclusions/Recommendations

That there be:

- provision of universal opportunity and selective experience in early education;
- abolition of Grade XII departmental examinations;
- inauguration of the Alberta Academy, Early Ed and the supporting ACCESS network;
- extension of opportunities in further education;
- modification in certification requirements for teachers in early and basic education;
- reorganization of the Department of Education and Department of Advanced Education;
- revision of funding arrangements for all levels of recurrent education, including provisions for life experience and student assistance;
- modification of the school year and of procedures for the transfer of credits;
- reduction in the length of all general and most professional first-degree programs in universities;
- preparation of an integrated Provincial Development Plan.

References

Alberta, *Report of the Commission on Educational Planning*, 1972.

285 SPECIAL COMMITTEE ON ASSESSMENT AND TAXATION
(Special Committee)

Appointed May 7, 1969

Reported March, 1970

Committee Nine members; Ralph Brown (President, Alberta Association of Municipal Districts and Counties) chairman

Purpose To study and make recommendations regarding real property assessment and taxation, and assessment equalization practices and procedures for the purpose of requisitions upon municipalities for school foundation and hospital levies.

Conclusions/Recommendations

That all dwellings including detached and multiple residences, and farm residences, should be treated alike: dormitories should be exempt only when used in the primary and secondary school systems and nurses' training institutes but not for colleges and universities;

That the power of a municipal council to classify property and provide a special portion of fair actual value for assessments be replaced with a power to classify properties and provide a special *exemption from taxation,* relating to the municipal rates, or the school or hospital requisitions, or provincial requisitions, or any combination of them.

References

Alberta, *Report of the Special Committee Appointed by the Government of Alberta to Study Assessment and Taxation,* March, 1970.

286 TASK FORCE ON INTERCULTURAL EDUCATION
(Departmental Committee)

Alberta / 286

Appointed 1971

Reported June, 1972

Committee Eight members; C.D. Ledgerwood (Coordinator, Athabasca Regional Office of Education) chairman

Purpose To collect and summarize data to be used by the government as a basis for establishing policies and practices that will serve the educational wants and needs of cultural minorities.

Conclusions/Recommendations

That the Alberta Government encourage and support a revitalization of Native cultures;

That Natives and Whites join forces in cooperatively designing programs to fulfill the educational wants and needs of Alberta's Native peoples;

That one objective of the cooperative effort be to generate educational alternatives from which Native peoples can choose;

That, since Metis receive no special considerations by the Federal Government, the interests of Metis people be of particular concern to the Government of Alberta;

That education that is representative of both Indian and White culture be provided for Native people;

That there be more selective preparation and screening of teachers for Native students;

That grants and bursaries be made available for Native peoples wanting to train as teachers and teacher aides.

References

Alberta, *Native Education in the Province of Alberta,* June, 1972.

287 RED DEER COLLEGE INQUIRY
(Judicial Commission)

Appointed March 21, 1972

Reported May 11, 1972

Commission One member; T.C. Byrne (President, Athabasca University)

Purpose To inquire into the administration, organization and operation of Red Deer College; the relationships between the Colleges Commission, the College Board, staff, Faculty, students and the community, and the range of programs offered or planned by the college.

Conclusions/Recommendations

That, for at least a year, the affairs of the College be placed in the hands of an Administrator;

That the Administrator act as President of the College as well during his term of office making the present position of president redundant;

That legislation be enacted to facilitate the establishment of different governing structures for Red Deer College if these are deemed desirable;

That the Administrator shortly after his appointment establish a search and selection committee for a president to assume office with the restoration of college self-government.

References

Alberta, *Report of The Red Deer College Inquiry*, May, 1972.

288 INQUIRY INTO SCHOOL AFFAIRS: BONNYVILLE AREA
(Departmental Committee)

Appointed September 8, 1972

Reported January, 1973

Committee One member; W.H. Swift (former Deputy Minister of Education)

Purpose To inquire into and report upon school matters in respect of the Bonnyville Centralized High School.

Conclusions/Recommendations

That the most salient fact, and the genesis of a number of school problems that have arisen over the years, is that although the population of the area is heterogeneous in respect to ethnic origins, religions and other factors, there is one fact that predominates; namely, the presence of a very considerable cohesive population of French ancestry who maintain a strong allegiance towards their mother tongue and towards the Roman Catholic religion;

That despite the problems arising from the nature of the agreement which brought the high school into existence, the internal operation of the high school was not, in general, the subject of criticism;

That in addition to any other virtues the school may have it is a strong force in the direction of understanding, co-operation and mutual respect; and hence any solution to the legal problem which surrounds it must be with intent to maintain such excellence, pedogogical and sociological, as it possesses.

References

Alberta, *Inquiry into School Affairs: Bonnyville Area*, January, 1973.

289 STUDY GROUP ON NORTHLAND SCHOOL DIVISION (Departmental Committee)

Appointed August 9, 1974

Reported July, 1975

Committee — Three members; W.H. Swift (former Deputy Minister of Education) chairman

Purpose — To inquire into and report upon matters related to the Northland School Division No. 61.

Conclusions/Recommendations

That Northland School Division prepare and adopt a statement of purposes and philosophy;

That the board of trustees consist of nine members, all appointed by the Minister of Education;

That Treaty Indians resident in communities served by Northland be eligible for appointment;

That the superintendent of schools be the chief executive officer, and that he be a resident of Peace River;

That the development and use of materials in harmony with the children's environments be encouraged;

That teachers and school programs adopt a positive attitude towards the pupils antecedents.

References

Alberta, *Report of the Northland School Division Study Group*, July, 1975.

290 ALBERTA SCHOOL DISCIPLINE STUDY
(Special Committee)

Appointed — 1975

Reported — May 12, 1977

Committee — Eight members; S.C.T. Clarke (Director, Special Sessions, University of Alberta) chairman

Purpose To study the current state of school discipline, what school discipline should be like, and what assistance could be provided to practitioners in the field.

Conclusions/Recommendations

That the responses of the participants were spread across the spectrum of possible views on most matters of school discipline;

That the reaction of the largest single group, a plurality of 41% of all participants, was that school discipline as it was in 1975-76 was just about right. Among the various groups polled, parents especially endorsed this position;

That the next most commonly held view was that school discipline was a bit too lenient. Trustees and teachers especially endorsed this position;

That 32% of participants perceived discipline as being a bit too lenient and 34% called for it to be stricter.

[No recommendations were presented as such.]

References

Alberta, *General Report of the Alberta Discipline Study 1975-76*, 1977.

[Sponsored by the Alberta Teachers' Association, the Alberta School Trustees Association, and the Department of Education]

291 PROJECT NORTH TASK FORCE
(Departmental Committee)

Appointed February, 1975

Reported November 30, 1976

Committee One member; Fred J. Dumont (School Superintendent) chairman

Purpose To do a comprehensive assessment of educational needs of Northern Albertans in order to fulfill planning and research obligations undertaken by the Department of Education under the terms of the Canada-Alberta North Agreement.

Conclusions/Recommendations

That a curriculum project be designed and operationalized to stimulate a concerted effort by school authorities to identify and collect pertinent curriculum materials;

That a sustained program of orientation of teachers to Northern people and the development of community relations skills be initiated;

That community commitment to schooling by direct, active involvement be increased;

That the Department of Education undertake an intensive analysis of the variables of remoteness, sparsity and isolation with the view to establishing means of quantifying them for translation into a grant support program;

That an in-depth study of the Northern Saskatchewan program be undertaken to determine whether or not the use of Cree in early grades contributed positively to school success, and that the Department of Education design a project similar to the Northern Saskatchewan program.

References

Alberta, *Report of an Assessment of Educational Needs of Northern Albertans*, November, 1976.

292 TASK FORCE ON THE EVALUATION OF STANDARDIZED ACHIEVEMENT TESTS FOR ALBERTA SCHOOLS
(Departmental Committee)

Appointed June, 1976

Reported 1977

Committee Twenty-three members; T. Mott (Guidance and Counselling Supervisor, Special Education Branch) coordinator

Purpose To evaluate commercial standardized achievement tests in terms of their congruency with Alberta curricula and their technical adequacy.

Conclusions/Recommendations

That findings indicated that some tests contained items that related well to specific strands of Alberta curriculum content in particular subject areas; however, none of the tests adequately covered the total spectrum of Alberta curriculum content.

References

Alberta, *Report of the Task Force on Evaluation of Standardized Achievement Tests for Alberta Schools*, Spring 1977.

293 MINISTER'S ADVISORY COMMITTEE ON STUDENT ACHIEVEMENT (Departmental Committee)

Appointed October, 1976

Reported May, 1979

Committee Nine members; James Hrabi (Associate Deputy Minister for Instructional Services) chairman

Purpose To review the quality and achievement standards of basic education in Alberta.

Conclusions/Recommendations

That MACOSA (Minister's Advisory Committee on Student Achievement) type tests be administered periodically at selected grade levels, but with sampling plans extended to permit generalization of results to school system populations;

That the proposed assessment program test curricular objectives selected from all domains (knowledge, attitudes and skills) and thought levels, and not only from the most easily tested areas;

That the tests developed by MACOSA investigators be revised as required, and that those tests which have not been given be normed in order that they may be used in subsequent assessments of student achievement;

That at some appropriate time the MACOSA Reading, Writing, Listening and Speaking tests be used to investigate relationships among various aspects of the language arts in order to determine recommendations about instruction;

That mandatory grade 12 departmental examinations for the purpose of awarding final marks not be reinstituted;

That grade 12 departmental examinations continue to be made available in January and June for school systems that wish to use them.

References

Alberta, *Student Achievement in Alberta,* May, 1979.

BRITISH COLUMBIA

294 SELECT COMMITTEE TO EXAMINE THE WORKINGS OF THE 1872 SCHOOL ACT
(Legislative Committee)

Appointed March 12, 1875

Reported January 24, 1976

Committee Six members; A. Rocke Robertson (Member for Esquimalt) chairman

Purpose To examine the workings of the 1872 School Act.

Conclusions/Recommendations

That compulsory education be made general throughout British Columbia, taking as a basis the compulsory clauses of the Ontario School Act, which make it obligatory on all children to attend some school, or be otherwise educated for four months in each year, from the age of seven to twelve years, inclusive;

That Clause 7 of the 'Public School Amendment Act, 1873,' be so amended as to make it obligatory on the Trustees to select and appoint their Teacher from among the duly qualified Teachers, whose names shall be submitted to the Trustees by the Board of Education;

That on complaint being made to the Board of Education, by any person resident in a School District, as to the moral conduct of the School Teacher in such District, the Board of Education should have power to investigate such charge;

and, upon being satisfied of its truth, if they shall deem it sufficient, to disqualify such Teacher from holding his position, the Board of Education should have power to cancel the certificate of such Teacher, and thereupon it should be the duty of the Trustees to dismiss such Teacher;

That power be given to the Board of Education to close Schools where the attendance falls below ten, if, in their discretion, they shall think fit.

References

British Columbia, *Sessional Papers*, 1875.

295 REPORT OF SELECT COMMITTEE ON PUBLIC SCHOOLS CONCERNING THE CACHE CREEK BOARDING SCHOOL
(Legislative Committee)

Appointed January 13, 1876

Reported January 24, 1876

Committee Six members; A.E.B. Davie (Member for Cariboo) chairman

Purpose To overhaul the working of Public Schools, including the *Cache Creek* Boarding School.

Conclusions/Recommendations

That it is advisable that boys and girls not be educated in the same establishment;

That the boarding and lodging of the children, and the washing of their clothes, be provided by some person or persons employed by the Master, if practicable, the remuneration of such person or persons to be in proportion to the number of scholars, and tenders to be invited for the performance of such duties;

That children not be required to perform menial duties;

That the following persons only shall be allowed to visit

the School, namely: Parents or relatives of the children, Judges of the Supreme or County Courts, Ministers of any religious denomination, members of the Legislative Assembly, Justices of the Peace, Government Agents, and such other persons as may be introduced to the Master by any of the above functionaries;

That no balls or political meetings be allowed in the school building;

That the teacher superintend the conduct of the scholars out of school hours;

That the school for boys be presided over by a Master and Matron, being husband and wife;

That the school for girls be presided over by a Mistress and, if necessary, a Matron in addition;

That it is advisable that the appointment and dismissal of Teachers be vested in the Lieutenant-Governor in Council;

That a Deputy Superintendent be appointed for and to reside on the Mainland at some central point; the Provincial Secretary to act as Superintendent on the Island.

References

British Columbia, *Sessional Papers*, 1876.

296 COMMISSION OF INQUIRY INTO THE SOUTH PARK SCHOOL DRAWING BOOKS
(Judicial Commission)

Appointed — November 29, 1905

Reported — 1906

Commission — One member; Peter S. Lampman (County Court Judge, Victoria)

Purpose — To inquire into all matters pertaining to the action of the Board of Examiners, the

Department of Education and the Principal of the South Park School at Victoria, in connection with the drawing books submitted by the pupils of the said South Park School at the High School Entrance Examination held in the month of June, 1905.

Conclusions/Recommendations

That it appears there was a great deal of ruling which in the opinion of the Commissioner was ample to justify the examiners and the Department in the course they took.

References

British Columbia, 'Report on South Park School Drawing Books', 1906.

297 COMMISSION OF INQUIRY INTO CHARGES AGAINST THE DEPARTMENT OF EDUCATION BY MISS GERTRUDE DONOVAN OF VICTORIA (Judicial Commission)

Appointed January 8, 1908

Reported [ ]

Commission One member; Harold Bruce Robertson (Victoria Barrister)

Purpose To inquire into charges against the Department of Education by Miss Gertrude Donovan of Victoria.

Conclusions/Recommendations

References

British Columbia, Order in Council, January 8, 1908.

298 COMMISSION TO SELECT A SITE FOR THE UNIVERSITY OF BRITISH

COLUMBIA
(General Commission)

<u>Appointed</u> February 25, 1910

<u>Reported</u> June 28, 1910

<u>Commission</u> Five members; R.C. Weldon (Dean of Law, Dalhousie) chairman

<u>Purpose</u> To visit and make a careful examination of the several cities and rural districts in the Province suggested as suitable University sites, and to select as a location for the University that city or rural district best suited for University purposes, which selection when made to be final.

<u>Conclusions/Recommendations</u>

That the University not be placed on a site which may in time be completely surrounded by a city;

That not less than 250 acres be set apart for the University campus and 700 acres for experimental purposes in agriculture and forestry, exclusive of a forest reserve for forestry operations on a large scale;

That the most suitable site is at Point Grey, unless the soil there and that of the delta land adjacent are found to be unsuitable for the experimental work of the College of Agriculture;

That should Point Grey prove impossible, the next choice is a site along the shore west of North Vancouver, provided the tunnel and bridge are constructed;

That the third choice is St. Mary's Hill overlooking the Pitt, Fraser, and Coquitlam Rivers, provided residences are erected for the students;

That Central Park, though conveniently located, will probably be surrounded by the Cities of Vancouver and New Westminster, and because of this and of the absence of outstanding scenic advantages is undesirable.

References

British Columbia, *Statutes*, 10 Edw. VII, chap. 51.

British Columbia, *University Site Commission Report*, 1910.

299 COMMISSION OF INQUIRY INTO MUNICIPAL MATTERS OF THE CORPORATION OF THE DISTRICT OF SOUTH VANCOUVER
(Judicial Commission)

Appointed May 16, 1912

Reported May 16, 1913

Commission One member; Matthew Joseph Crehan (Chartered Accountant)

Purpose To enquire into all Municipal matters of the Corporation of the District of South Vancouver which relate to contracts and dealings of and with the Municipal Council of the said Corporation or any member thereof, and contract of and with the Board of School Trustees or any member thereof, since the 1st day of January, 1908.

Conclusions/Recommendations

That, although nothing very seriously wrong was found, the Board should be more businesslike and should recognize their responsibility in handling school affairs and in disposing of the ratepayers' money;

That the purpose of supplies, construction of School buildings and works of a like character should be undertaken by the proper Departments of the Municipality, as the Trustees have not the machinery to carry out so much public work and get full value for every dollar expended.

References

British Columbia, Order in Council 583/12, May 16, 1912.

British Columbia, 'Report on South Vancouver Investigation,' 1913.

300 COMMISSION OF INQUIRY INTO MATTERS RELATING TO THE SECT OF DOUKHOBORS IN THE PROVINCE OF BRITISH COLUMBIA
(Related Commission)

Appointed August 15, 1912

Reported December 21, 1912

Commission One member; William Blakemore (Mining Engineer)

Purpose To inquire into matters relating to the Sect of Doukhobors in the Province of British Columbia.

Conclusions/Recommendations

That with reference to schools, the Doukhobors take the ground that education unfits the young for the pursuits of the peasant, and that this has become a problem already in nearly all countries;

That they believe their children are being educated in the best sense of the word, in their homes and on the soil, by being held down to the simple beliefs and traditions of their forefathers;

That they also fear that education will inoculate their children with the ideas of their educators, which they claim are alien to the Doukhobor belief.

References

British Columbia, *Report of Royal Commission on Matters Relating to the Sect of Doukhobors in the Province of British Columbia,* 1912.

301 COMMISSION OF INQUIRY INTO THE AFFAIRS OF THE PRESENT BOARD

AND PAST BOARDS OF SCHOOL TRUSTEES OF THE CITY OF VANCOUVER
(Judicial Commission)

Appointed February 11, 1913

Reported May, 1914

Commission One member; Henry Osborne Alexander (Vancouver Barrister)

Purpose To inquire into the affairs of the present Board and past Boards of School Trustees of the City of Vancouver, such inquiry to include the purchase and sale of school sites and school property, the purchase of furniture and other supplies, and generally all matters coming under the jurisdiction of the Vancouver School Board.

Conclusions/Recommendations

That some system of auditing be adopted by the Department of Education;

That a standard set of books be instituted for the use of school boards throughout the Province.

References

British Columbia, Order in Council 194/13, February 11, 1913.

Marjorie C. Holmes, *Royal Commissions and Commissions of Inquiry under the 'Public Inquiries Act' in British Columbia: 1872-1942*, [1950]

302 COMMISSION OF INQUIRY INTO THE AFFAIRS OF THE PRESENT BOARD AND PAST BOARDS OF SCHOOL TRUSTEES OF THE CITY OF NELSON AND COMPLAINTS REGARDING THE PRINCIPAL OF NELSON PUBLIC SCHOOL
(Judicial Commission)

Appointed February 19, 1913

Reported March 12, 1913

Commission One member; P.S. Lampman (Victoria Judge)

Purpose To inquire into the affairs of the present board and past boards of school trustees of the City of Nelson and complaints regarding the principal of Nelson Public School.

Conclusions/Recommendations

That the principal's certificate be suspended.

References

British Columbia, Order in Council 232/13, February 13, 1913.

British Columbia, 'Report on Board of School Trustees of the City of Nelson', 1913.

303 SURVEY OF THE SCHOOL SYSTEM
(Departmental Committee)

Appointed 1924

Reported May 30, 1925

Committee Two members; J. Harold Putman (Senior Inspector of Schools, Ottawa) and George M. Weir (Professor of Education, University of British Columbia)

Purpose To enquire into all matters pertaining to state education.

Conclusions/Recommendations

That a central Canadian research bureau be established to make possible educational development in accordance with scientifically determined educational objectives;

That school boards not have the option of charging fees

except for non-resident pupils;

That the public school system provide for elementary schools from six to twelve years of age, middle schools from twelve to fifteen, and high schools beyond that;

That high school streams lead to a graduation diploma, normal school entrance, commercial specialization, or university matriculation;

That teacher training institutions include more on the psychology of the various subjects and on the use of tests and measurements;

That student teachers have a rich experience of observation and practice-teaching, and all schools of the province be available when required;

That the grade eight formal examination be done away with and a gradual introduction of the accrediting system be accomplished;

That the City of Vancouver be granted considerable educational autonomy, by statute if necessary;

That consolidation of assisted schools be carried out wherever it seems educationally or financially desirable, with the approval of local boards if possible, but in face of their disapproval if necessary.

References

British Columbia, *Survey to the School Systems*, 1925.

304 SPECIAL COMMISSION TO INQUIRE INTO THE SALE OF GOVERNMENT LANDS IN THE UNIVERSITY SUBDIVISION
(Departmental Committee)

Appointed May, 1929

Reported February 25, 1930

Committee One member; A.N. Daykin (Vancouver Barrister)

Purpose To inquire into the sale of Government lands in the University subdivision.

Conclusions/Recommendations

References

British Columbia, Order in Council 749/29, May 20, 1929.

305 SPECIAL INQUIRY INTO THE AFFAIRS OF THE UNIVERSITY
(Special Committee)

Appointed April, 1932

Reported [ ]

Committee One member; Peter S. Lampman (Victoria Judge)

Purpose To inquire into the affairs of the university.

Conclusions/Recommendations

References

British Columbia, (*Victoria Daily Times*, April 30, 1932).

306 COMMITTEE APPOINTED BY THE GOVERNMENT TO INVESTIGATE THE FINANCES OF BRITISH COLUMBIA
(Special Committee)

Appointed April 15, 1932

Reported July 12, 1932

Committee Five members; George Kidd (President, B.C. Electric) chairman

Purpose To investigate the finances of British Columbia.

Conclusions/Recommendations

That free education be provided up to a pupil's fourteenth birthday only; that to age sixteen he pay 50 per cent of the entire cost of his education, and that after age sixteen he pay 100 per cent of the entire cost;

That teachers salaries be reduced by 25 per cent;

That should it eventually be found that the financial resources of the University are so meagre as to impair its efficiency, the question will have to be considered whether it may not be in the best interests of higher education to close the University and rely on the proposal to establish scholarships to furnish the means of attending a University elsewhere in the Dominion.

References

British Columbia, *Report of the Committee Appointed by the Government to Investigate the Finances of British Columbia,* 1932.

307 COMMISSION ON SCHOOL FINANCE IN BRITISH COLUMBIA (Departmental Committee)

Appointed June, 1934

Reported March 22, 1935

Committee Report written by 'Technical Advisor' H.B. King (Principal, Kitsilano High School) and presented to the two 'Commissioners', George Weir (Minister of Education) and John Hart (Minister of Finance)

Purpose To survey the whole field of educational financing.

Conclusions/Recommendations

That the Provincial Government assume almost complete financial responsibility for education;

That there be a uniform Provincial tax upon real property of from 3 to 4 mills;

That equalization of assessments be put upon a scientific basis;

That administrative reorganization into large school units be carried out.

References

British Columbia, *School Finance in British Columbia*, 1935.

308 COMMISSION OF INQUIRY INTO THE ADMINISTRATION AND METHODS OF DISCIPLINE OF MOUNT VIEW HIGH SCHOOL
(Judicial Commission)

Appointed July 6, 1943

Reported September 4, 1943

Commission One member; John Owen Wilson (County Court Judge, Cariboo)

Purpose To inquire into the administration and methods of discipline of Mount View High School.

Conclusions/Recommendations

That, in the opinion of the Commissioner, no person administering a unit the size of Mount View should be expected to teach for more than a very small portion of his working hours, if at all; and that he should be free to devote most, if not all of his time, to study, administration and supervision.

References

British Columbia, *Report of John Owen Wilson, Commissioner re Mount View High School*, 1943.

309 COMMISSION OF INQUIRY INTO EDUCATIONAL FINANCE
(General Commission)

Appointed November 27, 1944

Reported October, 1945

Commission One member; Maxwell A. Cameron (Faculty of Education, University of British Columbia)

Purpose To inquire into the existing distribution of powers and responsibilities between the Provincial Government and the school districts and to appraise the present fiscal position of the school districts in British Columbia.

Conclusions/Recommendations

That consolidation discussion be encouraged, but that implementation should proceed without seeking local approval;

That there be equalization of standards and equalization of assessments;

That the basic or Provincial programme be supported by basic grants consisting of a Provincial salary schedule, an allowance for posts of responsibility, a bonus for teachers in especially remote schools, and an allowance for current expenditures other than teachers' salaries, transportation, and debt charges.

References

British Columbia, *Report of the Commission of Inquiry into Educational Finance*, 1945.

310 COMMISSION ON PROVINCIAL-MUNICIPAL RELATIONS IN BRITISH COLUMBIA
(Related Commission)

Appointed February 16, 1946

Reported January 20, 1947

Commission One member; Carl Goldenberg (Montreal Barrister)

Purpose To investigate provincial-municipal relations.

Conclusions/Recommendations

That the principle of equalization recommended by the Cameron Report is sound and the Government is to be commended for accepting it and implementing the recommendations so promptly;

That the system will, however, lose some of its effectiveness if the grants are not reviewed from time to time and adjusted to meet changing conditions.

References

British Columbia, *Provincial-Municipal Relations in British Columbia,* 1947.

311 COMMISSION ON SCHOOL TAXATION
(General Commission)

Appointed August 9, 1947

Reported 1948

Commission Six members; H. Alan Maclean (Assistant Deputy Attorney General) chairman

Purpose To inquire into and report upon the following matters.

1. The performance of assessment functions for school taxation purposes within the Province, and particularly in the unorganized and organized areas of large municipal school districts.

2. The degree to which land and improvements are

being assessed in accordance with the definitions thereof in the 'Public Schools Act' for school taxation purposes in the unorganized and organized areas of certain large municipal school districts.

3. The applicability and suitability of the definitions of 'land' and 'improvements' in the 'Municipal Act', the 'Village Municipalities Act', 'Public Schools Act' and the 'Taxation Act'.

4. The general incidence of taxation under the 'Public Schools Act'.

5. All matters relevant to the present system of school cost sharing.

Conclusions/Recommendations

That an authority be established which might be called an Assessment Commission, to bring about a provincial wide equalization of assessments.

References

British Columbia, 'Report of the Commission on School Taxation,' 1948.

312 ROYAL COMMISSION ON DOUKHOBOR AFFAIRS
(Related Commission)

Appointed September 12, 1947

Reported January 10, 1948

Commission One member; Harry J. Sullivan (New Westminster Judge)

Purpose To inquire into and concerning the recent disturbances in the Doukhobor settlements in British Columbia, to hear representatives from the factions concerned and to recommend possible remedial action.

Conclusions/Recommendations

That a new plan for the education of Doukhobor children be worked out immediately for School Districts 7, 8, 9, 12 and 13 comprising the Grand Forks and Kootenay areas; and that much permanent benefit would result from a consolidation of schools in these Districts;

That the only real and permanent solution of the Doukhobor problem lies in education and assimilation;

That opportunity must be provided the Doukhobor children to participate in all the educational, cultural and recreational activities which the larger schools afford.

References

British Columbia, Order in Council 2309/47, September 12, 1947.

313 SPECIAL COMMITTEE ON DOUKHOBOR AFFAIRS
(Special Committee)

Appointed 1950

Reported March 29, 1952

Committee Thirteen members; Harry B. Hawthorn (Department of Anthropology, University of British Columbia) chairman

Purpose To inquire into the problems besetting the Doukhobors.

Conclusions/Recommendations

That the opposition to schooling is composed in part of objections to education in any form, and in part of objections to the Canadianizing influence of public schools.

References

British Columbia, *Report of the Doukhobor Research Committee*, 1952.

314 ROYAL COMMISSION ON EDUCATION
(General Commission)

Appointed January 17, 1958

Reported December 29, 1960

Commission Three members; S.N.F. Chant (Dean of Arts & Science, University of British Columbia) chairman

Purpose To enquire into the various phases of the provincial educational system with particular attention to programmes of study and pupil achievement.

Conclusions/Recommendations

(Included in the 158 formal recommendations were the following:)

That religious instruction in the schools not be extended beyond the present provisions;

That Grade VII be returned to the elementary school level;

That the six-three-three grade sequence be replaced by a seven-three-two (or three) sequence;

That the holding power of the rural schools be improved;

That instruction in the elementary schools be intensified and the secondary school day be lengthened;

That the school year be lengthened to a minimum of 200 days;

That elementary schools planned in future not exceed 600

pupils, and schools of any other type not exceed 1,200 pupils;

That more attention be given to school libraries;

That kindergartens be established at the discretion of local boards;

That pupil/teacher ratios be studied;

That persistent efforts to recruit young people of high ability be continued and intensified;

That teacher certification be upgraded;

That the commencing salaries of fully qualified teachers continue to be set at a level that is comparable to those paid in other professions that require equivalent qualifications;

That a one-year period of internship be introduced between the second and third years of the elementary teacher training programme;

That objective examinations be used more sparingly, and more essay-type questions be used in subjects that stress the understanding of knowledge rather than the recall of items of information;

That the spiral of learning principle be abandoned, and more emphasis be placed upon mastery of the courses of instruction at each grade level;

That the use of instructional time for extra-curriculum activities be kept to a minimum;

That the possibility of procuring more Canadian and British text-books be thoroughly canvassed;

That pupils be required to devote more time to their school work out of school-hours;

That counselling services be improved;

That boards be explicitly empowered to impose regulations

regarding school clothing or the adoption of a school uniform;

That community organizations and groups be encouraged to make greater use of school facilities;

That the primary or general aim of the educational system of British Columbia be that of promoting the intellectual development of the pupils, and that this should be the major emphasis throughout the whole school programme.

References

British Columbia, *Report of the Royal Commission on Education*, 1960.

315 SURVEY OF HIGHER EDUCATION IN BRITISH COLUMBIA AND A PLAN FOR THE FUTURE
(Special Committee)

Appointed [not an official inquiry]

Reported 1962

Committee One member; John B. Macdonald (President, University of British Columbia)

Purpose To survey higher education in British Columbia and provide a plan for the future.

Conclusions/Recommendations

That three types of institutions be provided for higher education: universities able to concentrate on the expensive areas of graduate studies, research, and special professional preparation, as well as undergraduate preparation; four-year degree granting colleges; and two-year regional colleges;

That, for the present, the University of British Columbia be *the university*.

That Victoria College have the privilege of deciding to

become an independent degree-granting college;

That a four-year degree-granting college be established in the western Lower Fraser Valley;

That the school districts of the Okanagan Valley co-operate in establishing a two-year regional college with the expectation of its becoming a four-year degree-granting college by 1970;

That a two-year regional college be established in the vicinity of Castlegar to serve the school districts from Trail to Nelson;

That a two-year regional college be established in metropolitan Vancouver;

That, in addition, two-year regional colleges be planned for operation by 1971 in the following regions: Central Vancouver Island Region; Kamloops and South Cariboo Region; Central Interior (Prince George); Eastern Lower Fraser Valley.

References

John B. Macdonald, *Higher Education in British Columbia and a Plan for the Future*, 1962.

316 SURVEY COMMITTEE ON SCHOOL LIBRARIES
(Departmental Committee)

Appointed 1963

Reported November 1, 1964

Committee Six members; Franklin P. Levirs (Assistant Superintendent of Education, Instructional Services) chairman

Purpose To survey school libraries in British Columbia and to make recommendations.

Conclusions/Recommendations

That except in the smallest schools of one or two teachers, classroom collections should be used only to supplement the central library of the school;

That the basic responsibility for the development of the library in any school must rest with the school librarian under the general supervision of the principal;

That although full use of external library services available should be made, a school district should undertake the development of its own school library service as a primary function.

References

British Columbia, *Survey of British Columbia School Libraries*, 1964.

317 BCTF COMMISSION ON EDUCATION
(Special Committee)

Appointed July, 1967

Reported September, 1968

Committee Four members; D.B. MacKenzie (former Vancouver Assistant Superintendent) chairman

Purpose To stimulate and provoke a study and debate within the teaching profession in British Columbia of major educational issues in the hope that out of such study and debate will emerge guidelines for the future design of education; and in particular to identify for study and debate issues related to: purposes and objectives in education, the need for change in the existing school system, directions for change that seem likely to produce quality education, and implications for the teaching profession as related to teacher preparation, continuing education of teachers, and deployment of teachers.

Conclusions/Recommendations

[The Report included 189 recommendations on a very wide range of educational issues; beginning with, 'Top priority should be given to the elementary schools in terms of educational planning and financial assistance.']

References

Involvement: The Key to Better Schools: The Report of the Commission on Education of the British Columbia Teachers' Federation, 1968.

[Sponsored by the British Columbia Teachers' Federation]

318 COMMITTEE ON SCHOOL UTILIZATION
(Departmental Committee)

Appointed January 19, 1968

Reported October, 1969

Committee Four members; J.L. Canty (Superintendent, Administrative Services) chairman

Purpose To investigate the extent to which public school facilities are utilized within the present framework of organization, the possible alternative organizational patterns which might increase the utilization, and the implications of such alternatives.

Conclusions/Recommendations

That an extended day of operation in the senior secondary school be adopted;

That there be developed a semester system of organization throughout the secondary school, with an extension of the summer organization as an introductory step;

That positive steps be taken to integrate planning of school and other community developments by those communities not already doing so.

References

British Columbia, *Report of the Committee on School Utilization,* 1969.

319 SELECT STANDING COMMITTEE ON SOCIAL WELFARE AND EDUCATION (Legislative Committee)

Appointed	February 2, 1968
Reported	April 3, 1968
Committee	Fourteen members; J.D. Tisdalle (Member for Saanich) chairman
Purpose	To survey the extent to which marijuana, LSD, and other lysergic drugs are available to our young people, and to study the cause and effect of such drugs. [Motion of February 15]

Conclusions/Recommendations

That research be conducted to determine the individual, social, and physiological reasons for persons misusing drugs and how this misuse can be contained and reversed;

That a department of Government establish a bibliography of acceptable and accredited research materials;

That suitable materials be drawn from such bibliographies and included in travelling libraries of videotapes, films, and filmstrips to be circulated to School Boards and used at the discretion of the Boards in relation to their local needs and in conjunction with local schools and individual teachers;

That the Department of Education circulate with the material a list of Provincial resource people available to assist in dissemination or elaboration of such materials;

That each School Board be encouraged to make full use of

their own community resource people.

References

British Columbia, *Journals*, 1968.

320 ADVISORY COMMITTEE ON INTER-UNIVERSITY RELATIONS
(Departmental Committee)

Appointed May 23, 1968

Reported March 7, 1969

Committee Five members; G. Neil Perry (Deputy Minister of Education) chairman

Purpose To investigate inter-university relations and those issues which have frequently appeared to be a cause of friction between the Universities or between the Universities and the Provincial Government.

Conclusions/Recommendations

That the Provincial Government consider the replacement of the existing Academic and Advisory Boards by a new intermediary body;

That this intermediary body be given the task of developing a capital budget for the university system.

References

British Columbia, *Report of the Advisory Committee on Inter-University Relations*, 1969.

321 SELECT STANDING COMMITTEE ON SOCIAL WELFARE AND EDUCATION
(Legislative Committee)

Appointed February 1, 1971

Reported March 24, 1971

Committee Eleven members; J.D. Tisdalle (Member for Saanich) chairman

Purpose To examine the provisions and practices relating to the security of tenure for teachers in the public schools of British Columbia [Motion of February 9]

Conclusions/Recommendations

That the function of tenure provisions is to indicate those conditions under which a teacher may be assured of continuing employment by a school district; that it is desirable that there be such provisions; but that it is essential that these provisions apply only to those teachers who have proven themselves capable of performing their duties satisfactorily, and who continue to perform them at that level;

That there be some form of review provided in cases of dismissal;

That a teacher be notified immediately whenever performance of his duties is evaluated as unsatisfactory; that he be notified of improvements considered necessary; that if, after a reasonable period of time, he did not effect these improvements, he be subject to dismissal on the grounds of inefficiency.

[Specific recommendations for changes to the *Public Schools Act* were given.]

References

British Columbia, *Journals*, 1971.

322 SELECT STANDING COMMITTEE ON SOCIAL WELFARE AND EDUCATION (Legislative Committee)

Appointed February 1, 1972

Reported March 23, 1972

Committee — Sixteen members; J.D. Tisdalle (Member for Saanich) chairman

Purpose — To report on the definition of the tenure of office of the members of the teaching staffs in the universities and on procedures followed by the universities relating to this matter, and to make recommendations. [Motion of February 11]

Conclusions/Recommendations

That the practice followed by universities in granting 'appointments without term' be continued;

That the three public universities of the Province work together to agree on a common definition of 'appointment without term';

That there be no discrimination, in terms of race, religion, sex, or politics.

References

British Columbia, *Journals*, 1972.

323 COMMITTEE ON TEACHER EDUCATION
(Departmental Committee)

Appointed — 1973

Reported — June 27, 1974

Committee — Thirty-three members; John Bremer (Commissioner of Education) chairman

Purpose — To conduct an inquiry into the state of teacher education in British Columbia.

Conclusions/Recommendations

That changes be made in the procedures followed by the membership of such teacher education policy-making bodies as currently exist, so as to provide for more consultation with legitimate groups, including students, whose point of view they should reflect;

That immediate constitution and funding of a continuing representative advisory committee on teacher education be made, to include three members from each of the following groups: Trustees, Public, Parents, Universities (Faculties of Education), Teachers, Students, and the Provincial Department of Education;

That representation to the Advisory Committee from community colleges be included when it becomes appropriate;

That two members from the Teacher Education Advisory Committee serve on the Joint Board of Teacher Education (one student and one public).

References

British Columbia, *Teacher Education in British Columbia: Final Report*, 1974.

324 COMMITTEE TO EXAMINE SERVICES FOR THE COMMUNICATIVELY IMPAIRED OF BRITISH COLUMBIA
(Departmental Committee)

Appointed — February, 1973

Reported — October, 1973 [to Minister of Health]

Committee — Twelve members; J.H.V. Gilbert (Faculty of Medicine, University of B.C.) chairman

Purpose — To examine, report and make recommendations on service for the prevention and amelioration of communication disorders in British Columbia.

Conclusions/Recommendations

That individuals with communication impairments be assured access to the necessary educational, social and rehabilitative supports to enable them to function and participate *as equals* in the formal and informal institutions of our society and that this be achieved by means of integration into, rather than segregation from, social, educational and work institutions within his or her community.

References

British Columbia, *Recommendations on Services for the Communicatively Impaired in British Columbia,* 1973.

325 SELECT STANDING COMMITTEE ON SOCIAL WELFARE AND EDUCATION (Legislative Committee)

Appointed February 7, 1973

Reported April 18, 1973

Committee Fourteen members; Rosemary Brown (Member for Vancouver-Burrard) chairman

Purpose To inquire into the question of the advertising of alcohol and tobacco products in the Province and legislation and regulations with respect thereto, and the effects of such advertising on the consumption of alcohol and tobacco products. [Motion of February 19]

Conclusions/Recommendations

That the Committee was more concerned by the growth in the number of young people who were beginning to drink and smoke than it was by the veteran smokers and drinkers cognizant of the fact that the young people were more vulnerable and susceptible to the wiles of advertising than were the veterans;

That representation be made to the Federal Government immediately, asking that it implement its ban on the advertising of these products, and work towards supporting a national and international advertising ban.

References

British Columbia, *Journals*, 1973.

326 ROYAL COMMISSION ON POST SECONDARY EDUCATION IN THE KOOTENAY REGION
(General Commission)

Appointed	April 25, 1973
Reported	February 13, 1974
Commission	Seven members; Ian McTaggert-Cowan (Dean of Graduate Studies, University of B.C.) chairman
Purpose	To examine post-secondary educational needs in the Kootenay region of the Province, to examine the respective roles and opportunities of Selkirk College and Notre Dame University in meeting these needs, and to attempt to identify within the Province unique educational needs which might effectively be met in the Kootenay region.

Conclusions/Recommendations

That an institution to be known as the Kootenay Institute for Post Secondary Studies be created in the Kootenay region of British Columbia and that it provide courses and, as may be appropriate, diploma, certificate and degree programs in the fields of vocational education, technological education, academic education, community service and cultural activities;

That the Governing Council provide, forthwith, post secondary educational services for the East Kootenay Region;

That Notre Dame University of Nelson be replaced by a four-year College concerned with liberal studies within the Kootenay Institute for Post Secondary Studies;

That Selkirk College become a College within the Kootenay Institute;

That the Government of the Province undertake a review of

vocational training and particularly apprenticeship training within the Province.

References

British Columbia, *Report of the Royal Commission on Post Secondary Education in the Kootenay Region*, 1974.

327 COMMITTEE ON UNIVERSITY GOVERNMENT
(Departmental Committee)

Appointed August, 1973

Reported May 2, 1974

Committee Five members; first John Bremer (B.C. Commissioner of Education) and then Walter Young (Political Science Department, University of Victoria) chairman

Purpose To consider the internal and external forms of university governance, with particular reference to the relationship between the Universities and the Provincial Government, and to make recommendations to the Minister of Education for appropriate changes in the Universities Act.

Conclusions/Recommendations

That the size of the Boards of Governors be increased to fifteen members;

That the membership be as follows: the Chancellor, the President, six appointed by the Lieutenant-Governor in Council, three members of faculty elected by and from the faculty at large, two students elected by and from the Alma Mater Society or its equivalent, two members of the Alumni Association elected by and from the Alumni Association;

That the present bi-cameral Senate/Board structure be retained;

That the Act specify those powers of Board and Senate that are exclusive and those that are joint;

That a basic structure be established for the composition of Senate, but that beyond this, that the membership of Senate for each university be modified appropriately;

That the basic structure include: (a) the President, Academic Vice President, Chancellor, Deans of Faculties, Librarian, Director of Continuing Education (or equivalent), one representative of the Community Colleges; (b) a number of faculty twice the number in 'a'; and (c) a number of students equal to the number in 'a';

That the University Council consist of eleven members appointed by the Lieutenant-Governor in Council, and that the following be excluded from membership; Members of Parliament, Members of the Legislative Assembly, Presidents, members of the Board of Governors, Faculty members and students of any of the provincial universities, and employees of the Department of Education.

References

British Columbia, *Report of the University Government Committee*, 1974.

328 TASK FORCE ON THE COMMUNITY COLLEGE
(Departmental Committee)

Appointed November, 1973

Reported March, 1974

Committee Thirteen members; Hazel l'Estrange (Douglas College Council) chairman

Purpose To examine college-government relationships, college-university relations, the problems of college financing, the role of community colleges in British Columbia, and to recommend changes in legislation leading to the creation of a Community College Act.

Conclusions/Recommendations

That every area of the province be included in a college region;

That 100% funding by the provincial treasury of capital costs be continued;

That colleges be granted corporate status;

That the college councils be charged with the responsibility of establishing a democratic system of internal governance ensuring effective involvement by all elements of the internal college community in the decision-making process;

That a provincial continuing education advisory committee be established to advise the Department of Education on the needs for continuing education;

That all citizens 65 years of age and older and all those who qualify for mincome may enrol in any college programme tuition free;

That admission policies be standardized for all colleges;

That the department of education initiate a feasibility study of worker study-leave for British Columbia;

That priority be given to the employment of Canadian citizens within the college system;

That a concerted effort be made to establish policies to increase the number of women hired by colleges so that the sex ratio of college personnel at all levels will better reflect the balance between men and women in the labour force.

References

British Columbia, *Towards the Learning Community: Working Paper on the Community College in British Columbia*, 1974.

329 STUDY COMMITTEE ON THE SMALL SENIOR SECONDARY SCHOOL (Departmental Committee)

Appointed November, 1973

Reported August 27, 1974

Committee Six members; William D. Reid (Superintendent, Field Personnel) chairman

Purpose To study and report upon the small senior secondary school in British Columbia.

Conclusions/Recommendations

That correspondence courses be placed more directly under individual school control;

That counselling services for small secondary schools be improved;

That itinerant specialists be made available to small secondary schools to provide instruction, clinics, and workshops in highly specialized activities;

That special education services be provided for small secondary schools on the basis of need rather than numbers;

That immediate provision be made for a professional development workshop for principals of small secondary schools;

That immediate provision be made for a professional development program for teachers currently working in small secondary schools and also for teachers who will be working in this type of school;

That special consideration, in financial terms, be given to small secondary schools by the Department of Education.

References

British Columbia, *Interim Report of the Small Senior Secondary School Study Committee*, 1974.

330 JERICHO HILL SCHOOL INQUIRY
(Departmental Committee)

Appointed June 18, 1974

Reported September 4, 1974 [to Provincial Secretary]

Committee One member; B. Chud (School of Social Work, University of British Columbia)

Purpose To examine certain aspects of Jericho Hill School.

Conclusions/Recommendations

That the Department of Education remove Jericho Hill School and other activities related to the deaf and blind from the office of Supportive and Integrated Services except as specified;

That the Department of Education allocate the provincial resources commensurate with the costs involved in providing the very best education for children suffering from hearing or eye impairment;

That in other respects the Department of Education relate to the educational needs of these children as it does to other children living and studying in the school districts of British Columbia;

That the Department of Health consider the creation of a Registry for Children at Risk in the Province of British Columbia;

That a British Columbia Board for the Education of Deaf and Blind Children be established;

That the present transportation system be critically reviewed;

That every effort be made to get away from institutionalized living for these children.

References

British Columbia, *Report of Inquiry: Jericho Hill School* [1974]

331 SURVEY COMMITTEE ON COMMUNITY COLLEGES IN THE LOWER MAINLAND OF BRITISH COLUMBIA
(Departmental Committee)

Appointed September, 1974

Reported January, 1975

Committee Three members; Leonard Marsh (Emeritus Professor of Education, UBC) chairman

Purpose To study the total college system in the Lower Mainland, to assess the desirability of reorganization, and to make specific recommendations for the development of smaller and administratively simpler college structures to serve the people of the Lower Mainland.

Conclusions/Recommendations

That community colleges in the Lower Mainland not operate exclusively within specific school district boundaries;

That vocational training be accorded equality of recognition and support with all other types of college instruction;

That social as well as instructional and study facilities be considered an integral part of college development;

That the Department of Education initiate a detailed study of the role, philosophy, organization and financing of adult and continuing education in British Columbia;

[Several recommendations dealt with the role of present and future colleges and institutions; namely Vancouver Community College, 'Langara Community College', Vancouver School of Art, 'Vancouver Vocational College', 'Burnaby Vocational College', 'Richmond Vocational College', Fraser Valley College, Capilano College, Douglas College,

Haney Correctional Institute, 'Green Timbers Community College', and future community colleges in Delta and Langley.]

References

British Columbia, *Report of the Survey Committee on Community Colleges in the Lower Mainland,* British Columbia, 1975.

332 STUDY OF RESEARCH AND DEVELOPMENT IN BRITISH COLUMBIA (Departmental Committee)

Appointed January 23, 1975

Reported August 31, 1975

Committee Five members; K. George Pedersen (Dean of Education, University of Victoria) chairman

Purpose To conduct a survey of the current status of practice-oriented research and development divisions in various governmental and other agencies (with an obvious emphasis on education), to determine the perceptions of the various educational interest groups in British Columbia regarding research and development, and to consider the local feasibility of alternate approaches.

Conclusions/Recommendations

That a research and development competence be supported within the B.C. Department of Education;

That the modest beginnings of a research and development unit be focused on satisfying the internal service needs of the Department of Education;

That a representative advisory committee to the Minister be established for the purpose of assisting in the establishment of overall school system's goals and objectives;

That the Division of Communications with the Department of

Education assume responsibility for developing, in consultation with the various educational vested interest groups, an adequate dissemination consultative service, primarily for the use of the school systems of this province.

References

British Columbia, *A Study of Research and Development in British Columbia*, 1975.

333 SELECT STANDING COMMITTEE ON HEALTH, EDUCATION, AND HUMAN RESOURCES
(Legislative Committee)

Appointed March 13, 1975

Reported April 30, 1975

Committee Fourteen members; Rosemary Brown (Member for Vancouver-Burrard) chairman

Purpose To examine into and study the subjects of school district organization and administration and the system of teacher salary bargaining, including learning and working conditions contracts.
[Motion of March 26]

Conclusions/Recommendations

That both trustees and teachers take advantage of the opportunities which the Department of Labour intends to provide in training personnel to be more effective in the collective bargaining process;

That in the event the parties fail to establish an arbitration board, the Department of Labour appoint an arbitrator;

That the final resolution of disagreements in the bargaining process be through the form of arbitration after a full process of negotiation and conciliation has been attempted.

References

British Columbia / 332

British Columbia, *Journals*, 1975.

334 ROYAL COMMISSION OF INQUIRY ON PROPERTY ASSESSMENT AND TAXATION
(Related Commission)

Appointed April 24, 1975

Reported July 30, 1976

Commission Seven members; Robert A. McMath (former Richmond Alderman) chairman

Purpose To inquire into all ramifications of the implementation of an assessment system based on actual value, and to review all aspects of real property taxation procedures.

Conclusions/Recommendations

That the Provincial Government should consider committing itself publicly to paying 75 percent of the current and capital cost of the public school system as a whole in British Columbia within a period of five years, and that equalization grants should continue;

That the Government require the universities to pay full property taxes with respect to land and improvements used for commercial purposes, and that the Government tax university residences on the same basis as other residential property in the same local taxing jurisdictions;

That the Department of Municipal Affairs and the Department of Education jointly study alternatives to taxing or continuing to exempt private schools.

References

British Columbia, *Commission of Inquiry on Property Assessment and Taxation: Preliminary Report*, 1976.

335 COMMISSION OF PUBLIC INQUIRY IN THE MATTER OF VANCOUVER COMMUNITY COLLEGE
(Departmental Committee)

Appointed May 15, 1975

Reported July, 1975

Committee Three members; George Suart (Vice-President of Administration, Simon Fraser University) chairman

Purpose To examine the overall administrative, operational and financial processes utilized in the operation of Vancouver Community College Technical and Vocational Institute and the impact of these processes on the delivery of College service to the community.

Conclusions/Recommendations

That Vancouver Community College continue to develop accounting procedures which will provide a workable management information and control system;

That the Department of Education ensure that all procedures developed for the control and funding of college programmes are clearly understood by all parties;

That the Department of Education initiate plans for the development of a long-range planning capability for colleges so that preliminary budget forecasting can be begun two to three years before a budget becomes operational;

That the College Council thoroughly study and unequivocally decide what is to be the nature of Vancouver Community College;

That the Vancouver School of Art be separated from Vancouver Community College and established as an institution in its own right;

That the college principal and administration recognize the need for a change in administrative style.

References

British Columbia, *Report of the Public Inquiry Commission Appointed to Examine Certain Aspects of Vancouver Community College*, 1975.

336 COMMISSION ON UNIVERSITY PROGRAMS IN NON-METROPOLITAN AREAS (Departmental Committee)

Appointed May 5, 1976

Reported September 2, 1976

Committee One member; William C. Winegard (former President, University of Guelph) chairman

Purpose To advise on all matters related to the delivery of academic and professional programs outside of the Vancouver and Victoria metropolitan areas, and academic transfer programs and their articulation.

Conclusions/Recommendations

That a multi-campus university be established by 1990 to serve the non-metropolitan areas of British Columbia;

That the new university begin as a separately funded Division of Simon Fraser University charged with the responsibility to provide a comprehensive outreach degree-credit program;

That the Division be headquartered in Vernon and have four small University Centres in Prince George, Kamloops, Kelowna and Nelson;

That the Division offer upper level degree-completion programs in Arts, Science and Education;

That the new University College of Simon Fraser University be funded by the Universities Council of British Columbia separately from the main campus of Simon Fraser University;

That the University of British Columbia and the Association of Professional Foresters jointly assess the need for Forestry courses in various parts of the Province;

That the University of British Columbia and the University of Victoria cooperate in the delivery of degree-completion programs in Nursing to the non-metropolitan areas.

References

British Columbia, *Report of the Commission on University Programs in Non-Metropolitan Areas*, 1976.

337 COMMITTEE ON CONTINUING AND COMMUNITY EDUCATION IN BRITISH COLUMBIA
(Departmental Committee)

Appointed June, 1976

Reported December, 1976

Committee Twenty-three members; Ronald Farris (Superintendent of Communications) chairman

Purpose To study continuing and community education in British Columbia, and to recommend future policy on funding, administration, and programming in this field.

Conclusions/Recommendations

That the concept of life-long learning be adopted as basic to the planning of the total public educational system in British Columbia;

That the government place in statute a statement of purposes and goals with respect to the development of adult education in the province;

That a mechanism be established to provide more vigorous provincial leadership and co-ordination for adult education;

That a provincial 'open college' be established to satisfy

a wide range of adult education needs, especially those in non-metropolitan areas;

That every citizen be given the opportunity, on a tuition-free basis, for educational upgrading, up to and including the grade 12 level or its equivalence.

References

British Columbia, *Report of the Committee on Continuing and Community Education in British Columbia*, 1976.

338 ADVISORY COMMISSION ON VOCATIONAL, TECHNICAL AND TRADES TRAINING IN BRITISH COLUMBIA
(Departmental Committee)

Appointed July 14, 1976

Reported January 31, 1977 [to Minister of Education and Minister of Labour]

Committee Six members; Dean H. Goard (former Principal, B.C. Institute of Technology) chairman

Purpose To study and report on vocational, technical, and trades training in British Columbia.

Conclusions/Recommendations

That an Occupational Training Council be established;

That the proposed new B.C. Occupational Training Council establish occupational counselling centres throughout the province, and that these centres provide information and guidance on vocational programs (selection procedures, entrance qualifications, and course prerequisites), as well as on the labour market (current or future demand for specific occupations);

That the new council provide qualified counselors to the secondary schools as requested by them;

That the new council be provided with the resources to do

research;

That vocational preparation programs, such as English-language training, employment orientation for women, programs on deafness, and trained community aids, be recognized as vocational and continue to receive funding and support;

That the Occupational Training Council ensure that federal participation in the field of adult vocational training be coordinated with and in controlled support of provincial efforts to guarantee that the interests of the students are best served, and that the provincial government affirm, both legislatively and administratively, its paramountcy in the educational and training fields.

References

British Columbia, *Report of the Commission on Vocational, Technical, and Trades Training in British Columbia,* 1977.

339 COMMITTEE ON THE EDUCATION AND TRAINING OF TEACHERS (Departmental Committee)

Appointed September 21, 1977

Reported June 16, 1978

Committee Five members; Malcolm F. McGregor (former Professor of Classics, University of British Columbia) chairman

Purpose To conduct a thorough examination of the programs for the preparation of teachers.

Conclusions/Recommendations

That the Joint Board of Teacher-Education be eliminated and that a Council for the Education of Teachers be established;

That the Council be advisory to the Faculties of Education and that it serve as a co-ordinating authority for

Continuing Education throughout the Province;

That a Board of Certification be established;

That greater rigour than is now employed be applied to the granting of admission to the Faculties of Education; that completion of at least one academic year in an academic Faculty with an average of 70% be a prerequisite for admission to a Faculty of Education; that the student be required to submit a letter of application, stating his qualifications and aims; that each applicant be interviewed; and that each applicant be required to write a test in English usage;

That the Standard Certificate for elementary teachers be abolished, and that every teacher have a degree;

That during the last two years of training in the elementary program at least sixteen weeks be spent in the schools and that the final practicum comprise at least eight continuous weeks;

That the secondary programme require five years of study, of which four will be devoted to academic education and one to professional training; and that students prepare themselves in two Teaching Fields from the subjects taught in the secondary school;

That the secondary practica require a minimum total of twelve weeks, and the final practicum demand a minimum of eight continuous weeks.

References

British Columbia, *The Education and Training of Teachers in British Columbia*, 1978.

CANADA

340 ROYAL COMMISSION ON INDUSTRIAL TRAINING AND TECHNICAL EDUCATION
(General Commission)

Appointed June 22, 1910

Reported March 28, 1911, and May 31, 1913

Commission Seven members; James W. Robertson (Principal, Macdonald College) chairman

Purpose To inquire into the needs and present equipment of the Dominion as respects industrial training and technical education, and into the systems and methods of technical instruction obtaining in other countries.

Conclusions/Recommendations

That all children to the age of 14 years receive the benefits of elementary general education, but after 12 years of age, for the children whose parents expect or desire them to follow manual occupations, the content of the courses, the methods of instruction and the experience from work undertaken at school should have as close relation as practicable to the productive, constructive and conserving occupations to be followed after the children leave school;

That advanced vocational training and technical education be provided at a higher level;

That interest and financial support be shared by individuals, corporations and associations, and by local, provincial, and federal governments;

That overall organization be carefully planned with development boards and administrative commissions at all levels;

That the sum of $3,000,000 be provided annually for a period of ten years by the Parliament of Canada and paid annually into a Dominion Development Fund.

References

Canada, *Sessional Papers*, 1913, vol. 28.

341 ROYAL COMMISSION ON RADIO BROADCASTING
(Related Commission)

Appointed December 6, 1928

Reported September 11, 1929

Commission Three members; John Aird (President, Canadian Bank of Commerce) chairman

Purpose To examine into the broadcasting situation in the Dominion of Canada and to make recommendations to the Government as to the future administration, management, control and financing thereof.

Conclusions/Recommendations

That broadcasting be placed on a basis of public service and that the station providing a service of this kind be owned and operated by one national company; and that provincial authorities have full control over the programs of the station or stations in their respective areas;

That the company be known as the Canadian Radio Broadcasting Company; that it be vested with all the powers of private enterprise and that its status and duties correspond to those of a public utility;

That time be made available for firms or others desiring to put on programs employing indirect advertising; that no direct advertising be allowed; that specific time be made available for educational work; that where religious broadcasting is allowed, there be regulations prohibiting statements of a controversial nature or one religion making an attack upon the leaders or doctrine of another; that the broadcasting of political matters be carefully restricted under arrangements mutually agreed upon by all political parties concerned; that competent and cultured announcers only be employed.

References

Canada, *Report of the Royal Commission on Radio Broadcasting*, 1929.

342 ROYAL COMMISSION ON DOMINION-PROVINCIAL RELATIONS
(Related Commission)

Appointed August 14, 1937

Reported May 4, 1940

Commission Five members; Newton W. Rowell (Chief Justice of Ontario [When Chief Justice Rowell resigned because of ill health, Joseph Sirois (Law Department, Laval University) replaced him as chairman]

Purpose To re-examine the economic and financial basis of Confederation and of the distribution of legislative powers in the light of the economic and social developments of the last seventy years.

Conclusions & Recommendations

That the quality of education and welfare services is no longer a matter of purely provincial and local concern;

That in Canada today, freedom of movement and equality of opportunity are more important than ever before, and these depend in part on the maintenance of at least minimum national standards for education, public health, and care of the indigent;

That the most economically-distressed areas are the ones least capable of supporting these services, and yet are also the ones in which the needs are likely to be greatest;

That not only national duty and decency, if Canada is to be a nation at all, but equity and national self-interest demand that the residents of these areas be given average services and equal opportunities.

References

Canada, *Report of the Royal Commission on Dominion-Provincial Relations*, 1940. Book I & II.

343 ROYAL COMMISSION ON NATIONAL DEVELOPMENT IN THE ARTS, LETTERS AND SCIENCES
(Related Commission)

Appointed April 8, 1949

Reported May, 1951

Commission Five members; Vincent Massey (Chancellor, University of Toronto) chairman

Purpose To examine and make recommendations upon:

(a) the principles upon which the policy of Canada should be based, in the fields of radio and television broadcasting;
(b) such agencies and activities of the government of Canada as the National Film Board, the National Gallery, the National Museum, the National War Museum, the Public Archives and the care and custody of public records, the Library of Parliament; methods by which research is aided including grants for scholarships through various Federal Government

agencies; the eventual character and scope of the National Library; the scope or activities of these agencies, the manner in which they should be conducted, financed and controlled, and other matters relevant thereto;

(c) methods by which the relations of Canada with the United Nations Educational, Scientific and Cultural Organization and with other organizations operating in this field should be conducted;

(d) relations of the government of Canada and any of its agencies with various national voluntary bodies operating in the field with which this inquiry will be concerned.

Conclusions/Recommendations

That in addition to the help already being given for research and other purposes the Federal Government make annual contributions to support the work of the universities on the basis of the population of each of the provinces of Canada;

That these contributions be made after consultation with the government and the universities of each province, to be distributed to each university proportionately to the student enrolment;

That these contributions be sufficient to ensure that the work of the universities of Canada may be carried on in accordance with the needs of the nation;

That all members of the National Conference of Canadian Universities be eligible for the federal grants mentioned above;

That scholarships in the natural sciences continue, and machinery be set up to make advance scholarships available in the humanities, the social sciences and in law.

References

Canada, *Report: Royal Commission on National Development in the Arts, Letters and Sciences*, 1951.

344 SURVEY OF SOCIAL AND ECONOMIC CONDITIONS OF THE INDIANS OF BRITISH COLUMBIA
(Departmental Committee)

<u>Appointed</u> 1954

<u>Reported</u> 1955

<u>Committee</u> Three members; Harry B. Hawthorn (Department of Anthropology, University of British Columbia) chairman

<u>Purpose</u> To survey the social and economic conditions of the Indians of British Columbia, and in particular to study community and family life, resources, employment, education, relations with the law, social welfare needs, and administration.

<u>Conclusions/Recommendations</u>

That teachers accept the continued existence of an Indian life which is different, and understand that race does not imply intellectual or moral attributes;

That teachers not try to remake the child beyond the recognition and acceptance of his community;

That the school not be made the vehicle of postponed social reform;

That community reform be undertaken at the adult level, and to that end, teachers take part (in an informed and responsible manner) in community affairs and adult education;

That with the ultimate aim of giving every person the possibility of integrating favourably into Canadian life, the principle of joint education of Indian and White children be followed wherever possible.

<u>References</u>

Canada, *The Indians of British Columbia: A Survey of Social and Economic Conditions*, 1955.

345 SURVEY OF THE EDUCATIONAL FACILITIES AND REQUIREMENTS OF THE INDIANS IN CANADA
(Departmental Committee)

Appointed January, 1955

Reported July 26, 1956

Committee Three members; G.G. Brown (former Municipal Inspector of Schools) chairman

Purpose To survey the Indian day schools and residential schools in order to assess the present facilities and to ascertain the future needs and educational requirements of the Indian children and to establish, as far as possible, a priority rating indicating about when the respective requirements should be met.

Conclusions/Recommendations

That the overall aim of any really functional program is to give the Indian children a second educational foundation extending into secondary and higher education for increasing numbers, to develop good standards of health, social and moral attitudes, and to equip them to adjust themselves competently, on an equal footing with white youths, in Canadian society as self-reliant and self-supporting citizens.

References

Canada, *Survey of the Educational Facilities and Requirements of the Indians in Canada,* Part I, General Report, 1956.

346 ROYAL COMMISSION ON CANADA'S ECONOMIC PROSPECTS
(Related Commission)

Appointed June 17, 1955

Reported 1957

Commission — Five members; Walter Lockhart Gordon (Chartered Accountant) chairman

Purpose — To inquire into and report upon the long-term prospects of the Canadian economy, that is to say, upon the probable economic development of Canada and the problems to which such development appears likely to give rise, and without limiting the generality of the foregoing, to study and report upon:

(a) developments in the supply of raw materials and energy sources;
(b) the growth to be expected in the population of Canada and the changes in its distribution;
(c) prospects for growth and change in domestic and external markets for Canadian productions;
(d) trends in productivity and standards of living; and
(e) prospective requirements for industrial and social capital.

Conclusions/Recommendations

That the functions of the universities touch every facet of our society. Through the preservation of our heritage they maintain our way of life, and through the interest they generate in the arts, they enrich it. They enliven the perception of social processes, and contribute to the orderly development of social institutions and relations. It is incredible that we would allow their services to society in these ways to lapse or to lag;

That, in relation to the increase in the national productivity and wealth of the country, Canadian universities occupy a key position. They are the source of the most highly skilled workers, whose knowledge is essential in all branches of industry, and, in addition, they make a substantial contribution to research and in the training of research scientists.

References

Canada, Order in Council P.C. 1955-909.

Canada / 347

Canada, *Royal Commission on Canada's Economic Prospects*, 1957.

347 ROYAL COMMISSION ON BROADCASTING
(Related Commission)

Appointed	December 2, 1955
Reported	March 15, 1957
Commission	Three members; Robert MacLaren Fowler (Barrister; President, Canadian Pulp and Paper Association) chairman
Purpose	[Keeping in mind that the reconsideration of television should be based upon the principles that the grant of the exclusive use of certain frequencies or channels for broadcasting shall continue to be under the control of the Parliament of Canada, and that the broadcasting and distribution of Canadian programmes by a public agency shall continue to be the central feature of Canadian broadcasting policy] to examine television broadcasting and the aspects of sound radio broadcasting which are related to television broadcasting.

Conclusions/Recommendations

That in Canada there appear to be four principal functions which we expect our broadcasters to discharge. These are, first, to inform (news, public events, the reporting of facts); secondly, to enlighten (interpretation of the news, education, discussion, debate on the facts); thirdly, to entertain (enjoyment, relaxation); and fourthly, to sell goods (advertising, distribution of goods and services);

That concerning broadcasting generally, a surprising amount of interest was shown in educational broadcasts. Most witnesses recognized that radio, and more particularly television, are tremendously influential instruments, and many would like to see greater use made of these instruments in the realm of formal education. The value of the present school broadcasts was stressed by many witnesses from all parts of Canada. The general view was that the Canadian Broadcasting Corporation could advantageously expand its activities in this field, without in any way impinging on provincial rights, simply by cooperating fully with, or by having educational programmes prepared entirely by, the various provincial ministries of education.

References

Canada, *Report: Royal Commission on Broadcasting*, March 1957.

348 JOINT COMMITTEE ON INDIAN AFFAIRS
(Legislative Committee)

Appointed: April 29, 1959 (House of Commons); May 5, 1959 (Senate)

Reported: July 8, 1961

Committee: Twelve Senators and twenty-four Members of Parliament: Senator James Gladstone (Senator) and Lucien Grenier (M.P. for Bonaventure) joint-chairmen

Purpose: To investigate and report upon Indian administration in general and, in particular, on the social and economic status of the Indians.

Conclusions/Recommendations

That education is the key to the full realization by Indians of self-determination and self-government;

That education of Indian children in schools under the jurisdiction of the provinces be continued and expanded;

That kindergarten facilities for Indian children be provided;

That the provincial authorities be approached to ensure that a more comprehensive and accurate account of the

Indian people is used and described in history courses and texts;

That agreements be entered into with provincial authorities to extend adult education facilities to Indians with the program expanded;

That travelling library facilities to Indian communities be expanded wherever possible;

That academic upgrading and social orientation courses to prepare young Indians for placement or specialized training be greatly expanded;

That full support and encouragement be given to formation of Home and School or Parent-Teacher Associations;

That the fullest possible encouragement and incentive be given to Indian children to go as far as they can in school;

That in addition to an intensive educational program, the economic opportunities and environment of the Indian people be developed;

That the Canadian Broadcasting Corporation and other agencies prepare factual presentations of the Indians' way of life and their contribution to the development of Canada.

References

Canada, *Joint Committee of the Senate and the House of Commons on Indian Affairs*, 1959.

349 COMMITTEE ON EDUCATION FOR THE YUKON TERRITORY (Departmental Committee)

Appointed April 14, 1960

Reported August 26, 1960

Committee Three members; G.G. Brown (former Municipal Inspector of Schools) chairman [Upon the death of Mr. Brown, J.C. Jonason (School Inspector) assumed the chairmanship]

Purpose — To prepare recommendations relative to:

1. The School Ordinance, including the function and responsibility of the office of Commissioner and of Superintendent of Schools; the establishment of school districts; and the advisability of establishing separate schools for religious minorities.
2. School Facilities, Elementary and Secondary.
3. Curriculum.
4. Pupils.
5. Teachers.
6. Adult Education.
7. Advisability of Territorial supervision of Old Crow School and Mission Schools.
8. Advisability of having both Territorial and Mission schools.
9. Cost Analysis.
10. School Administration.

Conclusions/Recommendations

That in recent years there has been a growing interest by Canadians in the problems of integrating Canadian Indians with the life of Canadians in general;

That the traditional policy in Canada has been to regard Indians as wards of the state, to maintain them on Indian reserves and to see that they did not suffer unduly from privation;

That undoubtedly there was a time when the building of large residential schools or schools with hostels was justified by circumstances, but the Committee questioned the need for and the advisability of continuing the policy of racial segregation by the maintenance of these large establishments.

References

Canada, *Report of the Committee on Education for the Yukon Territory*, 1960.

350 ROYAL COMMISSION ON PUBLICATIONS
(Related Commission)

Appointed September 16, 1960

Reported May, 1961

Commission Three members; M. Grattan O'Leary (President, *Ottawa Journal*) chairman

Purpose To inquire into and report upon the recent and present position of and prospects for Canadian magazines and other periodicals with special but not exclusive consideration being given to problems arising from competition with similar publications which are largely or entirely edited outside of Canada or are largely or entirely foreign in content.

Conclusions/Recommendations

That every nation must provide within itself the means of maintaining stability. In North America today this function is largely directed and exercised through the communications media. No technique of social control could be more reflective of our ideals of freedom and competition. Here is no coercion. The teacher explains, the politician proposes, the salesman displays, and society -- when it is satisfied acts. It is a process of suggestion and of persuasion, the very essence of democracy;

That in this role, communications are the thread which binds together the fibres of a nation. They can protect a nation's values and encourage their practice. They can make democratic government possible and better government probable. They can soften sectional asperities and bring honorable compromises. They can inform and educate in the arts, the sciences and commerce. They can help market a nation's products and promote its material wealth;

That, while Canada and the United States may have the same basic cultures, they each at the same time have domestic and other tasks and problems -- political, social and economic -- which differ widely. Canada's particular responsibilities, her government, her constitutional structure, her ideals and aspirations, her memories and milestones, even her discords, are facts in her existence which cannot be approached understandingly or usefully by communications media owned or controlled in another country, even though that country be friendly.

References

Canada, *Report: Royal Commission on Publications*, May, 1961.

351 ROYAL COMMISSION ON BILINGUALISM AND BICULTURALISM (Related Commission)

Appointed July 19, 1963

Reported February 1, 1965 ('Preliminary Report') and October 8, 1967, May 23, 1968 ('Education'), September 19, 1969, October 23, 1969, February 14, 1970

Commission Ten members; Davidson Dunton (President, Carleton University) and Andre Laurendeau (Editor in Chief, Le Devoir) co-chairmen

Purpose To inquire into and report upon the existing state of bilingualism and biculturalism in Canada and to recommend what steps should be taken to develop the Canadian Confederation on the basis of an equal partnership between the two founding races, taking into account the contribution made by the other ethnic groups to the cultural enrichment of Canada and the measures that should be taken to safeguard that contribution.

Conclusions/Recommendations

That it would appear from what is happening that the state of affairs established in 1867, and never since seriously challenged, is now for the first time being rejected by the French Canadians of Quebec;

That we are going to have to put our country's divisions on display, and we appreciate the dangers of doing so, but the feeling of the Commission is that at this point the danger of a clear and frank statement is less than the danger of silence;

That, above all, the Commissioners are convinced that they are demonstrating a supreme confidence in Canada; because to tell a people plainly, even bluntly, what you believe to be the truth, is to show your own conviction that it is strong enough to face the truth. It is in fact to say to the country that you have faith in it and in its future;

That, since language is the basic ingredient of culture, a major concern has been the opportunities for each of the two main linguistic groups in Canada to have access to an education which would allow the fullest expression and development of the mother tongue, and at the same time ensure an adequate communication between the two societies;

That it is the right of Canadian parents to have their children educated in the official language of their choice, and the opportunity to learn the second language;

That citizens of a country with two official languages should be provided with an education which allows them to participate in either society;

That the Commissioner's interpretation of bilingualism in Canada means that the major social and political institutions will function in the two languages, but that individual Canadians will not be required to know the second language;

That, in order to have a true opportunity of decision, all children must be given an introduction to the second language through the school system.

References

Canada, *A Preliminary Report of the Royal Commission on Bilingualism and Biculturalism*, 1965.

Canada, *Report of the Royal Commission on Bilingualism and Biculturalism*, vol. 2, 1968.

352 STUDY OF UNIVERSITY GOVERNMENT IN CANADA
(Special Committee)

Appointed November, 1963

Reported August, 1965

Committee Two members; Sir James Mountford and Robert O. Berdahl (Political Science Department, San Francisco State College) [Sir James Duff (former Chancellor, University of Durham) replaced Sir James Mountford who resigned because of ill health.]

Purpose To make a dispassionate examination and evaluation of the present structure and practices of the government of both the English- and French-language universities of Canada, including provincial, church-related and independent institutions.

Conclusions/Recommendations

That if tension levels are already high at many Canadian universities, it seems likely that future developments will only serve to heighten them;

That the rapid rate of expansion planned for higher education in most provinces points to increasing pressures on the President to obtain rapid decisions at the very time that the teaching faculties are asking for more and more of a share in these decisions;

That the two-tier pattern of university government be retained but with an almost fundamental alteration; that is, in place of the assumed separation of powers between Board and Senate, a system be introduced whereby they are brought into much closer contact at many stages.

References

University Government of Canada, 1966.

[Sponsored by Canadian Association of University Teachers, the Association of Universities and Colleges of Canada, and the Ford Foundation]

353 COMMISSION ON FINANCING HIGHER EDUCATION IN CANADA (Special Committee)

Appointed 1964

Reported June 30, 1965

Committee Four members; Vincent W. Bladen (Dean of Arts & Science, University of Toronto) chairman

Purpose To study, and report and make recommendations on the financing of universities and colleges of Canada with particular reference to the decade ending in 1975.

Conclusions/Recommendations

That the Federal Government review annually with the Provincial Governments the adequacy of the federal contribution to the cost of higher education;

That such federal support be in a form which avoided any invasion of the provincial right;

That a Minister of the Crown be given responsibility for coordinating university assistance from all federal agencies;

That there be an increase in the federal per capita grants to $5 for the year 1965-66, and a further increase of $1 each year thereafter until appropriate revision has been achieved;

That a Capital Grants Fund be established into which $5 per head of the Canadian population would be paid each year and that federal grants for research be greatly increased;

That the Student Loans Plan be continued and expanded as necessary;

That provincial governments adopt long-range planning for

higher education and that the essential role of university research and good research libraries be recognized;

That for the next decade, popular pressure for the abolition of fees be resisted;

That universities coordinate and cooperate with other universities for the sake of economy and efficiency;

That universities continue to pursue excellence without extravagance;

That individual and corporate donors be aware that continued and indeed increasing private support is necessary.

References

Financing Higher Education in Canada: being the Report of a Commission to the Association of Universities and Colleges of Canada, 1965.
[Sponsored by the Canadian Universities Foundation and the Ford Foundation]

354 COMMITTEE ON BROADCASTING
(Departmental Committee)

Appointed May 25, 1964

Reported September 1, 1965 [to the Secretary of State and Registrar General of Canada]

Committee Three members; Robert M. Fowler (Barrister; President, Canadian Pulp and Paper Association) chairman

Purpose To study, in the light of present and possible future conditions, the purposes and provisions of the Broadcasting Act and related statutes and to recommend what amendments, if any, should be made to the legislation.

Conclusions/Recommendations

That the federal government, although concerned neither with curriculum nor directly with cost, has an undoubted obligation, as the owner of the public sector of broadcasting and the controller of the private sector, to ensure that the facilities of the entire broadcasting system are placed at the disposal of the provincial educational authorities to the greatest practical extent;

That the closed-circuit technique is better suited to purely scholastic programming, because it affords greater flexibility and adaptability to differing regional and provincial requirements; and that for adult school courses and at the university level, for which evening courses are numerous and available space limited, broadcasting would reach a larger number of students;

That the educator must try to understand the nature of broadcasting, and the broadcaster must accept the authority of the educator with respect to program content and scholastic presentation;

That there is no justification for permitting television broadcasts to start earlier than noon, except in very special circumstances, and that the morning hours could be put to more important national use in transmitting school and university broadcasts.

References

Canada, *Report of the Committee of Broadcasting*, 1965.

355 ROYAL COMMISSION ON THE STATUS OF WOMEN IN CANADA (Related Commission)

Appointed February 16, 1967

Reported September 28, 1970

Commission Seven members; Florence Bird (Writer, Lecturer, Broadcaster) chairman

Purpose To inquire into and report upon the status of women in Canada, and to recommend what steps

> might be taken by the Federal Government to ensure for women equal opportunities with men in all aspects of Canadian society, having regard for the distribution of legislative powers under the constitution of Canada, particularly with reference to federal statutes, regulations and policies that concern or affect the rights and activities of women.

Conclusions/Recommendations

That equal opportunity for education is fundamental; that education opens the door to almost every life goal; and that wherever women are denied equal access to education they cannot be said to have equality;

That changes in education could bring dramatic improvements in the social and economic position of women in an astonishingly short time;

That federal Crown Corporations and agencies make clear to educational institutions, and to the public, that career opportunities within their organizations are open to women and that they are encouraging women to prepare themselves for such careers;

That the provinces and territories adopt textbooks that portray women, as well as men, in diversified roles and occupations;

That the federal government provide special funds for young women and young men to acquire university education leading to a degree in fields designated to be of special interest for aid to developing areas;

That the provinces and territories provide co-educational guidance programmes in elementary and secondary schools;

That the provinces and territories set up courses in co-educational family life education, including sex education;

That the current educational needs and interests of women in rural areas be studied;

That Eskimo and Indian women be encouraged to take training in adult education for work in the northern communities.

References

Canada, *Report of the Royal Commission on the Status of Women in Canada,* 1970.

356 SPECIAL SENATE COMMITTEE ON A SCIENCE POLICY FOR CANADA (Legislative Committee)

Appointed	November, 1967
Reported	December 17, 1970, December 17, 1971, September 11, 1973
Committee	Twenty-two members; Maurice Lamontagne (Senator) chairman
Purpose	To consider and report on the science policy of the Federal Government with the object of appraising its priorities, its budget and its efficiency in the light of the experience of other industrialized countries and of the requirements of the new scientific age.

Conclusions/Recommendations

That the university is where a man starts to become a scientist or technologist, and whether he then builds a university career or works outside the academic world, his university education will have been a significant influence on the whole country's relations with the world of science and technology;

That if Canada moves ahead in the international science and technology race, the universities will deserve much of the credit, and if we fall behind, or if the population comes to consider the scientist as an ivory-tower isolationist and science as a sinister force, the universities will have to accept much of the blame.

References

Canada / 360

Canada, *A Science Policy for Canada: Report of the Senate Special Committee on Science Policy*, vol. 1, 1970.

357 COMMISSION ON THE RELATIONS BETWEEN UNIVERSITIES AND GOVERNMENTS
(Special Committee)

Appointed May, 1968

Reported October, 1969

Committee Two members; René Hurtubise (Faculty of Law, Université de Montreál) and Donald C. Rowat (Political Science Department, Carleton University) co-chairmen

Purpose To consider the distinctive role of universities in the changing Canadian society, particularly with respect to their responsibilities for the development of this role at the various levels of society; community, provincial, regional, national and international; to determine the need, nature and extent of university autonomy and of government and public control of universities; and to recommend the appropriate instruments by which relations between universities and governments can be established that do justice to their responsibilities.

Conclusions/Recommendations

['Concluding Reflections' included the following:]

That the university, a many-sided reality in time and space, should be envisaged as making a constant effort to reach an equilibrium between the poles of socialization and critical research;

That it is necessary to reach a basic consensus on the functions and responsibilities appropriate to a university with respect to: other levels of teaching; centres and agencies of research; and the obligations which are incumbent on other social institutions;

That the university of the future will tend to democratize itself;

That the university of the future will be permanent;

That the university will be creative;

That the university will look to the future.

References

The University, Society and Government: The Report of the Commission on the Relations between Universities and Governments, University of Ottawa Press, 1970.

[Sponsored by the Canadian Association of University Teachers, the Association of Universities and Colleges of Canada, the Canadian Union of Students, and the Union générale des étudiants du Québec.]

358 SPECIAL SENATE COMMITTEE ON POVERTY
(Legislative Committee)

Appointed November 26, 1968

Reported November 10, 1971

Committee Sixteen members; David A. Croll (Senator) chairman

Purpose To investigate and report upon all aspects of poverty in Canada, whether urban, rural, regional, or otherwise, to define and elucidate the problem of poverty in Canada, and to recommend appropriate action to ensure the establishment of a more effective structure of remedial measures.

Conclusions/Recommendations

That education is one of the keys to social and occupational mobility; and for the individual, education can mean an escape from poverty, access to meaningful and steady employment, and full participation in the social and political life of the nation;

That without in any way interfering with or limiting or denying the constitutional and traditional prerogatives of the provinces in education, the Government of Canada establish a National Office of Education with the following functions:

a) to develop and articulate national educational goals;
b) to co-ordinate the distribution of federal investments in education and training;
c) to sponsor and support educational research at the national level;
d) to provide a national centre for information and data on education throughout the country;
e) to sponsor and support action-research programs;
f) to support local communities and organizations, including those of Canada's native people, in achieving their participation in local educational systems.

References

Canada, *Poverty in Canada: Report of the Special Senate Committee on Poverty*, 1971.

359 COMMITTEE ON YOUTH
(Departmental Committee)

Appointed August, 1969

Reported December 18, 1970 [to Secretary of State]

Committee Three members; David Hunter (Parole Officer) chairman

Purpose To undertake a study of the aspirations, attitudes and needs of youth and the government's present role in this area.

Conclusions/Recommendations

That traditionally, the involvement of Canadian governments in the field of youth has revolved primarily around the question of education;

That over the past 50 years, more and more aspects of a young person's life have become an institutional responsibility shared by federal, provincial and municipal governments, and private organizations;

That the federal government undertake a detailed appraisal and evaluation of its entire system of support to post-secondary institutions;

That the federal government undertake a thorough evaluation of its student aid program, and that the Canada Student Loans Plan be revised immediately;

That the federal government drastically revise and restructure its method of training and recruiting officers for the Canadian Armed Forces;

That the existing Youth Allowance program be thoroughly evaluated to determine its effectiveness in encouraging the 16-18 age group to stay in school;

That the program of Summer Language Courses include financial credit and be broadened to include more students and more universities;

That in cooperation with provincial governments the Occupational Training for Adults program be assessed, re-evaluated and reworked;

That the Canada Council expand its present program to include new emphasis on innovative and experimental cultural and artistic programming for young people.

References

Canada, *It's Your Turn: A Report to the Secretary of State by the Committee on Youth* (revised report dated July 26, 1971).

360 SURVEY OF EDUCATION IN THE NORTHWEST TERRITORIES
(Departmental Committee)

Appointed 1970

Reported February 29, 1972

Committee Professional staff of the Territorial Education System; B.C. Gillie (Director of Education, N.W.T.) chairman

Purpose To examine the evolution of the present education system in the Northwest Territories; to obtain opinions and consider views of the staff impinging on the type of education offered; and to develop objectives for education which will reflect the stated wishes of the northern population served by the Territorial Department of Education.

Conclusions/Recommendations

That the Purpose of Education is to provide for all people opportunity for maximum development of their aptitudes, skills and competencies along with an understanding and appreciation of the sum total of human experience; and that such development should enable each individual to choose freely between different courses of action in such a manner that he can live a satisfying personal life while discharging his responsibilities as a participating member of a complex society.

[The 223 recommendations were apportioned as follows:]
Purpose, Objectives and Goals of the Territorial Educational Programme (Recommendation 1)
Pre-School Education (2-11)
Elementary Education (12-29)
Secondary Education (30-43)
Continuing and Special Education (44-92)
Curriculum Development (93-100)
Student Residence Programme (101-134)
School Building-Construction, Management and Maintenance (135-141)
Teaching Personnel and Staff Training (142-176)

Classroom Assistants Program (177-189)
Educational Resources (190-198)
Financial Resources and Administration (199-213)
Local Involvement in Education (214-219)
Territorial Schools Ordinance (220-223)

References

Canada, *Survey of Education: Northwest Territories*, 1972.

361 COMMITTEE ON EDUCATION FOR THE YUKON TERRITORY
(Departmental Committee)

Appointed 1972

Reported September 22, 1972 [to Commissioner of the Yukon Territory]

Committee Three members; Franklin P. Levirs (former Superintendent of Schools, Yukon) chairman

Purpose To inquire into education in the Yukon Territory and to make recommendations concerning the School Ordinance, with special reference to its revision; public participation in school administration and school affairs at the school level; the financing of education; the administration of the school system; the curriculum of the elementary and secondary schools; special needs of Yukon Indians; special education of handicapped children; vocational education; adult education; the future of post-secondary education; the employment and supervision of the teaching staff; and other related matters.

Conclusions/Recommendations

That the revised School Ordinance establish the general powers and duties of all officers concerned in the school systems, as well as the general policies under which the system is to be operated;

That consideration be given as to whether it might be preferable in the Yukon to establish some sort of readiness test;

That the present local School Advisory Committee be reconstituted as Citizens' School Committees with definite powers and duties under the School Ordinance;

That each Indian village form an Education Committee of its own for purposes of encouraging an active interest and participation of Band members in school affairs;

That no school boards be established at this time;

That the Department of Education take whatever steps are necessary to establish at both the elementary and secondary levels appropriate studies on the history and culture of the Yukon including that of the native peoples.

References

Canada, *Report of the Committee on Education for the Yukon Territory*, 1972.

362 COMMISSION ON CANADIAN STUDIES
(Special Committee)

Appointed June 28, 1972

Reported October, 1975

Committee One member; T.H.B. Symons (President of Trent University)

Purpose To study, report, and make recommendations upon the state of teaching and research in various fields of study relating to Canada at Canadian universities.

Conclusions/Recommendations

That there be a major expansion in the attention given to Canadian studies in the university curriculum in many academic areas at both the undergraduate and graduate levels;

That a variety of approaches be followed in the development of Canadian studies, depending upon the needs and circumstances of individual disciplines and institutes;

That Government departments and agencies, both federal and provincial, adopt an open door policy to the fullest extent possible to assist those engaged in research;

That each university in Canada engage in some teaching and research about the area in which it is located;

That more attention be devoted, in all appropriate areas of the university curriculum, to study of the cultural life of Canada;

That a particular effort be made in teacher education to ensure that future teachers in the elementary and secondary schools of this country are given greater opportunity to acquire a fuller knowledge of Canadian society, culture, institutions and circumstances than is now provided in the curriculum of teacher education programmes.

References

To Know Ourselves: The Report of the Commission on Canadian Studies, Vol. I & II, 1975.

[Commissioned by the Association of Universities and Colleges of Canada.]

363 STUDY OF NORTHERN PEOPLE AND HIGHER EDUCATION (Special Committee)

Appointed January, 1974

Reported March, 1975

Committee One member; Del M. Koenig (Institute for Northern Studies, University of Saskatchewan)

Purpose To analyze the teaching and research programmes sponsored by Canadian universities in the North; to identify the main thrust of Canadian universities in the North, to note any gaps in their programmes, and to record regional and provincial variations in teaching programmes and research projects; to record the needs of northern people for higher education and to note how these needs are currently being met; and to recommend a set of guidelines for universities research projects to better fit the needs of northern peoples.

Conclusions/Recommendations

That the Association of Universities and Colleges of Canada facilitate the organization of a co-ordinating agency for all universities and other post-secondary institutions involved in northern activities;

That this proposed organization co-ordinate an on-going programme evaluation, definition of goals of northern involvement, and information exchange between member institutions;

That the government agencies involved in northern education programming conduct in-depth assessments of their programmes in relation to the factors discussed in this report;

That educators concentrate on listening to, and trying to understand, what it is that parents and students see as relevant northern content and try to adapt programmes to fit these needs.

References

Northern People and Higher Education: Realities and Possibilities, 1975.

[Sponsored by the Association of Universities and Colleges of Canada. A previous volume, prepared by W.O. Kupsch and taking the form of an inventory of existing programs, was published by AUCC in 1973.]

364 COMMISSION ON GRADUATE STUDIES IN THE HUMANITIES AND SOCIAL SCIENCES
(Special Committee)

Appointed January, 1974

Reported August, 1978

Committee Three members; Dennis Healy (Principal, Bishop's University, Lennoxville, Que.) chairman

Purpose To enquire into and report upon the nature, objectives and efficacy of Canadian graduate studies in the humanities and social sciences.

Conclusions/Recommendations

That the provinces initiate and administer a program to support studies at the Master's level in small universities;

That within each province or, for the Maritimes, within the region, committees be appointed to screen the Ph.D. candidates and to list the successful candidates in rank order;

That provincial governments meet a share of the costs of doctoral training;

That fellowship recipients be allowed to enrol in the doctoral program of their choice within the province;

That the Canada Council or its successor award a limited number of fellowships in the humanities and social sciences, tenable at any Canadian university and with a grant to that university to cover the full costs of tuition;

That such fellowships be tenable outside Canada only when it can be shown that the student has sound academic reasons for attending a foreign university;

That each university establish procedures to assess the academic validity, the relationship to the university's research objectives and the financial terms of all research contracts involving university personnel;

That research grants awarded by the Canada Council or its successor cover all indirect costs to the university and also an amount equivalent to the salary of the principal investigator;

That an additional 10 per cent be added to every federal grant or contract to a French-language university.

References

Canada, *Report of the Commission on Graduate Studies in the Humanities and Social Sciences*, August, 1978. [Appointed by the Canada Council; Report received by the Social Sciences and Research Council of Canada.]

365 THE MACKENZIE VALLEY PIPELINE INQUIRY
(Related Commission)

Appointed March 21, 1974

Reported April 15, 1977

Commission One member; Thomas R. Berger (British Columbia Supreme Court Judge)

Purpose To inquire into and report upon the terms and conditions that should be imposed in respect of any right-of-way that might be granted across Crown lands for the purposes of the proposed Mackenzie Valley Pipeline having regard to the social environmental and economic impact regionally, of the construction, operation and subsequent abandonment of the proposed pipeline in the Yukon and the Northwest Territories.

Conclusions/Recommendations

That one of a society's purposes in requiring formal education for its children is to preserve and transmit to the next generation its history, language, religion and philosophy -- to ensure a continuity of the beliefs and knowledge that a people holds in common. But the purpose of the education provided to northern native people was to erase their collective memory -- their history, language, religion and philosophy -- and to replace it with that of the white man;

That it is particularly important to understand the impact of the present education system on the native languages. When young men and women cannot understand their parents and grandparents, they learn little about their own people and their own past; nor do they acquire the confidence that comes with adult understanding;

That the Dene and the Inuit today are seeking to reclaim what they say is rightfully theirs. At the core of this claim, and basic to their idea of self-determination, is their right to educate their children -- the right to pass on to them their values, their languages, their knowledge and their history.

References

Canada, *Northern Frontier, Northern Homeland: The Report of the Mackenzie Valley Pipeline Inquiry*, 1977.

366 COMMITTEE OF INQUIRY INTO THE NATIONAL BROADCASTING SERVICE (Departmental Committee)

Appointed   March 14, 1977

Reported   July 20, 1977 [to the Prime Minister]

Committee   Seven members; Harry J. Boyle (Chairman of Canadian Radio-television and Telecommunications Commission) chairman

Purpose   To inquire into the manner in which the CBC is fulfilling its mandate, particularly with respect to public affairs, news, and information programming.

Conclusions/Recommendations

That in those huge areas of Canada which are sparsely populated, the CBC remains the major source of information and entertainment, and it is also the primary source of information and entertainment for minority English and French language groups in all parts of Canada;

That the effort needed to keep Canada together is at least as great as it was in 1867, and the communications media have a grave responsibility to keep Canadians fully informed in subjects on which they have to make fateful decisions. If we did not have the CBC, we should have to invent it;

That, as presented by the media, Canada is in a state of deep schizophrenia: if English and French Canada were on different planets there could hardly be a greater contrast of views and information;

That when the present issues in Canada are clarified, when the CBC has had a chance to show what it can do on its own initiative, when some firmer trends become apparent in technology, when Parliament has reconsidered its relations to the CBC and other cultural and communication agencies, a fuller inquiry will then be needed to provide a proper basis for future legislation.

References

Canada, *Report: Committee of Inquiry into the National Broadcasting Service*, July, 1977.

[Established by the CRTC]

367 TASK FORCE ON CANADIAN UNITY
(Related Commission)

Appointed July 5, 1977

Reported January, 1979

Commission Eight members; Jean-Luc Pepin (former Chairman of the Anti-Inflation Board) and John P.

Robarts (former Premier of Ontario) co-chairmen

Purpose — To enquire into questions relating to Canadian unity.

Conclusions/Recommendations

That the principle of the equality of status, rights and privileges of the English and French languages for all purposes declared by the Parliament of Canada, within its sphere of jurisdiction, be entrenched in the constitution;

That each provincial legislature have the right to determine an official language or official languages for that province, within its sphere of jurisdiction;

That linguistic rights be expressed in provincial statutes, which could include the entitlement recognized in the statement of the provincial first ministers at Montreal in February, 1978: 'Each child of a French-speaking or English-speaking minority is entitled to an education in his or her language in the primary or secondary schools in each province, wherever numbers warrant;' and that this right also be accorded to children of either minority who change their province of residence;

That the provinces review existing methods and procedures for the teaching and learning of both French and English and make greater efforts to improve the availability and quality of instruction in these languages at all levels of education;

That both the central and provincial governments meet to settle their respective areas of constitutional responsibility in the provision of essential services in the fields of health, social welfare, housing and education to status and non-status Indians, to Inuit, and to Metis on reserves, Crown lands, rural centres and large cities.

References

Canada, *A Future Together: The Task Force on Canadian Unity,* 1979.

Appendix

ROYAL COMMISSION ON OXFORD AND CAMBRIDGE UNIVERSITIES (PREAMBLE)

GEORGE THE FIFTH, by the Grace of God, of the United Kingdom of Great Britain and Ireland and of the British Dominions beyond the Seas, King, Defender of the Faith, to

Our Right Trusty and Well-beloved Counsellors:

Herbert Henry Asquith
Rowland Edmund, Baron Ernle
Robert, Baron Chalmers, Knight Grand Cross of Our Most Honourable Order of the Bath, late Secretary to the Treasury
Gerald William Balfour
Sir John Allsebrook Simon, Knight Commander of the Royal Victorian Order; and
Arthur Henderson; and

Our Trusty and Well-beloved:

Edward Gerald Strutt, Esquire (commonly called the Honourable Edward Gerald Strutt)
Thomas Banks Strong, Knight Grand Cross of Our Most Excellent Order of the British Empire, Doctor in Divinity, Dean of Christ Church, Oxford
Sir Howard Frank, Knight Commander of Our Most Honourable Order of the Bath
Sir Walter Morley Fletcher, Knight Commander of Our Most Excellent Order of the British Empire, Fellow of the Royal Society
Sir Horace Darwin, Knight Commander of Our Most Excellent Order of the British Empire, Fellow of the Royal Society

Sir Henry Alexander Miers, Knight, Fellow of the Royal Society, Vice-Chancellor of the University of Manchester
Sir John Hubert Oakley, Knight, Past-President of the Surveyors' Institution
William Henry Bragg, Esquire, Commander of Our Most Excellent Order of the British Empire, Fellow of the Royal Society; Quain Professor of Physics in the University of London
George Macaulay Trevelyan, Esquire, Commander of Our Most Excellent Order of the British Empire
Emily Penrose, Spinster, Officer of Our Most Excellent Order of the British Empire, Principal of Somerville College, Oxford
William George Stewart Adams, Esquire, Gladstone Professor of Political Theory and Institutions, Oxford
Hugh Kerr Anderson, Esquire, Doctor of Medicine, Fellow of the Royal Society
Blanche Athena Clough, Spinster, Vice-Principal of Newnham College, Cambridge
Herbert Mansfield Cobb, Esquire, Fellow and Member of the Council of the Surveyors' Institution
Montague Rhodes James, Esquire, Doctor of Letters, Provost of Eton
Albert Mansbridge, Esquire; and
Arthur Schuster, Esquire, Fellow and late Secretary of the Royal Society, Honorary Professor of Physics of the University of Manchester.

Great Britain, *Report of Royal Commission on Oxford and Cambridge Universities*, 1922. (The official appointment was made on November 14, 1919.)

EARLY PROVINCIAL PUBLIC INQUIRIES ACTS

Newfoundland	'An Act respecting Inquiries concerning Public Matters', 1888, Chapter 18
Nova Scotia	'An Act respecting Inquiries concerning Public Matters', 1876, Chapter 19
Prince Edward Island	'Public Inquiries Act', 1879, Chapter 17
New Brunswick	'An Act to Authorize the Issue of Commissions under the Great Seal in certain cases and for certain purposes', 1886, Chapter 4
Quebec	'An Act respecting inquiries concerning public matters', 1869, Chapter 8
Ontario	'An Act ... to make provision for Inquiries concerning public matters and official notices', 1868, Chapter 6
Manitoba	'An Act to make provision for Inquiries concerning Public Matters', 1873, Chapter 21
Saskatchewan	'An ordinance Respecting Commissioners to Make Enquiries Concerning Public Matters', *Ordinances of*

	the North-West Territories, 1895, No. 2
Alberta	'An Ordinance Respecting Commissioners to Make Enquiries Concerning Public Matters', *Ordinances of the North-West Territories*, 1895, No. 2
British Columbia	'An Act to make provision for Inquiries concerning Public Matters', 1872, Chapter 12
Canada	'An Act respecting Inquiries concerning Public Matters', 1868, Chapter 38

CHRONOLOGICAL TABULATION OF
47 'GENERAL' ROYAL COMMISSIONS
IN CANADIAN EDUCATION

DATE	PROV.	SUBJECT
1854-55	N.B.	King's College
1861-62	Ont.	Affairs and financial conditions of Toronto University and University College
1882-83	Que.	School Trust in the City of Montreal
1893-93	N.B.	Charges relating to Bathurst schools
1895-95	Ont.	Discipline in the University of Toronto
1897-98	Ont.	Cost of text books
1901-03	Man.	Establishing an Agricultural College
1902-02	N.S.	Teaching English in French speaking districts
1905-06	Ont.	University of Toronto
1906-07	Ont.	Cost and prices of text books
1907-09	Man.	University of Manitoba
1908-10	P.E.I.	Education
1909-11	Que.	Creating a board of Roman Catholic school commissioners for the City of Montreal
1910-10	B.C.	Site for the University of British Columbia
1910-12	Man.	Industrial education
1910-13	Canada	Industrial training and technical education
1912-14	Sask.	Agricultural and industrial education, and other school matters
1914-15	Alta.	Degree-conferring powers to Calgary College
1919-20	N.B.	Salaries of teachers
1920-21	Ont.	University finance
1923-25	Man.	Education

1924-24	Que.	Powers of R.C. school commissioners of Montreal, education of Jewish children, financial situation of Protestant schools
1929-30	P.E.I.	Education
1931-32	N.B.	Education
1933-34	Nfld.	Curriculum of colleges and schools
1944-45	B.C.	Educational finance
1945-47	Man.	Adult education
1945-50	Ont.	Education
1947-48	B.C.	School taxation
1953-54	N.S.	Public school finance
1953-55	N.B.	Financing of schools
1956-56	Nfld.	School tax at Corner Brook
1957-58	N.S.	School construction
1957-58	Alta.	Teachers' salaries
1957-59	Man.	Education
1957-59	Alta.	Education
1958-60	B.C.	Education
1959-60	P.E.I.	Educational finance
1961-62	N.B.	Higher education
1961-66	Que.	Education
1963-64	N.S.	Safe transportation of school children
1964-65	P.E.I.	Higher education
1964-67	Nfld.	Education and youth
1967-72	Alta.	Educational planning
1971-74	N.S.	Education, public service, and provincial municipal relations
1973-73	Sask.	University organization and structure
1973-74	B.C.	Post secondary education

INDEX OF COMMISSIONS AND COMMITTEES

R1 - General Commissions
R2 - Related Commissions
R3 - Judicial Commissions

L - Legislative Committees
D - Departmental Committees
S - Special Committees

NEWFOUNDLAND

			of Newfoundland with Canada (McNair) / 9
10	(R1)	1964-67	Royal Commission on Education and Youth (Warren) / 10
11	(R2)	1972-74	Royal Commission on Municipal Government in Newfoundland and Labrador (Whalen) / 11
12	(R2)	1972-74	Royal Commission on Labrador (Snowden) / 12
13	(R2)	1974-74	Commission of Enquiry into the St. John's Urban Region Study (Henley) / 14
14	(R3)	1974-75	Commission of Inquiry into the Closing of Upper Bullies School (Corbett) / 15
15	(D)	1977-78	Minister's Advisory Committee on Grade XII (Roebotham) / 16
16	(D)	1978-78	Task Force on Declining Enrolment in Education (Crocker/Riggs) / 16

NOVA SCOTIA

17	(L)	1825-25	Joint Committee of Council and Assembly on Education (Fairbanks) / 18
18	(L)	1848-48	Select Committee on Education (Young) / 19
19	(R1)	1902-02	Commission for the Purpose of Investigating the Best Methods of Teaching English in the Schools Situate in the French-speaking Districts of the Province (MacLellan) / 19
20	(S)	1921-22	Report on Education in the Maritime Provinces of Canada (Learned/Sills) / 20
21	(D)	1930-33	Committee on School Studies (Sexton) / 21
22	(D)	1938-39	Commission on the Larger School Unit (Munro) / 22
23	(R2)	1943-44	Royal Commission on Provincial Development and Rehabilitation (Dawson) / 22
24	(D)	-46	Commission to Investigate and Report

			on all Matters Affecting Teachers Salaries (MacGregor) / 23
25	(D)	1950-50	Commission on Teacher Education (Phillips) / 24
26	(S)	1952-54	Survey Project of the Joint Committee on Public Attitudes Towards Our Schools (Marshall) / 25
27	(R1)	1953-54	Royal Commission on Public School Finance in Nova Scotia (Pottier) / 25
28	(R1)	1957-58	Royal Commission on School Construction in Nova Scotia (Macnab) / 26
29	(S)	1963-64	Survey Report on Higher Education in Nova Scotia (MacKenzie) / 27
30	(R1)	1963-64	Royal Commission on the Safe Transportation of School Pupils (Rand) / 28
31	(D)	1969-69	Tribunal on Bilingual Higher Education in Nova Scotia (Munroe) / 28
32	(R3)	1969-69	Royal Commission on Section 3 of the Expired Collective Agreement between the Sydney School Board and the Nova Scotia Teachers' Union, Sydney Local (Moreira) / 29
33	(D)	1970-70	Survey of Digby School System (Keating) / 30
34	(D)	1970-71	Community College Planning Commission (Gaudet) / 31
35	(R1)	1971-74	Royal Commission on Education, Public Services and Provincial-Municipal Relations (Graham) / 32
36	(D)	1973-74	Committee on Pre-school Education and Social Development Programs (MacKenzie) / 33
37	(D)	1974-75	Federal-Provincial Study of Educational Technology in Nova Scotia (Duncan) / 34
38	(L)	1974-75	Select Committee on Education, Public Services and Provincial-Municipal Relations (Mooney) / 35
39	(L)	1974-75	Select Committee on the Nova Scotia Technical College Act (MacLean) / 36
40	(D)	1976-77	Cooperative Educational Survey (Walker) / 37

41	(R3)	1976-76	Royal Commission on the Board of School Commissioners for the Town of Mulgrave (Moseley) / 38

PRINCE EDWARD ISLAND

42	(L)	1834-34	Special Committee on Education (Dalrymple) / 40
43	(L)	1839-40	Special Committee on Education (Rae) / 41
44	(L)	1842-42	Joint Committee of Council and Assembly on Education (MacDonald) / 41
45	(L)	1851-52	Special Committee to Enquire into the Expediency of Making Education Free Throughout the Island (Coles) / 42
46	(R3)	1873-73	Commission to Investigate the Cases of Teachers Whose Salaries were in Dispute (Sinclair) / 43
47	(L)	1876-76	Special Legislative Committee to Investigate the Workings of the Education Law (Davies) / 43
48	(R1)	1908-10	Royal Commission on Education (McLeod) / 44
49	(R1)	1929-29	Royal Commission on Education (MacMillan) / 45
50	(R3)	1955-55	Commission on School Division No. 1 (Darby) / 46
51	(L)	1956-56	Select Standing Committee on Education (MacKay) / 47
52	(L)	1957-57	Select Standing Committee on Education (Large) / 48
53	(L)	1958-58	Select Standing Committee on Education (Bell) / 49
54	(R1)	1959-60	Royal Commission on Educational Finance and Related Problems in Administration (LaZerte) / 49
55	(R1)	1964-65	Royal Commission on Higher Education (Bonnell) / 50
56	(S)	1968-69	Province of Prince Edward Island: Provincial-Municipal Fiscal Study (Touche) / 51
57	(S)	1970-71	Committee on Teacher Education in Prince Edward Island (Smitheram)

			/ 52
58	(D)	1973-74	Evaluation of Elementary and Secondary Education in Prince Edward Island (Smitheram) / 54

NEW BRUNSWICK

59	(L)	1837-37	Committee on Education (Street) / 55
60	(L)	1842-42	Committee on Education (Wilmot) / 55
61	(S)	1844-45	Governor Colebrook's Elaborate Inquiry into Education (Brown) / 56
62	(L)	1845-45	Select Committee on Education (Wilmot) / 57
63	(R1)	1854-54	Royal Commission on King's College (Gray) / 57
64	(R3)	1886-86	Commission of Inquiry into the Conduct and Management of the Institution for the Deaf and Dumb, Fredericton (Mitchell) / 58
65	(R1)	1893-93	Commission of Inquiry into Charges Relating to the Bathurst Schools and Other Schools in Gloucester County (Fraser) / 59
66	(R1)	1919-20	Commission in Respect to the Salaries of Teachers in the Public Schools of the Province (Carter) / 60
67	(R1)	1931-32	Royal Commission on Education (McFarland) / 61
68	(S)	1937-37	Educational Survey of King's County (Plenderleith) / 62
69	(D)	1937-	Committee on Curriculum and Text Books (Peacock) / 63
70	(R1)	1953-53	Royal Commission on the Financing of Schools in New Brunswick (MacKenzie) / 64
71	(R1)	1961-62	Royal Commission on Higher Education in New Brunswick (Deutsch) / 65
72	(R2)	1962-63	Royal Commission on Finance and Municipal Taxation (Byrne) / 66
73	(R2)	1962-63	Royal Commission on Metropolitan Saint John (Goldenberg) / 67
74	(D)	1966-67	Committee on the Financing of Higher Education in New Brunswick (Deutsch) / 68

75 (S) 1968-69 Study of Teacher Education and Training (Duffie) / 69
76 (S) 1969-69 Study of High Education in the Atlantic Provinces for the 1970's (Crean/Ferguson/Somers) / 70
77 (D) 1970-71 Task Force on Social Development and Social Welfare (LeBlanc/Nutter) / 72
78 (D) 1971-72 Study Committee on Auxiliary Classes (MacLeod/Owens) / 73
79 (D) 1971-73 Committee on the Community Use of School Facilities (Ritchie) / 74
80 (S) 1972-73 Committee on Special Education (Kendall) / 75
81 (D) 1973-73 Committee to Examine Human Rights Education in New Brunswick (McNeilly) / 76
82 (D) 1973-73 Committee on Educational Planning (MacLeod/Pinet) / 78
83 (D) 1974-74 Task Force for Kindergarten Design (Smith/Roy) / 79
84 (S) 1974-75 Committee on Higher Education in the French Sector of New Brunswick (Lebel) / 80
85 (D) 1975-76 Task Force on School Food Service in New Brunswick (Johnston) / 81
86 (D) 1975-76 Task Force on Provincial Testing and Evaluation (Bruneau/Fontaine) / 82
87 (D) 1975-77 Task Force on School Libraries (Aiken) / 83
88 (D) 1976-76 Special Committee on Student Aid (Arsenault) / 84
89 (D) 1976-77 Task Force on School Year (Girouard/Kingett) / 85

LOWER CANADA/QUEBEC

90 (L) 1787-90 Committee of the Council on the Subject of Promoting the Means of Education (Smith) / 87
91 (R2) 1835-36 Royal Commission for the Investigation of all Grievances Affecting His Majesty's Subjects of Lower Canada (Gosford) / 88

92	(R2)	1838-39	Royal Commission on the Affairs of British North America (Durham) / 89
93	(L)	1853-53	Select Committee of the Legislative Assembly, Appointed to Enquire into the State of Education and the Working of the School Laws in Lower Canada (Sicotte) / 90
94	(R1)	1882-83	Commission of Inquiry into the School Trust in the City of Montreal (Coursol) / 92
95	(R2)	1883-83	Commission of Inquiry in All Departments of the Government / 93
96	(D)	1891-91	Committee on Agricultural Education (Ouimet) / 93
97	(R1)	1909-11	Commission of Inquiry into the Possibility of Creating A Board of Roman Catholic School Commissioners for the City of Montreal and its *Banlieue* (Dandurand) / 94
98	(R1)	1924-24	Commission of Inquiry into the Extension of the Powers of the Board of Roman Catholic School Commissioners of Montreal, the Education of Jewish Children in Protestant Schools or in Others, and the Financial Situation of the Protestant Schools of Verdun (Gouin) / 94
99	(S)	1937-38	Quebec Protestant Education Survey (Hepburn) / 96
100	(D)	1951-53	Sous-comité de Coordination de l'Enseignment à ses Divers Dégrés au Comité Catholique du Conseil de l'Instruction Publique (Désaulniers) / 97
101	(R2)	1953-56	Royal Commission of Inquiry on Constitutional Matters (Tremblay) / 98
102	(D)	1960-61	Comité d'Etude sur l'Enseignment Agricole et Agronomique (Regis) / 99
103	(D)	1961-62	Comité d'Etude sur l'Enseignment Technique et Professionnel (Tremblay) / 100

104	(R1)	1961-63	Royal Commission of Inquiry on Education in the Province of Quebec (Parent) / 101
105	(D)	1962-64	Comité d'Etude sur l'Education des Adultes (Ryan) / 104
106	(D)	1962-64	Comité d'Etude sur les Loisirs, l'Education Physique et les Sports (Bélisle) / 104
107	(R2)	1966-68	Commission d'Enquête sur l'Enseignement des Arts au Québec (Rioux) / 105
108	(D)	-67	Comité Interministériel sur l'Enseignement des Langues aux Néo-Canadiens (Gauthier) / 107
109	(D)	1967-68	Conseil de Restructuration Scolaire de l'Ile de Montréal (Pagé) / 108
110	(R3)	1968-68	Commission d'Enquête sur le Differend entre les Parties a la Negociation ... dans le Secteur Scolaire (Simard) /109
111	(R2)	1968-72	Commission of Inquiry on the Position of the French Language and on Language Rights in Quebec (Gendron) / 110
112	(D)	1970-71	Commission d'Etude de la Propagande Politique dans l'Enseignement (Dion) / 111
113	(D)	1972-73	Comité Interministériel pour entreprendre L'Etude du Probleme de la Distribution des Imprimès, Périodiques et Livres de Poche (Grandpré) / 112
114	(D)	1972-75	Commission d'Etude de la Tàche des Enseignants de l'Elementaire et du Secondaire (Faucher) / 112
115	(D)	1972-76	Comité Provincial de l'Enfance Inadaptée (Baron) / 113
116	(D)	1973-75	Commission d'Etude sur la Classification des Enseignants (Laberge) / 114
117	(D)	1973-75	Conseil Supérieur de l'Education sur l'Etat et les Besoins de l'Enseignement Collégial (Beauchemin) / 115
118	(D)	1974-74	Comité d'Etude sur la Recherche et

			l'Enseignement en Technologie du Bois (Poliquin) / 116
119	(D)	1974-74	Comité d'Etude sur la Création de l'Institut des Sports du Québec (Bouchard) / 117
120	(D)	1974-75	Groupe de Travail sur l'Education Physique et le Sport à l'Ecole (Beauregard) / 118
121	(D)	1975-75	Comité d'Etude sur la Réadaptation des Enfants et Adolescents Placés en Centre d'Accueil (Batshaw) / 119
122	(D)	1976-77	Groupe de Travail sur l'Institut d'Histoire et de Civilisation du Quebéc (Frégault) / 120
123	(D)	1976-77	Comité d'Etude sur la Situation des Enseignants Religieux (Monfette) / 121
124	(D)	1977-78	Commission d'Etude sur les Universités (Angers) / 122

UPPER CANADA/ONTARIO

125	(L)	1835-36	Committee on Education (Duncombe) / 124
126	(R2)	1839-40	Commission of Inquiry into the Public Departments of the Province (Sullivan/McCaul) / 125
127	(D)	1844-46	Ryersons' Report on a System of Public Elementary Instruction for Upper Canada (Ryerson) / 126
128	(S)	1848-51	Commission of Inquiry into the Affairs of King's College University and Upper Canada College (Workman) / 127
129	(R1)	1861-62	Royal Commission on Affairs and Financial Conditions of Toronto University and University College (Patton) / 128
130	(D)	1866-68	Special Report on Popular Education in Europe and the United States (Ryerson) / 129
131	(L)	1868-69	Select Committee to Enquire into the Management and Working of the

			Education Department (Cameron) / 130
132	(D)	1873-74	Provincial Farm Commission (Christie) / 130
133	(L)	1874-74	Legislative Committee to Enquire into the Management of the Agricultural College and Model Farm (Bethune) / 131
134	(R3)	1877-77	Commission of Inquiry into Charges Against the Central Committee of Examiners of the Education Department (Patterson) / 131
135	(D)	1881-82	Commission to Investigate Certain Charges Against Dr. Samuel May of the Education Department (Senkler) / 132
136	(R3)	1884-	Commission of Inquiry into an Incident at the Agricultural College (Winchester) / 133
137	(D)	1887-87	Special Inquiry into Conditions of the French Schools in the United Counties of Prescott and Russell (Dufort) / 133
138	(R3)	1888-	Commission of Inquiry into the Fire at the Government Farm (Blue/ Winchester) / 134
139	(D)	1888-89	Survey of Leading Schools of Technology in the United States (Ross) / 135
140	(D)	1889-89	Special Inquiry into the Schools in the Counties of Prescott, Russell, Essex, Kent, and Simcoe (Tilley) / 135
141	(D)	1893-93	Special Inquiry into the Schools in the Counties of Prescott, Russell, Essex, Kent, and Simcoe (Tilley) / 137
142	(R3)	1893-93	Commission of Inquiry as to the Ontario Agricultural College and Experimental Farm (Winchester) / 138
143	(D)	1895-96	Special Inquiry into the Separate Schools of Ottawa (Scott) / 138
144	(R1)	1895-95	Commission of Inquiry into the Discipline and Other Matters in the

			University of Toronto (Taylor) / 139
145	(R1)	1897-98	Commission of Inquiry into Cost of Text Books (Morgan) / 141
146	(R3)	1905-05	Commission of Inquiry into the Matters Referred to in a Resolution of the Senate of the University of Toronto (Meredith) / 141
147	(R1)	1905-06	Royal Commission on the University of Toronto (Flavelle) / 143
148	(R1)	1906-07	Commission of Inquiry into Cost and Prices of Text Books (Crothers) / 144
149	(R3)	1906-07	Commission of Inquiry to Investigate the Workings of the Blind Institute at Brantford, and the Deaf and Dumb Institute at Belleville (Snow) / 145
150	(D)	1909-	Survey of Technical Education in the United States and Europe (Seath) / 145
151	(D)	1910-12	Special Inquiry Into the English-French Schools, Public and Separate, in the Counties of Essex and Kent and Elsewhere in the Province (Merchant) / 146
152	(D)	1913-13	Survey of the Systems of Industrial and Technical Instruction in Europe (Merchant) / 147
153	(R2)	1915-17	Commission of Inquiry into Medical Education in Ontario (Hodgins) / 147
154	(R3)	1916-17	Commission of Inquiry into Certain Complaints Against the Internal Discipline and Management of the Ontario School for the Blind, Brantford (Gash) / 148
155	(R2)	1917-19	Commission of Inquiry into the Care and Control of the Mentally Defective and Feeble-Minded in Ontario (Hodgins) / 149
156	(R3)	1918-	Commission of Inquiry into the Building Department of the Board of Education of the City of Toronto (Lennox) / 150

			(MacLeod) / 167
174	(D)	1965-68	Committee on Aims and Objectives of Education (Hall/Dennis) / 169
175	(S)	1965-66	Commission to Study the Development of Graduate Programs in Ontario Universities (Spinks) / 172
176	(D)	1966-69	Minister's Committee on Religious Education (MacKay) / 173
177	(D)	1967-72	Task Force on School Health Services (Webb) / 175
178	(D)	1967-68	Committee on French Language Schools in Ontario (Bériault) / 176
179	(S)	1968-69	Commission on the Government of the University of Toronto (Lynch/ Webster) / 177
180	(D)	1969-72	Commission on Post-Secondary Education in Ontario (Wright/Davis) / 179
181	(D)	1969-70	Study Committee on Recreation Services in Ontario (Secord) / 180
182	(D)	1970-73	Task Force on Industrial Training (Dymond) / 181
183	(D)	1970-72	Committee of Inquiry into Negotiation Procedures concerning Elementary and Secondary Schools of Ontario (Reville) / 182
184	(R2)	1970-72	Royal Commission on Book Publishing (Rohmer) / 183
185	(D)	1971-72	Committee on Year-Round Use of Schools (Waldrum/Mannings) / 184
186	(D)	1971-72	Committee on the Costs of Education (McEwan) / 185
187	(D)	1971-72	Ministerial Commission on French Language Secondary Education (Symons) / 187
188	(D)	1971-73	Educational Resources Allocation System Task Force (Stephen) / 188
189	(L)	1971-73	Select Committee on Economic and Cultural Nationalism (Rowe) / 188
190	(L)	1971-73	Select Committee on the Utilization of Educational Facilities (McIlvene) / 190
191	(D)	1972-72	Task Force on the School Year (Fisher) / 191
192	(D)	1972-73	Study Team on the Sharing or

			Transferring of School Facilities (Christie/Marrese) / 192
193	(D)	1973-74	Ministerial Committee on the Teaching of French (Gillin) / 193
194	(D)	1973-74	Ministerial Commission on the Organization and Financing of the Public and Secondary School Systems in Metropolitan Toronto (Lowes) / 194
195	(R2)	1974-77	Royal Commission on Metropolitan Toronto (Robarts) / 195
196	(D)	1974-76	Task Force on the Educational Needs of Native Peoples of Ontario / 196
197	(D)	1975-77	Interim Committee on Financial Assistance for Students (Dupré/ Sisco) / 197
198	(D)	1975-75	Study of Women and Ontario Universities (McIntyre) / 198
199	(R2)	1975-77	Royal Commission on Violence in the Communications Industry (LaMarsh) / 199
200	(R3)	1976-76	Royal Commission of Inquiry on Algoma University College (Whiteside) / 200
201	(R2)	1976-77	Commission on the Reform of Property Taxation in Ontario (Blair) / 201
202	(D)	1976-77	Work Group on Evaluation and Reporting (Foisy-Moon) / 202
203	(D)	1977-78	Commission on Declining School Enrolments in Ontario (Jackson) / 203

MANITOBA

204	(R1)	1901-03	Commission of Inquiry into the Wisdom and Advisability of Establishing and Maintaining an Agricultural College (Patrick) / 205
205	(R1)	1907-09	Royal Commission on the University of Manitoba (Aikins) / 206
206	(R1)	1910-12	Commission of Inquiry into Aims and Methods in Industrial Education (Coldwell) / 207
207	(D)	1915-16	Special Report on Bilingual Schools

			in Manitoba (Newcombe) / 207
208	(R3)	1916-17	Commission of Inquiry into all Matters Pertaining to the Manitoba Agricultural College (Galt) / 208
209	(D)	1919-	Commission on Status and Salaries of Teachers (Hill) / 209
210	(S)	1923-23	Special Commission on the Possibility of Readjusting the Relations of the Higher Institutions of Learning (Learned) / 210
211	(R1)	1923-24	Royal Commission on Education (Murray) / 210
212	(R3)	1932-33	Commission of Inquiry into Impairment or Depletion of University of Manitoba Funds (Turgeon) / 211
213	(L)	1934-35	Select Committee to Enquire into the Administration and the Financing of the Public Educational System of the Province (Hoey) / 212
214	(S)	1937-38	Special Report on Education in Manitoba (Woods) / 213
215	(L)	1944-45	Special Select Committee on Education /(Schultz) / 214
216	(R1)	1945-47	Royal Commission on Adult Education (Trueman) / 216
217	(L)	1946-48	Select Special Committee Appointed to Study and Report on All Phases of the Pension Scheme for Teachers (Dryden) / 217
218	(R2)	1955-59	Greater Winnipeg Investigation Commission (Bodie) / 218
219	(D)	1956-56	Survey Covering Costs and Other Factors in Connection with the Establishment of a Dental College in the Province of Manitoba (Paynter) / 218
220	(D)	1957-58	Study Committee on Physical Education and Recreation (Kennedy) / 219
221	(R1)	1957-59	Royal Commission on Education (MacFarlane) / 220
222	(D)	1962-67	Survey of Reading (Sibley) / 221
223	(R2)	1963-64	Royal Commission on Local Government Organization and Finance (Michener) / 222

224	(S)	1963-65	Study of Education of Handicapped Children in Manitoba (Christianson) / 223
225	(D)	1966-70	Local Government Boundaries Commission (Smellie) / 224
226	(D)	1969-73	Core Committee on the Reorganization of the Secondary School (Bullock) / 225
227	(D)	1972-73	Task Force on Text Book Evaluation (Cramer) / 226
228	(D)	1972-73	Task Force on Post-Secondary Education in Manitoba (Oliver) / 227
229	(S)	1977-78	Task Force on Government Organization and Economy (Spivak/Riley) / 229

SASKATCHEWAN

230	(R2)	1906-07	Royal Commission on Municipal Organization (Smith/Ferguson) / 231
231	(R3)	1909-09	Commission of Inquiry into Morang Text Book Contract (Wetmore) / 231
232	(R1)	1912-13	Royal Commission on Agricultural and Industrial Education, Consolidation of Schools, Training and Supply of Teachers, Courses of Study, Physical and Moral Education (McColl) / 232
233	(S)	1917-17	General Survey and Investigation of the Incidence of Taxation in the Urban Municipalities of Saskatchewan (Haig) / 233
234	(S)	1917-18	Survey of Education in the Province of Saskatchewan (Foght) / 234
235	(R2)	1921-22	Commission of Inquiry to Study the Public Revenues Tax and to Inquire Generally into the Matter of Equalization of Assessments for Purposes of Provincial Taxation in the Municipalities of the Province, Urban and Rural (Armstrong) / 235
236	(L)	1923-23	Select Committee to Investigate the Advisability of Establishing the

			Rural Municipality as the Unit of Administration for Rural Schools (Finlayson) / 236
237	(D)	1932-33	Committee on School Finance and School Grants (Reid) / 237
238	(D)	1934-35	Debt Survey Committee (Estey) / 238
239	(R2)	1936-36	Commission of Inquiry into Provincial and Municipal Taxation (Jacoby) / 238
240	(D)	1938-39	Committee on School Administration (Martin) / 239
241	(D)	1943-44	Saskatchewan Reconstruction Council (Cronkite) / 240
242	(D)	1948-50	Committee on Provincial-Municipal Relations (Britnell) / 241
243	(R2)	1952-55	Royal Commission on Agriculture and Rural Life (Baker) / 242
244	(D)	1957-61	Continuing Committee on Local Government (McAskill) / 243
245	(D)	1962-63	Committee on Continuing Education (Archer) / 244
246	(R2)	1963-65	Royal Commission on Taxation (McLeod) / 245
247	(D)	1965-66	Committee on Instruction in Languages other than English (Tait) / 245
248	(S)	1965-67	Joint Committee on Higher Education (Spinks) / 246
249	(D)	1965-67	Committee on Teachers' Salary Negotiations: Legislation and Procedures (Moore) / 247
250	(D)	1967-69	Advisory Committee on Divisions Three and Four (Nicks/Gathercole) / 248
251	(D)	1969-70	Special Provisional Committee on Higher Education (Riederer) / 249
252	(D)	1971-72	Committee on Kindergarten Education (Fowlie) / 250
253	(D)	1972-72	Advisory Committee on Community Colleges (Faris) / 251
254	(D)	1972-73	Advisory Committee on Dental Care for Children (Paynter) / 252
255	(D)	1973-73	Advisory Committee on Physical Education (Campbell) / 252
256	(D)	1973-73	Task Force on the Status of Women in Saskatchewan (Hynd/Rocan) / 254

ALBERTA

273	(R2)	1954-56	Royal Commission on the Metropolitan Development of Calgary and Edmonton (McNally) / 272
274	(R1)	1957-58	Royal Commission on Teachers' Salaries (Blackstock) / 273
275	(R1)	1957-59	Royal Commission on Education (Cameron) / 274
276	(D)	1958-59	Hutterite Investigation Committee (Frame/Hayes) / 275
277	(D)	1960-61	Committee on Alberta School Bus Operations (Lawrence) / 276
278	(D)	1961-66	Survey Committee on Higher Education in Alberta (Hinman) / 277
279	(L)	1964-65	Special Committee on Collective Bargaining between School Trustees and Teachers (McKinnon/ Ludwig) / 278
280	(D)	1964-65	School Construction Inquiry (Badun) / 279
281	(R3)	1965-66	Public Inquiry into the Appointment by the Minister of Education of an Official Trustee for Fort Vermilion School Division #52 (Buchanan) / 280
282	(L)	1966-67	Special Committee on Centralization and Consolidation of Schools (Lamothe) / 281
283	(R2)	1966-67	Royal Commission on Juvenile Delinquency (Quigley) / 282
284	(R1)	1967-72	Commission on Educational Planning (Worth) / 283
285	(S)	1969-70	Special Committee on Assessment and Taxation (Brown) / 285
286	(D)	1971-72	Task Force on Intercultural Education (Ledgerwood) / 285
287	(R3)	1972-72	Red Deer College Inquiry (Byrne) / 287
288	(D)	1972-73	Inquiry into School Affairs: Bonnyville Area (Swift) / 287
289	(D)	1974-75	Study Group on Northland School Division (Swift) / 288
290	(S)	1975-77	Alberta School Discipline Study (Clarke) / 289
291	(D)	1975-76	Project North Task Force (Dumont) / 290

292	(D)	1976-77	Task Force on the Evaluation of Standardized Achievement Tests for Alberta Schools (Mott) / 291
293	(D)	1976-79	Minister's Advisory Committee on Student Achievement (Hrabi) / 292

BRITISH COLUMBIA

294	(L)	1875-76	Select Committee to Examine the Workings of the 1872 School Act (Robertson) / 294
295	(L)	1876-76	Report of Select Committee on Public Schools Concerning the Cache Creek Boarding School (Davie) / 295
296	(R3)	1905-06	Commission of Inquiry into the South Park School Drawing Books (Lampman) / 296
297	(R3)	1908-	Commission of Inquiry into Charges Against the Department of Education by Miss Gertrude Donovan of Victoria (Robertson) / 297
298	(R1)	1910-10	Commission to Select a Site for the University of British Columbia (Weldon) / 297
299	(R3)	1912-13	Commission of Inquiry into Municipal Matters of the Corporation of the District of South Vancouver (Crehan) / 299
300	(R2)	1912-12	Commission of Inquiry into Matters Relating to the Sect of Doukhobors in the Province of British Columbia (Blakemore) / 300
301	(R3)	1913-14	Commission of Inquiry into the Affairs of the Present Board and Past Boards of School Trustees of the City of Vancouver (Alexander) / 300
302	(R3)	1913-13	Commission of Inquiry into the Affairs of the Present Board and Past Boards of School Trustees of the City of Nelson and Complaints Regarding the Principal of Nelson Public School (Lampman) / 301

303 (D) 1924-25 Survey of the School System (Putnam/ Weir) / 302

304 (D) 1929-30 Special Commission to Inquire into the Sale of Government Lands in the University Subdivision (Daykin) / 303

305 (S) 1932- Special Inquiry into the Affairs of the University (Lampman) / 304

306 (S) 1932-32 Committee Appointed by the Government to Investigate the Finances of British Columbia (Kidd) / 304

307 (D) 1934-35 Commission on School Finance in British Columbia (King) / 305

308 (R3) 1943-43 Commission of Inquiry into the Administration and Methods of Discipline of Mount View High School (Wilson) / 306

309 (R1) 1944-45 Commission of Inquiry into Educational Finance (Cameron) / 307

310 (R2) 1946-47 Commission on Provincial-Municipal Relations in British Columbia (Goldenberg) / 307

311 (R1) 1947-48 Commission on School Taxation (Maclean) / 308

312 (R2) 1947-48 Royal Commission on Doukhobor Affairs (Sullivan) / 309

313 (S) 1950-52 Special Committee on Doukhobor Affairs (Hawthorn) / 310

314 (R1) 1958-60 Royal Commission on Education (Chant) / 311

315 (S) -62 Survey of Higher Education in British Columbia and a Plan for the Future (Macdonald) / 313

316 (D) 1963-64 Survey Committee on School Libraries (Levirs) / 314

317 (S) 1967-68 BCTF Commission on Education (MacKenzie) / 315

318 (D) 1968-69 Committee on School Utilization (Canty) / 316

319 (L) 1968-68 Select Standing Committee on Social Welfare and Education (Tisdalle) / 317

320 (D) 1968-69 Advisory Committee on Inter-University Relations (Perry) / 318

321	(L)	1971-71	Select Standing Committee on Social Welfare and Education (Tisdalle) / 318
322	(L)	1972-72	Select Standing Committee on Social Welfare and Education (Tisdalle) / 319
323	(D)	1973-74	Committee on Teacher Education (Bremer) / 320
324	(D)	1973-73	Committee to Examine Services for the Communicatively Impaired of British Columbia (Gilbert) / 321
325	(L)	1973-73	Select Standing Committee on Social Welfare and Education (Brown) / 322
326	(R1)	1973-74	Royal Commission on Post Secondary Education in the Kootenay Region (McTaggert-Cowan) / 323
327	(D)	1973-74	Committee on University Government (Bremer/Young) / 324
328	(D)	1973-74	Task Force on the Community College (L'Estrange) / 325
329	(D)	1973-74	Study Committee on the Small Senior Secondary School (Reid) / 327
330	(D)	1974-74	Jericho Hill School Inquiry (Chud) / 328
331	(D)	1974-75	Survey Committee on Community Colleges in the Lower Mainland of British Columbia (Marsh) / 329
332	(D)	1975-75	Study of Research and Development in British Columbia (Pedersen) / 330
333	(L)	1975-75	Select Standing Committee on Health, Education, and Human Resources (Brown) / 331
334	(R2)	1975-76	Royal Commission of Inquiry on Property Assessment and Taxation (McMath) / 332
335	(D)	1975-75	Commission of Public Inquiry in the Matter of Vancouver Community College (Suart) / 333
336	(D)	1976-76	Commission on University Programs in Non-Metropolitan Areas (Winegard) / 334
337	(D)	1976-76	Committee on Continuing and Community Education in British Columbia (Farris) / 335

338	(D)	1976-77	Advisory Commission on Vocational, Technical, and Trades Training in British Columbia (Goard) / 336
339	(D)	1977-78	Committee on the Education and Training of Teachers (McGregor) / 337

FEDERAL INQUIRIES

340	(R1)	1910-11	Royal Commission on Industrial Training and Technical Education (Robertson) / 339
341	(R2)	1928-29	Royal Commission on Radio Broadcasting (Aird) / 340
342	(R2)	1937-40	Royal Commission on Dominion-Provincial Relations (Rowell/Sirois) / 341
343	(R2)	1949-51	Royal Commission on National Development in the Arts, Letters and Sciences (Massey) / 342
344	(D)	1954-55	Survey of Social and Economic Conditions of the Indians of British Columbia (Hawthorn) / 344
345	(D)	1955-56	Survey of the Educational Facilities and Requirements of the Indians in Canada (Brown) / 345
346	(R2)	1955-57	Royal Commission on Canada's Economic Prospects (Gordon) / 345
347	(R2)	1955-57	Royal Commission on Broadcasting (Fowler) / 347
348	(L)	1959-61	Joint Committee on Indian Affairs (Gladstone/Grenier) / 348
349	(D)	1960-60	Committee on Education for the Yukon Territory (Brown/Jonason) / 349
350	(R2)	1960-61	Royal Commission on Publications (O'Leary) / 351
351	(R2)	1963-65	Royal Commission on Bilingualism and Biculturalism (Dunton/Laurendeau) / 352
352	(S)	1963-65	Study of University Government in Canada (Duff/Berdahl) / 354
353	(S)	1964-65	Commission on Financing Higher Education in Canada (Bladen) / 355
354	(D)	1964-65	Committee on Broadcasting (Fowler) / 356

355	(R2)	1967-70	Royal Commission on the Status of Women in Canada (Bird) / 357
356	(L)	1967-70	Special Senate Committee on a Science Policy for Canada (Lamontagne) / 359
357	(S)	1968-69	Commission on the Relations between Universities and Governments (Hurtubise/Rowat) / 360
358	(L)	1968-71	Special Senate Committee on Poverty (Croll) / 361
359	(D)	1969-70	Committee on Youth (Hunter) / 362
360	(D)	1970-72	Survey of Education in the Northwest Territories (Gillie) / 364
361	(D)	1972-72	Committee on Education for the Yukon Territory (Levirs) / 365
362	(S)	1972-75	Commission on Canadian Studies (Symons) / 366
363	(S)	1974-75	Study of Northern People and Higher Education (Koenig) / 367
364	(S)	1974-78	Commission on Graduate Studies in the Humanities and Social Sciences (Healy) / 369
365	(R2)	1974-77	The Mackenzie Valley Pipeline Inquiry (Berger) / 370
366	(D)	1977-77	Committee of Inquiry into the National Broadcasting Service (Boyle) / 371
367	(R2)	1977-79	Task Force on Canadian Unity (Pepin/Robarts) / 372

www.ingramcontent.com/pod-product-compliance
Lightning Source LLC
LaVergne TN
LVHW090800070826
844660LV00022B/1036

* 9 7 8 1 4 8 7 5 9 9 1 2 6 *